D1083398

THE TRADITION
OF MANUSCRIPTS

THE TRADITION OF MANUSCRIPTS

A STUDY IN THE TRANSMISSION OF

ST. CYPRIAN'S TREATISES

BY

MAURICE BÉVENOT, S.J.

PROFESSOR OF ECCLESIOLOGY AND
LECTURER IN PATRISTICS
AT HEYTHROP COLLEGE, OXON.

GREENWOOD PRESS, PUBLISHERS
WESTPORT, CONNECTICUT

Library of Congress Cataloging in Publication Data

Bévenot, Maurice.
   The tradition of manuscripts.

   "De ecclesiae catholicae unitate: the resultant
text": p.
   Reprint of the ed. published by the Clarendon Press,
Oxford.
   Bibliography: p.
   Includes indexes.
   1. Cyprianus, Saint, Bp. of Carthage--Manuscripts.
2. Transmission of texts. I. Cyprianus, Saint, Bp. of
Carthage. De ecclesiae catholicae unitate. 1978.
II. Title.
[BR65.C86B43 1978]   230'.1'3   78-14421
ISBN 0-313-20622-8

BR
65
.C86
B43
1979

© M. Bévenot 1961

This reprint has been authorized by the Oxford University
Press.

Reprinted in 1979 by Greenwood Press, Inc.
51 Riverside Avenue, Westport, CT 06880

Printed in the United States of America

10 9 8 7 6 5 4 3 2 1

ACKNOWLEDGEMENTS

THIS study was first taken in hand under the stimulus of Dom E. Dekkers, the editor of *Corpus Christianorum*, who recognized the need of a thorough revision of the works of St. Cyprian. But in a work of this kind one is indebted to more people than one can name. I should like to thank personally all the librarians of so many countries who have enabled me to secure details of the manuscripts in their care, but especially those of the Vatican, the Bibliothèque Nationale, the British Museum, and the Bodleian. For particular help in placing and dating many of the manuscripts, I am most grateful to Professor B. Bischoff of Munich, to Dr. R. W. Hunt, Keeper of the Western Manuscripts in the Bodleian, and to Mr. Neil Ker, lecturer in palaeography at the University of Oxford. At the same time, to be able to draw on the genial scholarship and stimulating encouragement of Professor R. A. B. Mynors, Corpus Professor of Latin, has been an experience for which I owe him more than I can say. But I must not omit to acknowledge the valuable assistance given me by the Institut de Recherche et d'Histoire des Textes in Paris, nor the timely contribution of the Pilgrim Trust which at a critical moment saved the enterprise from foundering altogether. Lastly, the unfailing interest of the Clarendon Press, and the meticulous care of its staff need no pointing out: they are manifest on every page.

MAURICE BÉVENOT, S.J.

September 1960

ERRATA

Page 13, number 590 should be *SALAMANCA, 2608 (olim Madrid, Bibl. Reg., II K 4)*

Page 14, last line should be *b 225 226 231 510 543 562*

Page 32, footnote 2, second line, *Avellana* should be *Avellao*

Page 69, line 13, should be *R, 59, K, and O*

Page 96, 10th line from the bottom, *8 ea] E; sed ea m²; ac non ea H¹T; om.* **L** *J²; et ea cett.* should be *8 ea] E; sed ea m²; ac nos et ea H¹T; om. J² et L; et ea cett.*

Page 105, 4th line from the bottom, *volatilibus W¹ Y BH¹ T* should be *volatilibus W¹ Y BeH¹ T*

Page 112, line 24, **224** *2 Marc. 12. 29-31* should be **224** *2 Marc. 12. 29 + Matt. 22. 37-40*

Page 159, after *Salisbury*, insert *Salamanca 2608*

CONTENTS

Contents

ABBREVIATIONS

A.C.O.	*Acta conciliorum oecumenicorum* (Schwartz)
A.C.W.	Ancient Christian Writers
C.L.A.	*Codices Latini antiquiores* (Lowe)
C.S.E.L.	*Corpus scriptorum ecclesiasticorum latinorum*
'*De Un.* MSS'	'St. Cyprian's *De unitate*, chap. 4, in the Light of the MSS' (Bévenot)
G.C.S.	*Griechische christliche Schriftsteller*
J.T.S.	*Journal of Theological Studies*
L.C.P.	*Latinitas christianorum primaeva*
M.G.H.	*Monumenta Germaniae historica*
Rev. Bén.	*Revue bénédictine*
T.L.L.	*Thesaurus linguae latinae*
T.u.U.	*Texte und Untersuchungen*
Z.N.T.W.	*Zeitschrift für neutestamentliche Wissenschaft und die Kunde der älteren Kirche*

Ur- prefixed to the siglum of a MS means an ancient ancestor, postulated as the source of that MS's chief characteristics

PT ('Primacy' Text): the version of *De unitate*, chap. 4, which contains the word *primatus*

TR (*Textus receptus*): the version of the same chapter as printed in *C.S.E.L.*

PT MSS: those apparently descended from an old collection, which contained the *De unitate* in its first edition. Similarly—

TR MSS: those descended from collections which contained it in its revised (TR) edition

GENERAL INTRODUCTION

1. *Purpose and plan*

THE present study was begun with a simple object in view: the preparation of a new critical edition of the treatises of St. Cyprian. Hartel's edition of Cyprian's works in the *C.S.E.L.* has long been recognized to be unsatisfactory: the MSS which he used were too few and not always the best; his use of them often showed inaccuracy and lack of judgement. But that was ninety years ago, when library catalogues were fewer and less informative, and before photography had revolutionized palaeography. Today, when higher standards prevail, a fuller study of the MSS is called for, so that the best use of the best materials should be made possible. It may be true that there are no 'good' MSS, nor 'bad' ones either, and that the 'best' MSS will have bad readings and the 'most corrupt' will preserve good ones, but an editor who is faced with a hundred or more MSS must make his choice of those which he will collate in detail, without prejudice to possible later 'finds' which he may have missed. His first problem is which MSS to choose.

Few scholars today would demand that every reading in every MS should be recorded in a critical edition: to collate all the MSS in detail would be impracticable and futile. One could mention works where for two lines of text there is a whole page of critical apparatus, an infinite succession of hieroglyphics in small type, but one may well ask whether such meticulous recording is of any use to anybody. The process may be justified where an ancient author survives in only a handful of MSS, otherwise a selection must be made.

With an author like Cyprian, the selection will vary according to the MSS available for any particular treatise or letter. Some of the letters survive only in very few MSS and those not of 'the best'; what has to suffice there will not suffice for the treatises, where we have a wider and a better choice open to us. Besides that, the letters, some eighty in all, seem to have been collected piecemeal, in ones and twos, or in small groups, and these appear in the MSS in almost any order, so that there is no uniformity of transmission. But the treatises appear in most of the MSS which contain collections of Cyprian's works; moreover, they are generally grouped together at the beginning, so that they seem to have formed a unity from the first, as is already suggested by Pontius's list, drawn up soon after Cyprian's death. It is for this reason that the scope of this study has been restricted to the treatises: they form a unity so that the MSS selected as 'the best' for one treatise can serve as 'the best' for the others too. For, *ceteris paribus*, in every MS the process of transmission which one treatise has been through, has likewise been gone through by all the others.

The treatise chosen to represent them all is the *De ecclesiae catholicae unitate*. It is to be found in at least 160 MSS, of which some are obviously more reliable than others. Can we select six, or ten, or a dozen of them, as providing between them the best text available today? If we can, it is reasonable to suppose that, other things being equal, these same MSS will provide an equally good text for the other treatises in them.

Such then, was the original plan and purpose of this study. But in the course of it, and in the very process of pursuing the problems which kept presenting themselves, the whole question of the transmission of ancient texts, especially of patristic texts, began to take on a new significance. It came by a slow, unconscious growth; indeed, it was only at the very end, when the data gathered in the collations of the *De unitate* came up for final appraisal, that the new view of the transmission of texts was even mentally formulated, a view which was then found to have repeatedly suggested itself in the earlier parts of the study, though its significance was not then realized.

The result is that this study has a dual purpose; the practical one of simplifying the editing of Cyprian's works, and the 'scientific' one of contributing, however slightly, to the historical question of the transmission of texts, a contribution which, if it is far from simplifying our approach to them, ensures its being more faithful to the facts. And so perhaps this study may, in its own modest way, also claim to be '*editorum in usum*'.

2. *Method: 'external' and 'internal' evidence*

It is necessary at the outset to explain the special meaning which is here attached to the terms 'internal' and 'external' evidence. Normally the distinction is used when discussing the date and authorship of a given work or of some part of it, but we are not concerned with such questions here. We are comparing MSS, and trying to assess their respective merits as witnesses to the text of Cyprian's treatises. But the evidence on which we rely in doing so seems to fall naturally into two classes: what the MSS can tell us about themselves *as MSS*, i.e. what we can learn from their physical constitution as codices: their script, date, place of origin, the order of their contents, &c.; and what *the text* in each of them reveals, i.e. what we are led to think of a MS from its mistakes, its peculiar but possibly correct readings, its agreements with and disagreements from the text of the other MSS. And since it is for the sake of the *text* of Cyprian that we are appraising the MSS of his works, it seems natural to call the evidence derived from the text itself the 'internal' evidence, and all the evidence that is non-textual the 'external' evidence. Another reason is that the latter provides a necessary background to the closer study of the text—an outer ring of evidence which must be worked through before we enter the inner maze of the countless variants in the MSS. This, then, will be the division and the order of our study.

Our work would be very much simplified if we knew all about the MSS which have survived and are available to us today. When was each of them written, and where, and by whom? What happened to it once it was written? Did it stay in the same place, or did it go from one place to another? If it travelled, where was it at different times, where and when was it available for further transcription or for the correction of another MS?

Very few of these questions can be answered for any of our MSS. For most of them the date can be given only to the nearest century; in some cases to the nearest half-century; there are very few that can be dated within a decade or two. Similarly for the place where they saw the light. In general the catalogues are silent, or at most say France, or Southern Italy, or Northern Italy, or the like. The process of comparison and sifting is going on year by year and materials are being accumulated which, in time, will enable the experts to determine date and place of origin more precisely. For Latin MSS before A.D. 800, Professor E. A. Lowe's series of volumes *Codices Latini antiquiores* (*C.L.A.*) have already provided invaluable help chiefly from the palaeographical point of view, and such a study as *Libri S. Kyliani* by Professor B. Bischoff and Dr. J. Hofmann, on the Scriptorium at Würzburg in the early ninth century, reveals the enormous labour involved in determining and classifying the extant MSS which came even from a single centre within a limited period. But until such studies are multiplied, so as to cover at least all the important scriptoria of the Middle Ages, questions as to time and place of origin of MSS can only be answered approximately—with varying degrees of approximation—and the wanderings of MSS in the different centuries will, even so, remain to be traced individually.

But what we should chiefly like to know is the ancestry of our extant MSS. What MSS were they copying, and where did those come from? How many links were there between them and the original? After all, even our oldest complete MSS of the treatises are dated six centuries after Cyprian's time: there may have been two or three links, there may have been twenty or more. There were periods in-between when culture was low and writing bad and careless: did the links in the chain ever miss those bad periods—a good MS surviving through them and being copied in the great Carolingian revival? Two ninth-century MSS may differ immensely in quality according to their ancestries, and even the eleventh and twelfth centuries have produced MSS as good as, if not better than, any of the ninth.

There are two ways in which our MSS of Cyprian can tell us something about their ancestors, apart from the text which they record. The fact that the order of the contents of two or more MSS is the same, is a prima facie reason for considering them to have come from a common source; small alterations of order need not necessarily affect such a conclusion. Lacunae in the text may also be revealing: MSS which have the same lacunae and are not derived from one another will owe the lacunae to a common ancestor. And certain types of lacunae, even in a single MS, can reveal the very construction and character of the codex from which it inherited them, and this in turn can help us to estimate the worth of the MS in our hands.

But none of this evidence: script, date, origin, wanderings of our MSS, character of their ancestors, takes us very far of itself. However, it provides an all-important background to our study of *the text* in our MSS, and the fuller it is, the better will be our judgement of the text. But it is all external to the text, and it is from the text itself that we get most help in assessing the value of our different MSS. It is with this that the present study is chiefly occupied.

Our central task is to establish a revised text of the *De unitate*. The method adopted is as follows: having, chiefly by the external evidence, divided our MSS into a considerable number of groups, we first take representatives of these and test them by thirty selected 'crucial passages' in our text where divergences have been observed in the MSS. Which of these representatives agree in the crucial passages? Do they form groups among themselves? And in those passages where we are sure of the true reading (as we sometimes can be), which of the MSS have preserved that reading, and which have blundered? On the basis of these tests, we choose some twenty or more MSS, all to be fully collated in preparation for our revision. This is carried out in the ordinary way, the different readings that confront us being weighed according to the 'authority' attaching to the various MSS, but also according to the immediate context and according to what we know of Cyprian's mind. The text cannot be established automatically by the majority votes of even the 'best' MSS; knowing the fallibility even of the 'best', an editor retains his freedom and submits his choice (along with the contrary evidence in the apparatus) to the judgement of his readers. However, no reading was adopted for the final text until *all* the MSS concerned had been collated.

The materials which have been collected in this way, and the relationship thus established between the resultant text and that of each of the MSS, constitute what we have called the 'internal evidence' for the quality of the MSS concerned. All that pertains to the *text* itself is 'internal', all that pertains to the *codices* as such, 'external'. Lacunae are on the borderline, for one is sometimes in doubt whether what looks like a lacuna in one MS may not be due to an interpolation in others. In that case it is the text that is in question. But usually lacunae can be recognized as due to carelessness of transcription—a word left out, or a line—or to the loss of folios in the model being copied. For this reason, lacunae are treated with the external evidence, where they can play a useful part in detecting a tradition in the MSS. So also quotations of Cyprian made by other authors not only tell us that they had a MS of his at hand (external evidence), but the text which they give can contribute to our revision and so to the 'internal' evidence we are looking for.

For the establishment of the text of the *De unitate* is not our final goal. It is from the combined evidence, external and internal, that we make our final choice among the MSS. When once the text has been established, it can in its turn be treated as a norm by which to estimate the MSS which have contributed to its making, with due regard for what the external evidence has already indicated. Those which are closest to the text of the revised treatise, and at the same time seem most independent of one another, will also be the most likely to provide, between them, the best materials available for a critical edition of the other treatises.

3. *Transmission and stemmata*

A word should perhaps be here added on what may be called the by-product of all this industry. It is customary to find in the preface to the critical edition of an ancient author, a stemma or family tree, designed to throw light on the relationship existing between the surviving MSS. Some of the latter may be placed below one of them to show that they have copied it, but the interest of the family tree lies in the ancestors whose presence must be postulated to explain the survivors. Some of the latter may form groups each with a common father, others are distinct from the groups and must be traced back to a more distant ancestry. But working back through the generations, one comes ultimately to the common archetype, if not to the original autograph itself.

Such a stemma gives one a certain confidence that the rejected readings found in the critical apparatus did indeed arise in this way, so that, if one took the trouble, one could put one's finger on the ancestor who was responsible for the mistakes transmitted to his surviving descendants. In fact, it is generally very difficult to do this, and often impossible. The reason is not far to seek. The construction of such a stemma depends on a certain view of the transmission of MSS: it adopts as basic the obvious fact that a copyist makes mistakes, and that his mistakes will be copied at the next generation or give rise to fresh mistakes. Thus MSS get worse and worse down the centuries, and therefore when we are postulating *ancestors*, we must suppose them to have been better and better up the centuries as we get nearer and nearer to the author himself. But such a stemma presupposes, though it rarely calls attention to the fact, that the various lines of descent have proceeded side by side, as it were, in water-tight compartments, so that the mistakes of one line—let alone the correct readings—never pass from one line to another. If, in fact, such exchanges have occurred, if, in other words, MSS of different lines have been compared and corrections made on any large scale, the construction of such a stemma becomes impossible. To overlook the fact of contamination or to treat it as negligible, and to construct a stemma in spite of it, is to print a stemma that is positively misleading.

'Contamination' among the MSS upsets all our calculations. It is one of the chief merits of Dr. Paul Maas's booklet *Textkritik*, that with his closing words he recognizes this by quoting the graphic comparison of Otto Immisch. As the chemical formula lays down inexorably the arrangement of the atoms in each compound, so too does the stemma lay down the relations between the MS readings for each passage—but only '*if* we have a virgin tradition. No specific has yet been discovered against contamination' (Paul Maas, *Textual Criticism* (1958), p. 49).

The reader will recognize that in the earlier part of this study there is a manifest groping after the construction of a stemma which should embrace all our data satisfactorily. Not all the checks which these efforts encountered are recorded here. It was only after the variant readings throughout the treatise had been compared, MS by MS, that the now obvious fact was recognized, viz. that there had been so much comparison and correction of readings *in the ancestors* of our MSS, that the creation of a stemma as ordinarily understood was now impossible.

There is no reason for thinking that this is something peculiar to the MSS of St. Cyprian; one might hazard the statement that it is equally true of all Latin patristic literature whose transmission depended equally on the monastic scriptoria of the Middle Ages. For the classics, and especially for the Greek classics, the situation may be different.

But it would seem wise at least seriously to face the possibility that the complications in the ancestry of our patristic MSS are such that we should lay aside the pretence of being able to reconstruct stemmata that really throw light on their descent. Perhaps some other way of expressing the relationship between our MSS can be found which will be more in conformity with the facts.

4. *The tables and the classification of the MSS*

The first table simply lists the MSS by centuries according to von Soden's system of numbering. Nos. 1–99 cover the first ten centuries thus:

Older than A.D. 700	1–9
Eighth century	10–39
Ninth century	40–69
Tenth century	70–99

Thereafter a hundred numbers are given to the MSS of each century, so that by adding 10 to the first digit we get the century to which they belong. Thus 205 is a twelfth-century MS.

If the number is in italics, it is either an addition to von Soden's list or it has been renumbered (in which case von Soden's number is also given in brackets).

The letter which follows the number in many cases, is the siglum of the MS either adopted from Hartel or from other scholars, or introduced for the purpose of this present study.[1] (Numbers are too cumbrous to be used in detailed collation.)

The present location of the MS follows.

---

[1] For convenience of reference an alphabetical list of the sigla of these MSS will be found in Table 3, p. 15, and also on the book-marker.

In the right-hand column is indicated the group to which the MS belongs, or was thought to belong, according to a rough classification made some years ago.[1] The basis of the classification was threefold: (1) the arrangement of the treatises among themselves; (2) the structure of chap. 4, according to the ways in which its two versions[2] were there represented—singly or variously combined; and (3) the textual variants in that same chapter.

Thus the chief arrangements of the treatises were distinguished by capital letters:

A   I IV VI V VII XI VIII X XII XIII
B   I IV VI V VII VIII XI X XII XIII
C   I IV VI V VII VIII XI XII XIII X
(C) I X IX 37 38 10 V VII VIII XI XII XIII IV VI
D   I IV VI VII V X VIII XI XII XIII

Nearly three-quarters of the MSS were included in these five groups. To the rest was assigned the letter X, which therefore represents (here) any arrangement of treatises other than the five just specified.

Preceding the capital letter will be found a number (from 1 to 7), which refers to the presentation in the MS of chap. 4; 1 represents PT alone, and 2 TR alone; 3 and 4 contain them both in succession, a small variation distinguishing them; 5 and 6 contain TR preceded by one (or two) sentences from PT; and 7 is an intricate interlacing of the versions (which originally prompted the accusation of 'Roman interpolations').

Most of the groups, thus characterized by a number and a capital letter, have been subdivided by the addition of small letters, a, b, c, &c., which indicate that the MSS in each subdivision have certain textual variants in common. This might occur even when the treatises did not preserve the order implied by the capital letter, but warning of this fact is given either by brackets (for a slight rearrangement), or by a dash (for a complete change) in Table 2 (p. 14), where all our MSS are listed in their 'family groups'.

It will be appreciated that this grouping is a very rough one. But it has been a useful guide in preparing the present study, and if for several MSS greater precision has now been reached, its general reliability has only been confirmed by closer acquaintance with the MSS and with the text of the *De unitate* as a whole.

[1] Cf. M. Bévenot, '*De Un.* MSS', pp. vi–ix. Also Table 2 below.
[2] The two versions are referred to as the 'Primacy' Text (PT) and the *textus receptus* (TR)—the first because it contains the word *primatus*, the second because it is the text printed in *C.S.E.L.*

In the first table all the MSS known to contain the *De unitate* are included together with a few others which have a direct bearing on our inquiry. These others are 3, 4, 5, 10, 15, 45, 56, 82, 85, 227.

The second table, 'The family groups of the MSS', presents the classification just referred to, increased and revised. It has served as a guide in the choice of the MSS to be consulted: save for the oldest MSS, which were all studied, it was possible to treat one or two of each group as representatives of the rest.

The third table (for convenience of reference) lists again the MSS most frequently referred to, in the alphabetical order of their sigla.

The fourth table is a list of the treatises as published by Hartel in the *C.S.E.L.*, together with those *spuria* to which it will be necessary to refer. They are in the Appendix to Hartel's edition.

TABLE I

Chronological list of MSS (by centuries)

		Family groups
1 V	Latino Latini's VERONENSIS	6 X e
(3	TURIN, Bibl. Naz., G V 37	
	Only XI and part of 63)	
(4 F	TURIN, Bibl. Naz., F IV 27 ⎫	
	MILAN, Ambros., D 519 inf. ⎬	1 A (?)
	VATICAN, Lat. 10959 ⎭	
	No treatises)	
(5	BRIT. MUS., 40165A	5 B (?)
	Fragments of three letters)	
7 S	PARIS, Lat. 10592	2 B a
(10 A	ROME, Bibl. Vitt. Emmanuele, 2106	
	Only the *Testimonia*)	
(15 X	MANCHESTER, John Rylands Lib., Lat. 15	
	No treatises)	
40 M	MUNICH, Lat. 208	3 D
41 Y	MUNICH, Lat. 4597	2 B a
44 (11) W	WÜRZBURG, Univ., Theol. fol. 145	2 B a
(45 L	VIENNA, Lat. 962	2 X c
	Contains second half of Cyprian's works. The first half, including the treatises, is lost)	
47 G	ST. GALLEN, 89	2 B b
50 R	VATICAN, Reg. lat. 116	2 X a

		Family groups
51 (80) T	VATICAN, Reg. lat. 118	4 A
55 P	PARIS, Lat. 1647A	2 (C) a
(56 C	PARIS, Lat. 12126	
	No treatises)	
58 J	ANGERS, 148	5 X f
59	TOURS, 256	5 (C) b
60 (20) Q	TROYES, 581	3 D
64 (91) K	LEYDEN, Univ., Voss. lat. fol. 40	5 X e
65 (95) O	OXFORD, Bod., Add. C 15	5 X b
66 (141) D	OXFORD, Bod., Laud Misc. 451	2 C a
67 (140) U	OXFORD, Bod., Laud Misc. 105	4 A
75	ST. GALLEN, 150	2 B b
(82 N	MONTE CASSINO, 204	
	No treatises)	
83	Latino Latini's BENEVENTANUS, or NEAPOLI-	
	TANUS	
	(Only a few collations)	
(85 E	PARIS, Lat. 17349	
	No treatises)	
100 B	BAMBERG, Patr. 63	6 X a
101	BAMBERG, Patr. 64	2 C a
110	VATICAN, Reg. lat. 117	5 (C) b
111 (211) p	VATICAN, Lat. 202	2 B c
115 m	MANTUA, B III 18	2 B c
122	PARIS, Lat. 1656A	2 C a
126 (102) k	METZ, 224	5 (C) a
130	BRUSSELS, 1052–3 (918)	5 X e
150 (90) h	LEYDEN, Univ., Voss. lat. oct. 7	7 A
200	BERLIN, Theol. lat. fol. 264	(5 X e)
201	BERLIN, Theol. lat. fol. 700	2 C a
202 (330) a	ADMONT, 587	2 X c
203	CUES, St. Nicolaus-Hospital, 36	((C))
204	ZWETTL, Cisterc.-Stift, 93	(7 A)
205	VIENNA, Lat. 850	2 X c
206 (236)	ADMONT, 136	2 X c
207 (235)	ADMONT, 381	2 X c
208 b	BERNE, Bibl. Bongarsiana, 235	5 X a
213	VATICAN, Lat. 6023	4 A
214 (517)	VATICAN, Reg. lat. 275	5 X c
216	TURIN, Bibl. Naz., D IV 37	(5 (C) b)
218 (320) t	PARIS, Lat. 1648	4 A
219 (420) g	PARIS, Lat. 1650	2 C a

		Family groups
221 ω	PARIS, Lat. 1656	5 B
223 o	PARIS, Lat. 17350	5 (C) b
225	PARIS, Lat. 1654	6 X b
226 i	PARIS, Lat. 14460	6 X b
(227	PARIS, Lat. 1655 No treatises)	
228 (120) H	PARIS, Lat. 15282	1 A
229	PARIS, Nouv. acq. lat. 1792	5 C a
231	CHARTRES, 36	5 (C) b
233	DIJON, 124	2 C a
234	TROYES, 37	3 C
237	TOURS, 257	5 (C) b
250	BRIT. MUS., Arundel 217	5 B
252 e	BRIT. MUS., Royal 6 B XV	5 B
253	LONDON, Lambeth Pal., 106	5 B
254	SALISBURY, Cathedral Lib., 9	2 B b
255	OXFORD, Bod., Bodley 210 (2037)	5 B
257	CAMBRIDGE, Pembroke Coll., 154	5 B
258	SHREWSBURY, School Lib., XXVI	5 B
270	MADRID, Bibl. Nacional, 199 (olim A 17)	7 A
305	VIENNA, Lat. 810	2 C a
306	VIENNA, Lat. 789	2 X c
321	PARIS, Lat. 1649	2 B c
324	PARIS, Lat. 1657	5 (C) b
325	PARIS, Lat. 1922	5 X c
331 β	TROYES, 442	2 C a
350	BRIT. MUS., Add. 21074	5 X c
354 (256)	OXFORD, Bod., New Coll. 130	5 B
355	CAMBRIDGE, Pembroke Coll., 161	7 A
369	LIÈGE, Univ., 70	(3 D)
370	ESCORIAL, S.I. 11	2 (C) b
400	ERFURT, Ampl. F. 90	(5 X e)
410	VATICAN, Ottob. lat. 600	2 C a
415	BOLOGNA, Univ., 2572	7 A
417	SIENA, F V 14	((C))
419	VOLTERRA, Bibl. Guanacci, 69 (6187)	(C b)
421 Z	PARIS, Lat. 1658	2 X b
430	ARRAS, 25	(X f)
435	CARPENTRAS, 31	3 C
440	LEYDEN, Univ., Voss. lat. qu. 19	(X e)
450	BRIT. MUS., Add. 21075 (A.D. 1396)	5 X e
470	BARCELONA, Univ., 574	(7 A)

500	BERLIN, Phillipps 1730	7 A
501	BERLIN, Hamilton 199	7 A
503	MUNICH, Lat. 18174	2 B a
504 μ	MUNICH, Lat. 18203	2 B b
505	MUNICH, Lat. 21240	5 (C) b
506	AUGSBURG, Lat. 65	(7 A)
507	VIENNA, Lat. 4704	(X)
508	CUES, St. Nicolaus-Hospital, 24	((C))
509	PRAGUE, Univ. III E 7	(2 C a)
510	VIENNA, Lat. 763	(6 X b)
511	VIENNA, Lat. 770	(X)
513	VIENNA, Lat. 14091	(6 X a)
514	VATICAN, Ottob. lat. 306	5 (C) b
515	VATICAN, Lat. 9943	6 X a
516	VATICAN, Urb. lat. 63	6 X c
518	VATICAN, Borgh. lat. 335	5 (C) b
519	VATICAN, Pal. lat. 159	5 X b
520	VATICAN, Lat. 195	6 X a
521	VATICAN, Lat. 197	2 B b
522	VATICAN, Lat. 198 (A.D. 1449)	2 B b
523 φ	VATICAN, Lat. 199 (A.D. 1454)	5 (C) b
524	VATICAN, Lat. 200 (A.D. 1456)	5 (C) b
525	VATICAN, Lat. 201	7 A
526	VATICAN, Lat. 5099	7 A
527	VATICAN, Pal. lat. 158	2 B b
528	VATICAN, Lat. 196	6 X a
529	VATICAN, Ottob. lat. 80	2 C b
530	FLORENCE, Laur., XVI 22	2 C b
531	FLORENCE, Laur., Gadd. 21	2 C b
533	FLORENCE, Laur., Fesul. 49	2 C b
534	FLORENCE, Laur., Med. Pal. 24	6 X c
536	TURIN, Bibl. Naz., E III 5 (A.D. 1469)	2 B b
537	TURIN, Bibl. Naz., H II 24	(5 (C) b)
538	CESENA, Bibl. Malatestiana, D XII 4	(3 D)
539	SIENA, F V 13	(X)
540	S. DANIELE DEL FRIULI, 22	(2 B b)
543	LUCCA, 1728	(6 X b)
546	VENICE, S. Marco, L II 23	2 C b
	(Valent., Lat. III 3)	

(Von Soden gives the references to the Venice
MSS according to Valentinelli's Catalogue.
These are now superseded)

		Family groups
547a	VENICE, S. Marco, Z L 41 (Valent., Lat. III 4)	5 X c
547b	VENICE, S. Marco, Z L 41 (Valent., Lat. III 4)	7 A
548	VENICE, S. Marco, Z L 39 (Valent., Lat. III 5)	5 (C) b
549	VENICE, S. Marco, L II 24 (Valent., Lat. III 6)	5 (C) b
550	VENICE, S. Marco, L II 59 (Valent., Lat. III 76)	3 D
551	BOLOGNA, Univ., 2364	7 A
552	MILAN, Ambros., A 122 sup. (A.D. 1464)	2 C b
553	MILAN, Ambros., C 131 inf.	5 (C) b
554	MILAN, Ambros., A 197 inf.	5 (C) b
555	MILAN, Bibl. Naz. Braidense, A.D. XIV 20	5 (C) b
556	VATICAN, Ross. 250	5 (C) b
557	VATICAN, Chigi A VI 177 (A.D. 1467)	2 B b
558	VATICAN, Lat. 10497	2 C a
559	ROME, Bibl. Vallicelliana, D 21	2 B b
560	PARIS, Nouv. acq. lat. 1282	7 A
561	PARIS, Lat. 13330	2 B d
562 (224) ρ	PARIS, Lat. 1659	6 X b
565	AVIGNON, 244	(2 (C) b)
566 r	RHEIMS, 370	5 X g
569	BRUSSELS, 365–79	2 X d
570	BRIT. MUS., Harley 3089	7 A
572	BRIT. MUS., Add. 21077	5 (C) b
573	BRIT. MUS., Harley 5005	2 C b
575	OXFORD, Bod., Laud Misc. 217	3 D
577	OXFORD, Bod., New Coll. 132	2 C b
578	OXFORD, Bod., Lincoln Coll. lat. 47	6 X a
579	OXFORD, Bod., Lat. th. d. 4	5 C b
580	CAMBRIDGE, Corpus Christi Coll., 25	5 B
581	CAMBRIDGE, Caius Coll., 114	5 X d
583 Ho	HOLKHAM HALL, 121	2 B d
585	CHELTENHAM, Phillipps, 4361 (So previously. Now untraceable)	2 C b
586	FRIBOURG, Cathedral Chapter (St. Niklaus)	7 A
590	MADRID, Bibl. Reg., II D 4	2 B b
594	COPENHAGEN, Gl. kgl., S 35 fol.	6 X d
595	CRACOW, Jagellonica, 1210 (A.D. 1435)	5 (C) b
640	BRUSSELS, 706–7	5 X e

		Family groups
641	BRUSSELS, 1075–8	2 X d
642	BRUSSELS, 9376	3 D
651	YORK, Cathedral, XVI I 1	5 B
700	MUNICH, 23756 (A.D. 1618)	X

TABLE 2

The family groups of the MSS of the De unitate

1 A	F (?) H
4 A	T U *213 218*
7 A	h *204* 270 355 415 *470* 500 501 506 525 526 547b 551 560 570 *586*
2 B a	S Y W 503
b	μ 521 522 527 *559* (536 540 *557* 590) — G 75 *254*
c	p m 321
d	Ho (*561*)
5 B	5 (?) 221 250 e *253* 255 *257 258 354* 580 *651*
2 C a	D *122 201 219* 233 305 331 410 *509* (101) — *558*
b	(419 529 530 531 533 546 *552* 577 *585*) — 573
3 C	234 — 435
5 C a	*229*
b	*579*
2 (C) a	P
b	*370 565*
5 (C) a	k
b	110 *216* 223 *237* 324 505 *514* 518 523 524 537 54*8 553 554 555 556 572 595* — 59 549 — 231
(C)	203 417 508
3 D	M Q *369 538* 575 642 — *550*
2 X a	R
b	421
c	a 205 *207 — 206 — 306*
d	569 641
5 X a	b
b	O 519
c	*214* 325 350 (547a)
d	581
e	K 130 400 440 450 (200) — 640
f	J — 430
g	566
6 X a	B 513 520 528 578 — *515*
b	225 226 510 *543 562*

```
c   516 534
d   594
e   V
X   83 507 511 539 700
```

TABLE 3

Alphabetical list of chief sigla

B	100	BAMBERG, Patr. 63
D	66	OXFORD, Bod., Laud Misc. 451
F	4	TURIN, F IV 27+MILAN, Ambros., D 519 inf.+VATICAN, Lat. 10959
G	47	ST. GALLEN, 89
H	228	PARIS, Lat. 15282
Ho	583	HOLKHAM HALL, 121
J	58	ANGERS, 148
K	64	LEYDEN, Univ., Voss. lat. fol. 40
L	45	VIENNA, Lat. 962
M	40	MUNICH, Lat. 208
N	82	MONTE CASSINO, 204
O	65	OXFORD, Bod., Add. C 15
P	55	PARIS, Lat. 1647A
Q	60	TROYES, 581
R	50	VATICAN, Reg. lat. 116
S	7	PARIS, Lat. 10592
T	51	VATICAN, Reg. lat. 118
U	67	OXFORD, Bod., Laud Misc. 105
V	1	'VERONENSIS' Collations
W	44	WÜRZBURG, Univ., Theol. fol. 145
X	15	MANCHESTER, John Rylands Lib., Lat. 15
Y	41	MUNICH, Lat. 4597
a	202	ADMONT, 587
b	208	BERNE, Bibl. Bongars., 235
e	252	BRIT. MUS., Royal 6 B XV
h	150	LEYDEN, Univ., Voss. lat. oct. 7
k	126	METZ, 224
m	115	MANTUA, B III 18
p	111	VATICAN, Lat. 202
μ	504	MUNICH, Lat. 18203

Collective sigla by 'family groups'

D = D+most of the 'Cistercians' (2Ca+3C+5Ca)
E = e+the rest of 5B
H = H+T+h and the other PT MSS (1A+4A+7A)
L = a and the rest of 2Xc

General Introduction

M = m+p+32I (2Bc)
P = P+k (and most of 2(C)a+2(C)b+5(C)a+5(C)b)
W = W+Y (and most of 2Ba+2Bb; but not S and G)

For the more precise meaning of these portmanteau sigla, as used in the actual collations, see pp. 94–95; as used in Appendix II, see p. 142.

Other abbreviations

Pel. readings given by Pelagius II (cf. p. 89)
Can. readings commonly found in the Canonist writings (1050–1150)
Flo. readings given by Florus of Lyons (cf. p. 90)
Wal. readings given by Walram of Nienburg (cf. pp. 90–91)
cett. the rest of the MSS collated

Critical Apparatus: The order of the MSS collated

m p W Y G a P k | S R J O D B e b V H T h
   M **W**   **L** **P** | **D** **E**   **H**

Certain MSS may be replaced by the collective siglum here indicated below them. Cf. pp. 94–95.

TABLE 4

List of treatises in Hartel's edition

   I   Ad Donatum
  II   Quod idola dii non sint (treated in the present study as *not genuine*)
 III   Ad Quirinum (Testimoniorum libri tres)
 IV   De habitu virginum
  V   De ecclesiae catholicae unitate
 VI   De lapsis
 VII   De dominica oratione
VIII   De mortalitate
 IX   Ad Fortunatum (De exhortatione martyrii)
  X   Ad Demetrianum
 XI   De opere et eleemosynis
 XII   De bono patientiae
XIII   De zelo et livore
XIV   Sententiae episcoporum de haereticis baptizandis (not a treatise, nor treated as such even in the MSS)

Spurious treatises referred to (as numbered in Hartel's Appendix)

App. ii   De bono pudicitiae
App. iii   De laude martyrii
App. iv   Ad Novatianum

App. vii   De duobus montibus (Sina et Syon)
App. xi   Oratio II: *Domine sancte*
App. xii   De duodecim abusivis saeculi

Spurious work (*not in Hartel*; cf. M.G.H., Poet. lat. iv. 2. 1, pp. 857–900)
cena   Cena Cypriani

PART I

THE 'EXTERNAL EVIDENCE'

T H E transmission of Cyprian's writings through the centuries bears certain characteristics which must be constantly kept in mind. Some of these they share with the works of other ancient authors, some are perhaps peculiar to his. In the first place, the corpus of his works is constituted by nearly one hundred items, of various length and character: 'treatises' (which are mostly addresses and sermons) and letters, mostly from him, but some addressed to him, and two or three merely connected with him. The century is completed and passed by a dozen or so further works: treatises, letters, and poems which came to be falsely ascribed to him. The transmission of his writings therefore differs from that of an author's large, single work, be it epic, history, or summa, in that from the first they were not published as one whole, but at most in groups of varying size, whose contents might overlap, and to which stray letters or groups of letters might be added in the course of time. This would in the first instance occur when a letter, or letters, received and preserved locally were found to be missing from the 'published' collection, and later when one collection was compared with another.

Whatever may have been the process, we have its results in our surviving MSS. Apart from a certain number of fragments our MSS, which date from about 800 onwards, present a bewildering number of different collections—differing both in what they contain and in the order in which the different items are arranged. In fact, not till the fifteenth century is there a single MS which includes the whole of the genuine corpus, and even then there is only one that succeeds in doing so, but at the price of incorporating a rich collection of *spuria* too (Turin, National Lib. E III 5).

It is obvious that a first step must be to gather together those MSS which have the same contents in the same order; in this way a certain number of groups of MSS can be formed. Of those remaining, some are seen to approach this group or that and may be linked up with them, others seem to be quite refractory or can only be associated with the previous ones on more or less violent hypotheses. One indication which often helps to place a MS is the presence of a spurious work in the midst of its other letters. There is then a probability that an ancestor of the MS originally ended before the *spurium*, for such an addition to an already constituted collection would normally be made not in the middle, but at its end. Hence what precedes a *spurium* or group of *spuria* will be an older collection; what follows it will be either part or whole of a distinct collection, and here we must be prepared both for the repetition of a letter already in the codex, and for the avoidance of such a repetition. In the first instance, it is likely that a whole block of letters has been taken from another codex; in the latter that we have a selection only from another codex, though usually in the same order as before. Of course, either of these procedures may have occurred without there being a *spurium* to make us suspect it, individual letters or blocks of letters being added to an already existing collection; it is such possibilities which make it so difficult to delimit original collections, and warn us against jumping too easily at recognizing dependence, or independence, between MSS without confirming evidence.

Though this study has been deliberately restricted to the treatises, it cannot altogether neglect the letters. The problem of the transmission of the letters was studied by Hans von Soden fifty years ago.[1] If he has not said the last word on the subject, his collection of materials must form the basis of any further study, as it has been an invaluable guide for the present work. But if the letters lie outside the scope of this study, they impinge on it in two ways: first in laying down the first rough grouping of the MSS, and secondly, because in at least one important group of MSS (P and its followers),[2] some letters have come to be placed among the treatises. If in general we find that the treatises usually form a group preceding the letters, then a MS which has three letters in the middle of the treatises presents a problem. Was it an accidental transference? Was it an original arrangement of the materials made independently of any other collections? Or was it merely a rearrangement of the materials in an already existing collection?

---

[1] H. von Soden, 'Die Cyprianische Briefsammlung: Geschichte ihrer Entstehung und Überlieferung', in *T.u.U.*, Neue Folge, X. Band, 3. Heft (1904), Leipzig.

[2] Paris, Bibl. Nat., Lat. 1647A (von Soden 55). For its contents see below, p. 29.

Von Soden, who deals with the treatises in an excursus to his great work, recognizes that the arrangement in P was no accident, such as he suggests for the slighter variations in the majority of the MSS (p. 201). It begins with two apologetic treatises I and X, followed by one in praise of martyrdom, IX, to which are attached the three letters on the same subject. For the moment that suffices to prove a deliberate arrangement. But von Soden treats it as if this proved that P in its treatises was independent from the other collections,[1] although he had clearly recognized earlier that the collection of letters in P agreed substantially with those of several other important MSS (pp. 73 ff.). The possibility that it was merely a rearrangement of contents in those MSS deserves attention; even if we have to reject it, its study will bring to light some interesting facts which help to assess the relations that exist between letters and treatises in general, and to improve our grouping of the MSS. This particular point, however, can only be presented as part of a complex whole, of which the data must be dealt with each in turn.

---

[1] Already before him Dom Ramsay had suggested that P's first part (i.e. the treatises with the three incorporated letters) came from a source different from that of its second part (which latter we can identify, viz. of the family of L, as we shall see presently), the inserted letters being passed over when the second part was copied (*J.T.S.* iii (1901–2) 590). However, the same result would occur if P simply transferred those three letters from the second part into the first.

CHAPTER I

Old Collections in Two Volumes

WE can understand that by the time that a considerable corpus of Cyprian's writings had been collected, it was difficult to contain it all in one volume. In any case it is clear that, at least in many cases, the corpus was divided between two volumes, the first consisting mainly of treatises, the second of letters. There exists, too, as we know, an eighth-century uncial volume containing the *Testimonia* (III) alone,[1] and the rest of the evidence makes it very probable that the corpus had already been formed (in two volumes) before the *Testimonia* was incorporated in it. It was generally included, if at all, at the beginning of the second volume.

The best-known case of an 'edition' in two volumes is that of L, the Lorsch MS of the ninth century, which contains the letters (preceded by *Test.*).[2] But luckily we have the old catalogue of the Lorsch library which, besides enabling us to identify this one, the second volume, also gives us the contents of the first volume, now lost.[3] This loss is in part compensated by some twelfth-century MSS which, having identical contents with those given in the catalogue, may be taken as derived from Lorsch's lost first volume. The most important of these is Admont 587, of the first half of the twelfth century, for which date I am indebted to the kindness of Professor B. Bischoff.

Other examples of separate second volumes are X of the end of the eighth century (Manchester, John Rylands Lib., Lat. 15);[4] E (Paris, Bibl. Nat., Lat. 17349; von Soden 85), of the ninth or tenth century; and N of the eleventh (Monte Cassino 204; von Soden 82).[5] We shall need to return to these more than once.

Of separate first volumes we have Y (Munich, Lat. 4597) and W

---

[1] Rome, Bibl. Vitt. Emmanuele 2106; originally Sessorianus 58 (von Soden places it in France, mistaking 'Sessorianus' for Soissons—pp. 197, 252, 254. He gives it the number 10; Hartel, A), cf. C. H. Turner in *J.T.S.* vi (1904–5) 246–7. (*C.L.A.* iv. 422.)

[2] Vienna, Staatsbibl., Lat. 962 (von Soden 45, Hartel L).

[3] Vatican, Pal. lat. 1877, fols. 1–34. The contents of the first volume of Cyprian are given on fol. 28.   [4] *C.L.A.* ii. 222.

[5] Cf. *Bibliotheca Casinensis*, iv. 165–9, and M. Inguanez, *Cod. Casin. MSS catalogus*, vol. ii, pp. 4–5. Hartel and von Soden date it tenth century: but besides the above see E. A. Lowe, *The Beneventan Script*, pp. 20, 346.

(Würzburg, Univ., Theol. fol. 145) of the early ninth century[1] both derived from the same parent MS; but they both give us the list of contents of their *whole* corpus, so that we know what was intended for their second volume. But we have no such help in S, a fragmentary uncial MS of about A.D. 500 (Paris, Bibl. Nat., Lat. 10592),[2] nor in J, of the first half of the ninth century (Angers Bibl. Munic. 148), or K of about the same date (Leyden, Voss. lat. fol. 40); no more than in O of the ninth (Oxford, Bod., Add. C 15), U, also of the ninth (Oxford, Bod., Laud Misc. 105), G, a selection of treatises of about the year 900 (St. Gallen, Stiftsbibl., 89), and b of the twelfth century (Berne, Bibl. Bongars., 235).[3] Some of these contain a few letters at the end, but they are all substantially collections of treatises, most of which probably had a corresponding volume devoted to the letters.

When writing came to be less spread out, it became possible to include all in one volume. Normally there would be a straightforward transcription, but if there were one or more letters at the end of the first volume, especially if the second volume began with the *Testimonia*, those letters might be transferred to the second part, proper to the letters. In such a case, of course, though rearranged, the contents of the whole would preserve the same tradition. But these collections in two volumes sometimes led to a confusion of traditions. Thus a monastery which had only a first volume might wish to produce a codex as complete as possible, and might borrow a second volume for the purpose. If this second volume belonged to a different tradition, the result would be a combination of traditions, likely to puzzle and even mislead the scholars of today. If the monastery's first volume was A and it borrowed from the fuller collection of $\alpha + \beta$, we can be tempted to suppose from the combination Aβ (which is perhaps all we have), that we are dealing with a single, uniform tradition. In fact, even if α survives separately, we might have no reason for connecting it with β. And transference of letters from one part to the other can have occurred here too, complicating the issue still further.

By a strange fortune, among the MSS of St. Cyprian we have the fullest evidence of such a combination of different traditions. It may be

---

[1] B. Bischoff u. J. Hofmann, *Libri Sancti Kyliani* (1952), pp. 33–34, 128. Y is of the first third of the century, W of the second third.

[2] *C.L.A.* v. 602.

[3] Some apology is due for indicating the Berne MS by 'b'. This siglum was used by Latino Latini for his Beneventanus (also called by him Neapolitanus, 'N'). The MS is now lost, and its readings (at least in the *De unitate*) are so uncertain or unimportant, that it has here been omitted as being unhelpful.

recalled that on the basis of a change of hands in the course of transcription of the treatises in the Cistercian MS H (Paris, Bibl. Nat., Lat. 15282), it was suggested that two different MSS were being copied, one of which provided the bulk of the treatises, the other the *Ad Donatum* and all the letters.[1] This suggestion was probably mistaken, as we shall see, but the principle invoked was sound, if incorrectly applied. The fact is that among the Cistercian MSS to which H belongs, the order of the *treatises* of H is unique, but it corresponds to that of the families of MSS which contain the 'Primacy Text' (in the *De unitate*, chap. 4) in some adulterated form. (Of these, T, of the ninth century—Vatican, Reg. lat. 118—may be taken as the type.) Let us suppose that A and B are two standard orders of treatises and a and b the corresponding orders of letters. The view then taken may be expressed schematically thus:

$$H = A + b$$
$$\text{Other Cistercians} = B + b$$
$$T = A + a$$

And to complete the picture, the Oxford MS, D (Bod., Laud Misc. 451) which like T is of the ninth century, combines the 'Cistercian' treatises with the letters of T, so that its contents are:

$$D = B + a^2$$

It is clear that we have here all the possible combinations of two editions, each of which was originally in two volumes, and that, *if our starting-point was correct*, the original editions consisted respectively of A+a and B+b—i.e. the contents of T and the contents of the Cistercians (exclusive of H). But if our starting-point was wrong, if after all H represented one of the editions (say, A+α), then D will represent the other edition (B+β), and we get:

$$H = A + \alpha$$
$$\text{Other Cistercians} = B + \alpha$$
$$T = A + \beta$$
$$D = B + \beta^3$$

This possibility was overlooked in the previous survey of the MSS, but a fresh appraisement of the evidence makes it by far the more probable one. As will be shown later (Chapter III), T's letters (apart from

---

[1] M. Bévenot, '*De Un.* MSS' (Rome, 1937), pp. xv–xvi.

[2] This schematization follows the conclusions arrived at by Chapman (cf. *J.T.S.* iv (1902–3) 121–2).

[3] Another Oxford MS, Bod., Laud Misc. 105, has the treatises of T, followed by three letters only and four *spuria*; therefore 'A + ?'.

a long appendix) belong to a well-established family with a recognizable order of contents, whereas H's letters belong to another ancient family, which has survived only in the Cistercian MSS proper. The conclusion seems inescapable. Just as the Cistercian MS H is unique in preserving the pure Primacy Text, it is unique too in having preserved *together* not only the collection of treatises, but the collection of letters that goes with it. It is not that H (among the Cistercians) borrowed its treatises elsewhere and followed the other Cistercians in the letters; it is rather that H represents an original edition and that other Cistercians borrowed their letters from *it* (or from its model). And, similarly, it is not D which has borrowed its letters from T, while in the treatises it corresponds to the Cistercians. As H represents an original edition, so too does D, and it is the other Cistercians and T which are different combinations of those two editions, each taking one-half from either.

This conclusion finds confirmation in the character of the collection of letters in H, which we have just said belong to a separate ancient family. This can best be treated now, as other elements will need consideration before we take up the question of the 'well-established family' to which the letters of T belong.

CHAPTER II

The Letters of H

WE have just seen four types of MSS, of which two must have been original and two derivative, the latter being formed by an interchange of the collections of the letters. We concluded that H and D were typical of the originals, and T and the Cistercians typical of the derivatives, thus:

$$\text{ORIGINALS}\begin{Bmatrix} H = A+\alpha \\ D = B+\beta \end{Bmatrix} \rightarrow \begin{Bmatrix} T = A+\beta \\ \text{Cist.} = B+\alpha \end{Bmatrix} = \text{derivatives.}$$

The basis of the β collection of letters can be traced well back, but for α we have apparently nothing earlier than the twelfth century. Can then α really be an old collection, and were we right in putting it with A, which certainly seems to be an old collection of treatises?

Hartel, in spite of his contempt for the 'Codices interpolati recentiores', grudgingly says of H 'non prorsus negligendum esse putavi' (p. lvii) because of its being more closely related to F, the Bobbio fragments, than any other MS.[1] Chapman saw the importance of this (cf. *J.T.S.* iv. 122) and called Turner's attention to it when the latter was preparing his account of F (cf. *J.T.S.* iii. 583). Building on their work von Soden concluded that H represented the contents of an ancestor of F (*Briefsamm-lung*, pp. 112–16). His chief argument, and it is a sound one, is that in F the contents are numbered in order, and ep. 47 is numbered as the 37th item. This corresponds exactly with its position in H.

But von Soden omits an important point and is mistaken in some of his calculations. Though he draws on Turner's article, he expressly leaves aside what Turner had said about the quaternions (p. 113, n. 1). This, however, is very pertinent to us, as it gives us a clue to the division of the Cyprianic corpus in two volumes.

To understand the situation, it will be necessary to lay out the data available (see p. 26).

The correspondences between F and H are obvious and striking. In the second gap can rightly be placed epp. 3 and 72. For it is most

---

[1] The remains of F (dated about the year 400) are today shared by three Italian libraries: Milan, Ambros., D 519 inf.; Turin, F IV 27; Vatican, Lat. 10959. For detailed descriptions see C. H. Turner in *J.T.S.* iii (1901–2) 582–4 and 576–8; *C.L.A.* iv. **458.

F *(the Milan–Turin–Vatican fragments) compared with H*[1]

F   ⌐ – – – – – MILAN – – – – – ⌐
57 *fin.*, 52, 47^{37}, 45^{38}, 44^{39} *init.*   4 *fin.*, 72 *expl.*, 61^{43} *init.*

one quaternion   three quaternions   leaf 1   6 leaves   leaf 8

quaternion xvii

H   (60) 57 < 59 > 52   47   45   44   13   43   65   66   4   3   72   61

F   61 *fin.*, 1^{44}, 46^{45}, 56^{46}, 54 *incip.*   ⌐ Vatican 54^{47} *init.*   54 *fin.*, 20^{48}, 30^{49}, 31^{50}, 12^{51} *incip.*
leaf 1   leaf 8

one quaternion   two quaternions

H   1   46   56   54   20   30   31   12

[1] What is not marked 'MILAN' or 'Vatican' is Turin. '*incip.*,' and '*expl.*' mean the rubrics 'Incipit . . .' and 'Explicit . . .' only; '*init.*' means the first part of the letter, '*fin.*,' its latter part. Each letter bears the number given in Hartel; the indices attached to most of them give their numeration in order, as entered by 'the (ninth-century?) corrector'. (Of course, he used Roman numerals.) The letters in H are given consecutively; the spaces between them do not mean omissions.

probable, as Turner said, that the end of 4 is on the first leaf of the quaternion of which the last leaf follows immediately (marked xvii), so that six leaves lie in-between. A leaf in this codex contains 27 or 28 lines of Hartel's text (not 22 as von Soden says (p. 113)) and those two letters contain about $82 + 78 = 160 =$ about 6×27 lines. That accounts for the second gap.

What of the first gap? Turner seems to imply that when 'the (ninth century?) corrector' numbered the letters, there was the same gap as there is today. That would be a mistake. Turner himself noticed that the end of 44 plus the beginning of 4 was insufficient to complete a quaternion, but he missed the fact that if, at that time, the beginning of 44 had been followed immediately by the end of 4, the corrector would have had no *heading* to which to assign the number 40 (we can presume that he had the headings of 3 and of 72 for the numbers 41 and 42).

Von Soden at least saw the difficulty of supposing that 13, 43, 65, and 66 were all there too, since the numeration would no longer correspond. Let us, however, suppose they were all there *originally*. With the missing parts of 44 and 4, they make up approximately 662 lines, which gives us almost exactly three quaternions (quaternion $= 8 \times 27\frac{1}{2} = 220$). The third of these quaternions would contain one and only one heading, viz. that of ep. 4, so that we have a simple explanation of the numbering by supposing the loss of only the first two of these quaternions *before* the corrector numbered the headings. The beginning of ep. 44 would run into the end of ep. 66, and so he would number ep. 4 '40'; then ep. 3 '41', and ep. 72 '42'.

We shall suppose that this was so in what follows, but it is by no means essential to the argument. The quaternion following the first gap is numbered xvii. The three that preceded it are now all missing, therefore our first quaternion must be numbered xiii. In other words, there were only twelve quaternions before (the latter part of) ep. 57. This presents a serious problem. For twelve quaternions represent only 12×220 lines $= 2,640$ lines: allowing 20–25 lines to a page in Hartel, that gives us only 106–32 of Hartel's pages. It is perfectly clear that the treatises in H (even supposing III to be a later addition) could not possibly fit in before the rest of the letters. In fact, there is only room for these letters.

What are we to conclude? Must we give up the idea that H gives us the original contents of F? By no means. The only proper conclusion is that F was in two volumes, but that the 'corrector', who in the ninth century put in the numbering of each item in order, had the two volumes before him and ran the numbering consecutively through the volumes. In this way, we have the numbering agreeing with the contents of H, and also the quaternions of F adapted to the second volume of the Cyprianic corpus. Of course, the quaternions of the second volume would begin their numbering again, but it would be natural for the corrector to number the contents of the two volumes consecutively.

We expected to find that the two original collections A+α and B+β were in two volumes, and to that extent our conclusion fits in. That we are right in placing A with α and B with β has at least this much in its favour that whereas B and β both conform to a well-established pattern, we now know that α has deep roots independent of β, and had with it a collection of treatises probably of a different character from those of B. It is reasonable to conclude that what went with α was not the common collection B but something *sui generis*. This is what A is: it is characteristic of the Primacy Text, and we therefore have good grounds for associating it with α, which derives from one of our very oldest witnesses, F.

Note. The absence of 59 in F (between 57 and 52) presents a problem which von Soden has probably solved correctly. Its presence seems to be demanded by the fact that epp. 47, 45, and 44 are headed by '*ad eundem* v, vi, and vii'. This is the end of the group of letters to Cornelius, which often runs (as in H) from 60 to 44, but includes 59. Its absence is not due to any lacuna in the MS, since the end of 57 and the beginning of 52 are on the same leaf.[1] We must recognize its omission (or displacement) in F, but its presence in the 'archetype' must be presumed owing to the explicit numbering of the last three letters to Cornelius.[2] Nor need we be surprised that 52 has not got '*ad eundem* iv', for its heading reads '*ad eundem [de] Novato*' where such a number might mislead.

That ep. 52 has no serial number might suggest a difficulty, since the ninth-century 'corrector' has numbered all the other letters of which the headings survive. But the Milan fragments have been used as guard-leaves in another codex, and were cut down to fit. Turner tells us explicitly: 'Ep. 52 has lost its number through the trimming of the page.' What is more regrettable is the absence, from whatever cause, of numbering to four of the quaternions, where we might expect it. We can be grateful that the signature of at least one of the gatherings has survived (xvii).

[1] In no other surviving MS is ep. 57 immediately followed by ep. 52.
[2] For this reason von Soden derives H not from F, but from one of F's ancestors.

CHAPTER III

A 'Well-established Family' of Letters and the Holkham MS

To appreciate the bearing of the order of the letters in T (and D) on the different collections of treatises, we have to review the contents of a number of MSS that are already well known and, following up various indications, especially those provided by the Holkham MS, we may thus be able to classify them a little better than has been done as yet.

Hartel had grouped, as his first family, L, N, and P. These were studied together, as to their contents and order, by Dom Ramsay in 1902.[1] His table may be usefully reproduced here (with two additions):

```
L   [I IV VI V XII XIII VII VIII X XI IX 58]              III  63  6
N                                       10 App. xi IX     III  63  6
P   I X IX 37 38 10 V VII VIII XI XII XIII IV VI          III  63  6

L   55 10 28 37 11 38 39    60 76 73 71 70 XIV 74 69ᵃ 69ᵇ 67 64 2 13 App. iii
N   55    28 37 11 38 39    60 76 73 71 70 XIV 74    69   67 64 2 13 App. iii
P   55    28    11    39 58 60 76 73 71 70 XIV 74 69ᵃ 69ᵇ 67 64 2 13

L   43 65 52 1 56 3 47 45 48 44 61 46 57 59 II 66    40  4 72 51 54 32 20 12
N   43 65 52 1 56 3 47 45 48 44 61 46 57 59          40  4 72 51 54 32 20 12
P   43 65 52 1 56 3 47 45 48 44 61 46 57 59    66 II 40 [4 72 51 54 32 20 12

L   30
N   30  II 66 cena App. xi
P   30] App. iii (imperfect)
```

The two additions (in square brackets) are (i) the list of contents of L's first volume (which explains, incidentally, the absence of 58 at least in L after 39, where it appears in P), and (ii) the eight letters at the end of P, which are all given in P's table of contents though absent in the body of the codex.[2]

---

[1] J.T.S. iii (1901–2) 585–94.

[2] The reason of this omission becomes obvious from a comparison of P with Metz, 224 of the eleventh century. Both were copying the same MS which had come to pieces at the end, losing a number of bifolia (including the last quire altogether), and mixing up the leaves that remained. Metz 224 copied what was left as it stood, regardless of the repeated lack of continuity (cf. von Soden, p. 257, for the essential data: a little ingenuity can restore the original layout of the quaternions). P (two centuries earlier!) recognized the situation and omitted the mutilated letters, but copied the *De laude martyrii*

No one will deny that the overwhelming correspondences in the letters point to a common source. App. iii, the *De laude martyrii*, is spurious and has been inserted in various places in different collections; here, in P, we find it at the end, as we might expect, but also (in L and N) after 13—a suitable place, since this letter opens with the praises of those who have suffered torture for the faith. If, as we saw, 37 and 38 were deliberately put by P among the treatises, their place in the original collection is clear from L and N. The positions of 10 and 58 will call for special consideration presently, as also the fact that in N ep. 69 is not divided in two, a very rare occurrence.

But so far we have nothing to suggest the contents of the first volume which went with that basic collection of letters. Dom Ramsay excludes the P treatises (and he may well be right in doing so) and suggests those of the lost first volume of the Lorsch Cyprian. As against both, it would seem that the Holkham MS has a claim to be heard, even though it is of the fifteenth century. The fact that it, and it alone among all the MSS of Cyprian, preserves a letter which, corrupt as it now is, appears to be genuine, suggests that it perpetuates a collection of Cyprian's works of the greatest antiquity.[1] As its letters follow those of N, the Monte Cassino MS, most closely, they can be profitably put side by side.

Ho   I IV VI V VII VIII XI X XII 58 *Silv.* 10   63 6 55 28
N   (*Silv.*) 10 App. xi IX III 63 6 55 28

Ho   37 11 38 39 60 76 73 71 70 XIV 74 69 67 64 2 13 App. iii 43 65 52 1
N   37 11 38 39 60 76 73 71 70 XIV 74 69 67 64 2 13 App. iii 43 65 52 1

Ho   56 3 47 45 48 44 61 46 57 59 40 4 72 51 54 32 20 12 30 II 66 *cena* IX
N   56 3 47 45 48 44 61 46 57 59 40 4 72 51 54 32 20 12 30 II 66 *cena* App. xi

From 63 to *cena* we have absolute identity of contents and order. Moreover, not only is 69 not divided, but in ep. 55 there is a big lacuna several pages long, identically, in the two MSS. It runs from 628. 12 to 639. 3; in N it is found on fol. 73^r, in Ho on the last line of fol. 60^r.

The next thing to notice is the combination '58 *Silv.* 10' in Ho, coming before the common succession of letters. In N, 10 precedes them too, but not in L, so that if the first half of L could explain the absence of 58

(App. iii) as far as it went, not noticing the lacuna of two folios which occurs near the start (26. 10–30. 6). This lacuna recurs exactly in the Metz MS, and together with the common loss of the end of that treatise (45. 13–52. 7), confirms the above reconstruction.

[1] Cf. M. Bévenot, 'A New Cyprianic Fragment', in *Bulletin of the John Rylands Library*, vol. 28 i (1944) 76–82. The new letter is referred to as '*Silv.*', being addressed to Silvanus and others.

among the letters in N as well as in L, it cannot explain the absence of 10 among those of N. Nor has 10 in N been merely transferred to the beginning from after 55 (where it stands in L), for it came from a MS in which the new letter, *Silv.*, preceded 10 as it does in Ho.

This is proved by the *incipit* to ep. 10 in N which reads as follows: 'Incipit epistula Cypriani ad Silvanum et Regianum martyres in metallo constitutos.' Anyone reading ep. 10 will be as puzzled as Dom Ramsay was in 1902 by this 'extraordinary, and as it would seem unique, title'. It is, in fact, the title of the new letter *Silv.* which precedes it in Ho. There the title reads '*Cipriani Silvano Regino et Donatiano incipit*'.[1] The simplest explanation of this mistake is that in some ancestor of N these two letters followed each other (as they do in Ho), and that while the insignificance or illegibility of *Silv.* led to its being omitted, its *explicit* was by mistake transformed into the *incipit* of ep. 10.

A final indication that Ho represents a basic order for these and many other MSS is the connexion that exists between 58 and 10. They are found together, breaking the sequence of letters, in M and Q; and if they are separated in L (58 at the end of the first volume, and 10 *inserted* after 55), we have evidence that this is the result of a forcible divorce. For the heading of 10 in L reads: '*Incipit Thibari ad martyras et confessores.*' Now ep. 58 is the letter '*ad Tibaritanos*' or, as Ho innocently expresses it '*Plebi Tibari constitutis*' (P has '*ad Thebaritanos*'). The heading of 10 in L can only be explained by its having picked up the name *Thibari* from the *explicit* of the preceding letter, viz. 58. The same hybrid heading for 10 is found also in W and Y, two MSS which must also be included in this group, as we shall see.

The evidence of these much earlier MSS (L, M, Q, W, Y, of the 9th cent.; N of the 11th), therefore confirms the basic nature of the order in Ho (15th cent.). The stages were (1) *Silv.* was dropped, but a trace of it was left in N; (ii) its removal brought 58 and 10 together, as we find them in MQ; but (iii) even in some MSS in which they are separated, they have left traces of their having once been together—so LWY. It is difficult to explain the facts otherwise.

If, then, we accept the order of Ho as basic, we may conclude that when it was in two volumes, the second began with 63. The tendency

---

[1] Dom Ramsay on discovering the new letter in Ho, immediately recognized the title which had puzzled him before. In a private letter to Mr. C. W. James, the librarian at Holkham, he wrote in 1919: 'N does not contain the letter which has been photographed; but curiously enough the Incipit of the unedited letter is attached in the Monte Cassino MS to Ep. 10 which follows in your MS.'

thereafter was to open the second volume with III (the *Testimonia*),[1] and to transfer the odd letters of the first volume to the second. Ep. 58 remained behind in L and presumably in the first volume of N, which must once have been in existence. IX (the *Ad Fortunatum* which has many affinities with III) does not belong to the basic order, which obviously finished before the spurious *cena*. It was tacked on to the end of Ho, just as it often ends the first volume (W, Y, M, Q, T, D, H—it is last but one in L); in N it joins III among the preliminaries to the common collection of letters; in P, as we saw, its subject-matter (*De exhortatione martyrii*) gave it an early place among the treatises.

So far, in this chapter, we have tried to establish the importance of the collection of letters in Ho, and especially the fact that the group 58 *Silv.* 10 originally lay outside the second volume so that its position after the treatises in Ho suggests that these three letters were in fact at the end of the first volume. That should mean that the treatises which precede these three letters are the treatises that correspond to the collection found in the second volume. The importance of this is obvious. If we find old collections of treatises in the same order as that of Ho, it is likely that they represent the first volumes of N and L, as well as those that should go with the second half of Pk, &c. Both L's (missing) first volume and the first half of Pk will then have to be considered either as independent first volumes, or as rearrangements of the order found in Ho.

Actually several notable MSS have this order in their treatises, and the first two, Y and W, which have already been mentioned, will throw fresh light on the collection of the letters too.

Ho   I IV VI V VII VIII XI X XII XIII

$\left.\begin{matrix} \text{Y} \\ \text{W} \end{matrix}\right\}$ I IV VI V VII VIII XI X XII XIII IX

To these must be added the pair p and m (**M**), of the eleventh century,[2]

---

[1] That III was not originally between treatises and letters is a likely deduction (i) from its separate existence in A and at the beginning of W (written a generation before the rest of the MS, cf. *Libri S. Kyliani*, p. 33); (ii) from its absence in the twelfth-century MS, Paris, Bibl. Nat., Lat. 1655, which is almost identical with the list of the second volume in W and Y; (iii) from its absence in k, the Metz MS which is a sister of P; (iv) from its place at the very end (after a *spurium*) in another sister of P, Cues 36. On the other hand, it is very long and rather dull, so that it may have been thrown out at any time.

[2] 'p' represents Vat. Lat. 202 (from the famous library of the hermits of the Holy Cross *de Fonte Avellana*, in the diocese of Gubbio); 'm' is Mantua, B III 18 (from the important Benedictine abbey of Padolirone, or Polirone, not far from Mantua; the village is today called S. Benedetto Po). These two often agree with Baluze's *Burgundicus*.

the group **E** of the twelfth century,[1] and μ with its numerous parallel MSS of the fifteenth century.[2] All these add IX at the end, but the ten preceding treatises have the order of Ho.

Ho, then, of the fifteenth century, does not stand alone, and its claim to be the original first volume can now be contrasted with those of P and L:

Ho I   IV VI V VII VIII XI X XII XIII
P   I X IX 37 38 10   V VII VIII XI   XII XIII IV VI

It is just possible that P represents merely a rearrangement of the old collection, at least from V onwards, but as Dom Ramsay pointed out and verification confirms, the text of 10 in P bears no affinity with that of L, and the same may be said of the letters 37 and 38. It looks, then, as if, at least for its first six items, P was drawing on a different tradition; as for the rest, the question can be left open for the present.

But if we compare the list of L's (missing) first volume with the contents of Ho, we are quite at sea after the first four items:

Ho   I IV VI V   VII VIII XI X   XII XIII   58
[L] I IV VI V XII XIII VII VIII   X XI   IX 58

There may be reminiscences here of the older order, but no one would suppose that this was the original order from which the others sprang.[3] For besides P and L, there is another large body of MSS (from the 9th cent. on) including the 'Cistercian' MSS, which only differ at one point from the order in Ho. The oldest is the Oxford MS D already mentioned.

Ho   I IV VI V VII VIII XI X XII XIII
D   I IV VI V VII VIII XI   XII XIII X IX

That these are related is clear; and the preceding evidence is in favour of regarding the order of D, &c., as depending on that of Ho, and not vice versa.

There is a piece of counter-evidence which would seem to upset our conclusions with regard to Ho, but which on closer scrutiny finally confirms them. At the same time it will explain why it was said above that T's letters [which are the same as D's] belonged to a 'well-established family, with a recognizable order of contents'.

We have seen that Y and W are early ninth-century MSS whose

---

[1] **E** represents a group of nine MSS—all but one in England—which will be dis‧cussed later. The most important are Brit. Mus., Royal 6 B XV, and Arundel 217; Lambeth 106; Oxford, Bod. 210—all of the twelfth century.

[2] μ is Munich, Lat. 18203. This bears corrections made at Tegernsee, but it came from Italy where several sister MSS survive, of which the most striking is 559 (Rome, Bibl. Vallicelliana, D 21).

[3] The constituent parts of [L] will be investigated later (cf. pp. 43–44).

treatises agree with those of Ho. Those MSS both contain a list of contents of their second volume (now lost), obviously copied out from their common source. There is no reason for supposing that the second volume was intruded from another tradition—quite the contrary, as we shall see. We should, therefore, expect these lists to agree with the contents of Ho. Actually we find wide discrepancies. It is not a question merely of a block of letters transferred from one position to another (as we notice in T and D, or again in M and Q), but of the presence of a block of letters also found together in many other MSS (T, D, M, Q, **E**, and all but one of the many 15th-cent. descendents of P, &c.), letters which are *scattered* in Ho. This block consists of the letters:

13, 43, 65, 1, 61, 46

(to which others might be added, but they are here neglected to simplify the presentation. Once the key is found, the further complications can easily be disentangled.)

This block (with two more) forms one of the 'groups' into which Dom Chapman divided the sources of our surviving MSS, in a pioneer article on the subject.[1] But his comment on it is significant: 'This is a scratch collection, if it is really a collection.' Von Soden, besides showing in his chart how often this block of letters recurs in the MSS, says no more than that these six are usually found together.[2] The temptation to treat them as an original, if haphazard, group is obvious. Actually it is a derivative group, and it is derived from the order of Ho. That it thereupon had such a wide vogue only enhances the antiquity of that order. The proof is simple.

It will be remembered that when we were dealing with the three letters which in P are inserted among the treatises, we were not surprised that there were corresponding gaps among the letters. Something similar has happened here, though we are unable to determine its every detail. An ancestor of W tried to collect together all the letters to Cornelius, scattered as they were in his model. That, with a certain rearrangement of matter, explains the creation of our block of letters.

Ho	64 2		13 App. iii 43 65 *52* 1 *56* 3 *47 45 48 44* 61 46 *57 59* 40
[W]	64 2 ad Corn. vii 13		43 65 1 61 46
Ho	4	72 . . . II	
[W]	4 II *56* 3 72		

The letters to Cornelius in Ho are italicized, and their transference

---

[1] *J.T.S.* iv (1902–3) 114–15.   [2] *Briefsammlung*, p. 102.

as a group to before 13 in [W] is the fundamental reason behind our new block. App. iii was probably not in the original ancestor of Ho, as we have already seen, and 56 and 3 have been transferred to the end. The essential points are (i) that there is nothing in [W] which was not in Ho's ancestor, and (ii) our block of letters is in the same order as they were there, the gaps being explained by the extraction of the Cornelius letters and by one other transference.[1]

One cannot explain it the other way round, viz. that W's was the original order and Ho a derivative from it. Besides the unlikelihood of the Cornelius collection being broken up once it was gathered together, we should have to suppose that its *disiecta membra* were then put in the positions where they occur not only in N and Ho but also in P (which had not yet collected the Cornelius letters). The conclusion can only be that our block of letters, found in so many important MSS, so far from undermining the originality of the contents and order of Ho, only enhances its importance as the most faithful descendant of the head and source of several distinct groups of MSS, each of which has, in its own way, contributed to establish the antiquity of that family of letters.

Anyone not yet convinced may care to read the next chapter. For others it may have an interest of its own, though it contributes little to the main purpose of this book. It deals with a certain technique useful for the reconstruction of lost ancestors of our MSS, and introduces an example of the 'second volume' of Cyprian's letters, which by its antiquity must play an important part in any future edition of the *Testimonia* and of the letters themselves. It adds another piece of the jig-saw puzzle to those which already fit about Ho, and gives final assurance that we have got Ho in its right place.

[1] The lists in WY give us no indication which of the letters to Cornelius were here collected nor how they were arranged. Actually there are nine in Ho. However, W and Y end with 72, and so may not have had 51 in their model. The other letter omitted was more probably 48 than 60, as 48 disappears from all the collections of letters made between the ninth and fourteenth centuries, whereas 60 is in all of them and generally heads the Cornelius group. The MS most like WY has a group of only six of these letters, those that have a group of seven are H and R. Thus:

Paris, Lat. 1655 (12th cent.)	60	57	59			47	45	44
H	60	57	59		52	47	45	44
R		57	59	60	52	47	45	44

CHAPTER IV

Lacunae: Clues to Older Non-extant MSS; the John Rylands Cyprian

DR. PAUL MAAS in his *Textkritik* (p. 9)[1] calls attention to the fact that, whereas one MS may often borrow readings from another (of perhaps a quite different tradition), it will hardly ever borrow a lacuna. Hence lacunae, especially if they are of some length, are an indication of direct transmission in one tradition. Not that direct transmission is necessarily involved between two surviving MSS; only that they must go back at least to a common ancestor. Thus if A and B are two surviving MSS with the same lacuna, their relationship may be not only:

A   B
| or |
B   A,

but they may also be related thus:

where X and Y are MSS no longer extant, and all four share the same lacuna which originated in X. This is the essential pattern of the relationship between N and Ho owing to the common lacuna in ep. 55, which we have already noticed (p. 30), N corresponding to A and Ho to B. Ho (15th cent.) was certainly not copying N (11th cent.), but somewhere they had a common source. Of course, X and Y may each represent several MSS in succession, and again Y may not have existed at all, if Ho leap-frogged back to the common source. This same lacuna in ep. 55 will return for consideration presently.

We must distinguish different kinds of lacunae. Some are quite short and may represent a line or two omitted owing to homoeoteleuton, or by sheer accident. Where they represent a folio, a double folio, or one or more quaternions, two cases must be carefully distinguished: (i) where

[1] *Textual Criticism*, p. 8.

the loss of folio, &c., has occurred in a MS which survives, and (ii) where the loss occurred in an ancestor of that MS, but was not noticed at the time of transcription. The text will run on, oblivious of any gap, on the same page. That is what we find in N and Ho for the lacuna in ep. 55. The merely material loss (i) simply deprives us of the text of the lacuna and does not otherwise help us;[1] but the evidence of loss in an ancestor may provide precious information about that ancestor and help us to place the MS which has provided that evidence in its proper relation to others.

Similar help can come from transpositions, which give rise to 'pseudo-lacunae', i.e. lacunae at one place of a MS which are made up for, later, in another place. If in both places the text runs on, unconscious of any break, we may be sure of what happened: not that the scribe, noticing his mistake, wrote in later what he had left out, but that a folio or folios in the model had got out of position in the binding process, and that the scribe was unaware of it.[2] Such occurrences may enable us to determine the amount which a folio, or a quaternion, contained in the non-extant model, and even at times to determine its quaternions and their order. And by 'model' we mean that MS in which the transposition of folios, &c., actually occurred, which may have been several generations before the MS we are now handling.

Our MS P of the ninth century provides examples both of lacunae and of pseudo-lacunae in its model. In the *Ad Donatum* near the beginning of the MS, there is a passage which has been misplaced. On fol. 2ᵛ, col. 1, the text having reached 5. 10 (Hartel's page and line) runs on imme-diately with 9. 1 to 10. 18, where it picks up 5. 10 again and continues without a break. [The scribe of P must have noticed the mistake in the course of his work, for when he reached 9. 1, he *re-wrote* 9. 1–10. 18 and placed '*Vacat*' alongside his first writing of the passage.] A comparison of the length of 9. 1–10. 18 with what precedes its first appearance (3. 3–5. 10) and what follows it (5. 10–9. 1), shows that in the 'model' the middle bifolium of the first quire had been placed beyond the next folio, i.e. the folios of the first quaternion had come to be arranged thus:

---

[1] This is true of an otherwise complete MS, but in the case of fragments more or less consecutive, the actual lacunae may tell us much of the constitution of the codex from which it came. We made use of them in reconstituting several quaternions of F (*c.* A.D. 400) and were thus able to relate these fragments to H (12th cent.) (cf. above, Chapter II).

[2] Examples of this are not uncommon; cf. A. C. Clark, *The Descent of Manuscripts*, pp. 270–1, 327, &c.

38   *Lacunae: Clues to Older Non-extant MSS;*

1 2 3 6 4 5 7 8. We are thus given the lengths of 6, and of 4+5, which are respectively 39 and 79 lines of Hartel's edition. This gives about 40 lines to the folio, which is exactly the amount which precedes the pseudo-lacuna. Hence fol. 3 will have contained the beginning of the *Ad Donatum*. Folios 1 and 2 were taken up with the long and detailed table of contents (which we find in P), and most probably with an elaborate *Incipit* for the first treatise. Hence fols. 3–6, in their original order contained the following:

3 Bene admones . . . (3. 3) – . . . vel usurpatum (5. 10)   = 40 lines
⎰ 4 (inter)diu senio . . . (5. 10) – .   .   .   .   .   ⎱
⎱ 5 .   .   .   .   – ut saginatus (9. 1) ⎰   = 79 lines
6 in poenam .   .   .   (9. 1) – . . . vitiis principem (10. 18) = 39 lines

We may take it, then, at least as a working hypothesis, that a folio of P's 'model' contained approximately 40 lines of Hartel's printed text.

This hypothesis is confirmed by other lacunae in P's 'model'. Thus on fol. 85^v, col. 2, the text runs from the middle of XIII, *De zelo et livore* (430. 7) into the middle of IV, *De habitu virginum* (197. 19), the missing parts adding up to about 326 lines. With about 40 lines to the folio, this gives us 8 folios, and we conclude that a quaternion of the model had been lost. Exactly the same amount is missing at fol. 161^r, col. 1, where the first part of ep. 6 (482. 10) runs into the middle of ep. 55 (636. 8). At fol. 255^r, col. 1, is the lacuna in the *De laude martyrii* already referred to as being two folios long.[1] What follows (and breaks off) comes to 285 lines (8×36—the print in Hartel's Appendix is smaller), and represents a quaternion. The fact that all these lacunae occur also in k (Metz 224) along with the dismemberment and confusion of the final letters there,[2] shows that that MS was copying the 'model' itself which P was following. There, the last four quaternions had suffered losses and rearrangements which can be reconstructed as follows:

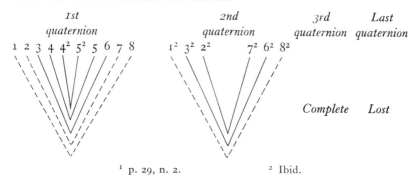

[1] p. 29, n. 2.   [2] Ibid.

Broken lines represent lost leaves; 1^2, 2^2, &c., represent the original folios of the second quaternion. The central bifolium of the second quaternion (4^2 5^2) had been inserted in the middle of the first, which had lost its two exterior bifolia. The second quaternion had also lost its external bifolium, and the two remaining bifolia interchanged places. *De laude martyrii* began on 6^2, so that both P and k here have a lacuna of two folios (7^2 8^2). But k actually contains the text of the first half of that lacuna, earlier on, since it copied 7^2 before 6^2.

This selection of lacunae in P—there is at least one more, from the *Testimonia* (87. 19–101. 19)—illustrates the value of such gaps in throwing light on lost ancestors, besides establishing the lengths of folio and quaternion in the model of Pk and the greater fidelity of k to that model.[1] It also prepares the way for the consideration of X (Manchester, John Rylands Lib., Lat. 15) and of its relation to Ho.

X is a MS of the late eighth century whose fortunes we can trace back to the fifteenth century when it was in the famous library of Murbach in Alsace, and it was probably written in the scriptorium there.[2] It is a 'second volume' of Cyprian's works, and save for the *Testimonia*, which was originally its opening piece, as we shall see, it contains nothing which is not in Ho, and its omissions are few. What is most striking is that the bulk of the letters follow the order of Ho, only about a dozen inserting themselves at different places in that order. The evidence that the MS which X was copying was in a dilapidated condition is sufficient to justify the conjecture that these 'insertions' were transferences within the same MS.

In the following comparison of the two MSS, the top line gives the contents of Ho; the second the contents of X which agree in having the same order, together with an indication (i) of the missing letters (marked o, and (ii) of those displaced (marked D); the third shows the new positions which the displaced letters took up in X.

[1] From the amount in a folio and the amount in the whole collection we can calculate the number of folios. P itself is a big codex with some 251 folios of writing, each of which contains about 58 of Hartel's lines. Its model had about 39 such lines to the folio. This means about 373 folios in the 'model'. Lacunae include five quaternions at least, i.e. another 40 folios. This dead reckoning gives a grand total of 413 folios. The probabilities are that it was in two volumes.

Further analysis of the contents of particular folios shows that scripture passages were *indented*. This was the normal practice in the fourth and fifth centuries, and was extremely rare later (cf. E. A. Lowe, 'More Facts about our Oldest Latin MSS', in *Classical Quarterly* xxii (1928) 43–62). It is therefore probable, to say no more, that the MS in question was a very early one.

[2] Cf. *C.L.A.* ii. 222.

Lacunae: Clues to Older Non-extant MSS;

Ho   10   63 6 55 28 37 11 38 39 60 76 73 71 70 XIV   74   69 67 64

X   ___ 10 ∧ III 63 6 55 28 37 11 38 D   D   76 73 71 70 XIV ∧ 74   69ᵃD D 64
39 67 69ᵇ   3

Ho 2   13 App. iii 43 65 52 1 56 3 47 45 48 44 61 46 57 59 40 4   72

X 2   13   0   43 65 52 1 56 3 47 45 D   44 61 46 D   D   40 4   D

72 12 32 20   57 59 48

Ho   51 54   32 20 12 30 II 66 *cena* IX

X   51 54 ∧   D   D   D   0 II 0   0   0
        60

We might have expected the absence of App. iii, which, as we have said, was an intrusion into the original collection, and still more that of *cena*, another *spurium* added at the end, so that IX too, though genuine, falls outside the original collection. Apart from these only 30 and 66 are missing.

We are left, then, with the possibility of displacements, since the lack of any system excludes the likelihood of deliberate rearrangement. Single letters or small groups appear in four or five places of the sequence common to X and Ho; if grounds can be found for considering these as mere displacements, no doubt will be left that X is derived from a MS which followed the order of Ho.

It was not uncommon for a monastery to borrow codices for transcription, and, if there was any hurry, to take them to pieces, distributing the quaternions to different scribes who could thus work simultaneously. For this or similar reasons, a codex when reassembled might have some of its quires displaced or lost, or double leaves and even whole quaternions folded the wrong way round, and though externally it would appear untampered with, its contents would in places be hopelessly confused. This confusion might or might not be noticed the next time it was copied (as we saw in the case of the end of P and of k). Unless the scribe were very intelligent and wide-awake, he would copy out the pages as they came, with the result that parts of the same letter might be separated from each other by parts of another letter, without any indication being left of what had happened.

This can be seen early on in X. Simply from James's Catalogue we can see at once that in the middle of 63 (fol. 76ᵛ) have been inserted the end of 74 and two bits of 69ᵃ—fragments missing from 74 and 69ᵃ, which letters are in their proper places in the series. It is not that leaves of X have been misplaced: the transference had occurred in the MS which X was copying. From the lengths of the bits here, we can reconstruct the original layout of those two letters:

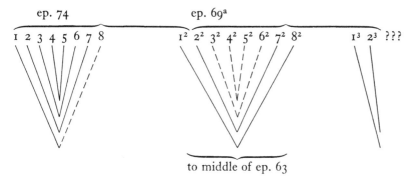

ep. 74   ep. 69ᵃ

1 2 3 4 5 6 7 8   1² 2² 3² 4² 5² 6² 7² 8²   1³ 2³ ???

to middle of ep. 63

The second quaternion came to pieces and lost its two middle double leaves (3^2–6^2); its two outer double leaves were transferred to ep. 63, carrying away the end of ep. 74 and two pieces of ep. 69ᵃ. The previous quire had lost its last leaf, so that its 7th leaf was now followed by 1³, the middle of ep. 74 running into the latter part of ep. 69ᵃ. What happened then, there is no means of telling, but as 69ᵇ and 67 follow 69ᵃ in Ho, and these two letters are found in X as an addition at the beginning, this suggests that the next two quires were also in pieces. We therefore turn now to the beginning of X.

Two things strike us at once: that the first twelve folios are in a different hand from what follows, and that the MS was originally meant to begin with fol. 13, with its fine heading to the *Testimonia*. Besides, fol. 12ᵛ is mostly blank. Those twelve folios are made up of parts of two quaternions, with seven in the first.[1] The next five folios have been bound in the wrong order: the true order is 11, 10, 9, 8, 12, the first three being single leaves, the last two a bifolium. This means that the quaternion originally ended with three blank folios (the last one carrying the no. ii), and that these three were later cut off, which explains why there is no quire-mark. (At a later binding the three loose leaves were put inside the only double-leaf (8–12) for safety, and thoughtlessly bound in there.)[2]

All this indicates that the first twelve folios were prefixed to the volume before the first binding. Combined with the other evidence, it can best

---

[1] The catalogue says that the first quaternion is missing. However, the number at the foot of fol. 7ᵛ is i and not ii (hence the confusion in the numbering of subsequent quires in the catalogue). The sixth folio of the quaternion was cut out before use.

[2] It must be noted that this description is of our present MS X, not of the MS which X was copying. But it throws light on the latter.

be explained by loose folios of the older MS whose proper place could not at first be determined. Thus 39, 67, and 69^b were eventually recovered and copied out. The last of these letters, joined to 69^a as a *single* letter in Ho and N (but nowhere else), follows 69^a in all the MSS we know: it doubtless followed 69^a originally in X's model. 10 was included among these stray letters; something has already been said of its transference from the first volume to the second. 58, a very popular letter, appears nowhere in X; it must have been still in the first volume, as in those of L and of N and, presumably, in that of the ancestor of Ho.

The lacunae and pseudo-lacunae found in X have enabled us to reconstruct in great part the MS which it was copying. Furthermore, they prove that it had the equivalent of about 30 lines of Hartel to the folio.[1] Is it merely a coincidence that from the analysis of the three lacunae in Ho (one of which it shares with N), we find that their common ancestor also had just over 30 Hartel lines to the folio? Was, then, X's immediate model the ancestor also of N and Ho? It is at least possible.

But there is a peculiar piece of evidence which may be significant. One of the many links between N and Ho was, as we noticed, a lacuna in ep. 55. This corresponds to (Hartel) 628. 12–639. 3, and occurs in N on fol. 73^r and in Ho on fol. 60^r. There is no such lacuna in X, yet something happened here which suggests that there was one in its model. The letter starts normally on fol. 85^v, but, soon after, the writing gets smaller and smaller, as if the scribe were trying to get it all into that quaternion—for someone else had already started the next letter (28) on a fresh quaternion. Eventually an extra quaternion was inserted, in *very large* writing, but that was now too much and a folio had to be cut out. The exact sequence of events cannot be determined, but it looks as if, at first, the lacuna was not noticed, then either the missing quaternion was found loose, or else its loss was noticed and made good from another copy. In other words, the trouble here manifest in X can be reasonably explained on the supposition that in the MS which X was copying some folios had gone astray, and if traced at the time were ultimately lost. For the lacuna, in N and Ho, comes to 244 lines in Hartel, which would correspond exactly to a quaternion in X's model.

---

[1] Professor A. Souter in a short, but valuable, article on the abbreviations in X (*Bulletin of the John Rylands Library*, vol. 5, 1918–19), suggests (p. 5 of the off-print) that 'the archetype consisted of short lines of seventeen letters or thereabouts' with 'two or three columns to the page'. With 30 lines of Hartel's edition to the folio, we can conclude: 2 columns to a page, 24 lines to a column, and 17 letters to a line.

CHAPTER V

A Common Ancestor: Ur-Ho

IF the preceding argumentation is well grounded, it leads to the conclusion that in the latter half of the eighth century, when X was written,
there was at Murbach, or in that region, an old MS—which we may be
permitted to call Ur-X—that was the ancestor of at least the second
volumes of LYWPN and Ho. It must have had a first volume, and if P
has an obviously secondary order of contents, we are left with three com-
petitors for the order of its first volume: YW, **L**,[1] and Ho. X, however,
has told us one thing, viz. that 58 was not in its second volume. One
might argue that it was lost along with its other missing folios and quaternions, but it is otherwise so close to HoN that it is reasonable to say that
58 was in its first volume, so that YW are eliminated. As between **L** and
Ho, which both have 58 in the first volume, a fresh piece of evidence
may now be decisive.

We have already noticed that **L** has a peculiar order in its treatises,
and that ep. 58 comes at the end. We know that order only from the old
catalogue of the Lorsch Library, but to compensate us for the loss of
that first volume of Cyprian's works, we have four MSS with precisely
the same contents, one now in Vienna, the other three in the Abbey of
Admont: Vienna, Lat. 850; Admont, 136, 381, and 587. All are of the
twelfth century, the last one belonging to its first half and certainly preserving the best text of the four. Admont 136 contains other works besides, including at the end a heterogeneous collection of Cyprian's letters,
among them ep. 58 again. It is clearly a secondary MS, but shows an
awareness of the loss of two-thirds of ep. 58 in its first transcription. This
defect will explain the absence of the letter in Admont 381, and this in
turn suggests the secondary character of that MS too.

But the two other MSS deserve our attention. They contain exactly
what is in the first volume of L, and in both ep. 58 has the lacuna just
mentioned (658. 22–665. 10).[2] But what is quite peculiar is that the

---

[1] **L** here represents the order of the first volume of L, as given in the Lorsch catalogue. It stands for the joint testimony of the four MSS which have preserved that
order, and which are indicated in the next paragraph.

[2] The lacuna comes to 168 lines in Hartel. From a pseudo-lacuna in L we can judge

treatises are divided into two groups. This is most patent in Admont 587 (henceforth called 'a'), where on fol. 35ʳ at the end of *De zelo et livore* (XIII) is written *Finit pars prior*. The lower part of that leaf has been cut away, and on the blank verso someone has written the first verse of the 'Veni Creator'. Folio 36ʳ begins again, in clear red uncials: 'Incipit altera pars epistolarum eiusdem Cypriani episcopi In primis de Dominica Oratione.' This same rubric is found in Vienna 850, fol. 147ᵛ, and the same division in two parts is implied in Admont 381, where the original table of contents on the first page only goes up to XIII, the rest having been added in subsequently.

Such a division implies that at one time this collection of treatises was itself in two separate volumes, which have otherwise left no trace of their existence.[1] There seems no reason to imagine that the well-established order which we have found in YWmp, &c., was rearranged and broken up into these two parts, so that we are driven to the conclusion that the lost first volume of Lorsch belonged to a *different* tradition from that of its second volume.

By the elimination of both YW and **L** as representative of the original first volume, we are brought back to Ho as representing, in *both* its parts, the original order that is at the back of so many of our important MSS. This is not to suggest that the *text* of Ho itself is of great consequence, in fact it leaves much to be desired even if it cannot be entirely neglected. But it means that the MSS, whose treatises are in the order of Ho, represent a very old tradition and should be treated together. These MSS are primarily Y and W, of the ninth century, m and p of the eleventh, and the English group **E** of the twelfth.[2]

It will be remembered that the starting-point of our study of the

that its predecessor, in which the inversion occurred, averaged 48 such lines to the folio. If the lacuna was due to the loss of folios in an ancestor, they were of a different size from this. For instance, if 4 folios were lost, that would mean their each containing only 42 of Hartel's lines (or even less, in view of the scripture quotations which Hartel spreads out). This would indicate that the volumes in which these lacunae first occurred were of different formats.

[1] If we pressed the meaning of *altera pars*, we might conclude that no volume of letters followed. This would confirm our conclusion that **L** and L did not belong to the one tradition.

[2] In making the collations, **E** was not linked with the others, chiefly because its letters differed almost entirely from those that normally go with its order of treatises. Actually this group **E** has textual peculiarities too that differ from those in the same order, as will be seen from the collations. Its character and importance will, therefore, be dealt with at a later stage. On the other hand, m and p were collated with the others, in spite of having a different collection of letters, because of a number of textual affinities which seemed to justify their inclusion.

division into two volumes was the assertion that D, whose *letters* are identical with those of T, represents 'an original edition' in the sense that both its treatises and at least the nucleus of its letters, come from one and the same tradition. Our study in the preceding chapters has provided the grounds for this assertion.

The letters of D, we then said, 'belong to a well-established family'. They are in fact derived from Ur-X, much as those of YW were. The letters to Cornelius have been grouped together, and have left the same gaps as before in what followed. The main difference is that the letters to Cornelius begin at the place in Ur-X where 60 (the first of these) stands, and the block of 10 letters that follows 60 there (viz. 76 . . . 2) has been put off till later. Thus:

YW   39 58 60 | 76 —— 2 | 'Cornelius letters' | 13 43 65 1 61 46 | . . . . .
DT   39 58 | 60 &c. (= 'Cornelius letters') | 13 43 65 1 61 46 | 66 54 | 76 —— 2 |

No one can doubt that here we have two arrangements of the same collection of letters, and that, as in both arrangements the block of letters 13 . . . 46 is formed by taking the sequence in Ur-X (or Ur-Ho) and extracting the Cornelius letters from it,[1] DT's collection of letters is one derived, at least in great part, from that same source. But if the *treatises* of YW came from that same source, as we have just seen, and those of T obviously do not, the likelihood remains that D's treatises did so too. In fact, as we saw when comparing various first volumes, the order of D's treatises is the same as that of Ho's, save for the shift of X to the end of the collection before the addition of IX.[2] Therefore, apart from the long supplement to be found at the end of D (as of T), D is a descendant, in *both* its parts, from a MS of great antiquity, which had substantially the order and contents of Ho, and which we may call Ur-Ho (identical with Ur-X, if the latter's conjectural first volume is included).[3]

The accompanying table attempts to reproduce our main conclusions. Only the 'second volume' appears in the table itself, the corresponding 'first volumes' being indicated below.

But what unresolved problems it leaves, with all its deceptive simplicity! To give only one instance: App. iii (*De laude martyrii*), found in

[1] Cf. pp. 34–35. It is quite likely that the order found in DT is a *rearrangement* of that found in YW.

[2] Cf. p. 33. That shift may have been due to hesitation caused by a lacuna here in D's model. There is such a lacuna in Ho (356. 16–370. 12) which coming to about 360 lines, would have been 12 folios in Ur-Ho (or Ur-X).

[3] This conclusion had not yet been come to when the collation was made, otherwise D would have been grouped with mpYW, &c.

L, N, and Ho after ep. 13, must have been in some common source, here indicated by (LNHo), but not in (HoX) since it is not found there in any of our other MSS. But then (LNHo) must have had the lacuna in ep. 55, since it is in Ho and N, and the trouble about it in X can be explained by a beginning of dilapidation in (HoX). But then L must have filled in the lacuna somehow—as is suggested in the note.

However, there is an alternative possibility, viz. that App. iii was in (HoX) from the first. If so, X might have lost it owing to the dilapidation, and YW likewise. (Pk) will then have thrown it out from among the letters to put it at the end (where (TD) has it before its long appendix of letters), and (MQ), which was using several sources, had it already when it reached ep. 13.

This simple example suggests of itself the difficulty of expressing the relations existing between MSS by means of conjectural ancestors and archetypes. There are so many unknown factors, that the evidence is capable of more than one interpretation, and any such tabulation will cut Gordian knots, not solve them. It may help to fix certain facts in the mind, but it will almost inevitably suggest relationships which may in fact be non-existent.

The conjectured descent of one of the 'second volumes'

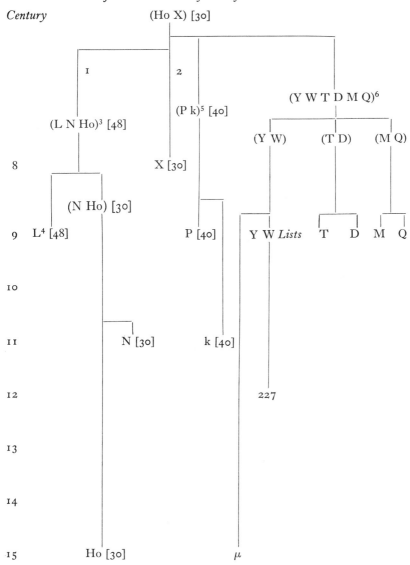

Conjectural MSS are in round brackets. Numbers in square brackets give number of Hartel lines per folio in conjectured ancestor.

1. Lacuna in ep. 55. 4. Lacuna in ep. 55 remedied?
2. Dilapidation of (Ho X). 5. Three letters early in vol. I.
3. Adds App. iii after ep. 13. 6. 'Cornelius' letters grouped.
N.B. A corresponding 'first volume' survives only for Y, W, μ, Ho, and D.

CHAPTER VI

Other Collections of Treatises

THE creation of a stemma such as we have just seen suggests the possibility of recovering the readings of the postulated common source, which
can then be compared with those of other hyparchetypes, as they may be
called, in hopes of discovering those of the archetype if not of the original autograph. It may suggest, too, the possibility of eliminating the
more corrupt members, and so of lessening the labour of collation. But
with the rest of the MSS of St. Cyprian, it must be confessed that there is
little hope of arranging them in similarly constructed stemmata, certainly
not on the basis which we have been chiefly using, viz. the order of contents. A good number of the later MSS can no doubt be classed under one
or other of the earlier ones, but the earlier ones themselves seem to
appear out of the blue, without clue to their relationships one with another. It will suffice to present the state of affairs as it appears in our surviving MSS, confining ourselves to our older ones, and to a few others
which at least keep the main treatises together.

As background we can first recall those with which we have already
dealt:

Collections of treatises

S, YW, mp, **E**, μ, Ho	I IV VI V VII VIII XI X XII XIII (IX)
D, 'Cistercians'	I IV VI V VII VIII XI XII XIII X (IX)
Pk	I X (IX 37 38 10) V VII VIII XI XII XIII IV VI
L (a, &c.)	I IV VI V XII XIII VII VIII X XI (IX 58)
HTh	I IV VI V VII XI VIII X XII XIII (IX)
MQ	I IV VI VII V X VIII XI XII XIII (IX)

In our treatment of these, we have tended to emphasize their differences, only allowing D to be a variation of the first list. But that there is
a general family resemblance among them cannot be denied. It is rather
otherwise in those that follow:

R¹ (Vatican, Reg. lat. 116)	I IV XIII XI VI (58) V VII VIII XII X (IX II) . . .
J² (Angers, Bib. mun. 148)	[I ?] X IV VI XII XIII VIII VII 63 V (IX) XI (10 III)
O³ (Oxford, Bod., Add. C 15)	I X IX VI XI VIII XII VII (63) IV XIII V (II 58 76 58!) . . .
K⁴ (Leyden, Voss. lat. fol. 40)	[I 13] IV (App. ii) VI V XII XIII VIII X IX (11 App. iv) VII . . .
59⁵ (Tours, 256)	I X XII XIII VIII IV V XI VI (58 IX) VII (II III) . . .
G⁶ (St. Gall, 89)	VII XII IX (App. xii–Greg. Naz.) VIII V
B⁷ (Bamberg, Patr. 63)	I IV VI V VIII X XIII XI XII VII (IX III) . . .
214⁸ (Vatican, Reg. lat. 275)	I X XI (IX) XIII XII VIII IV VII V VI . . .
208⁹ (Berne, 235)	I IV X VIII XI XIII XII VI V VII (IX 58 II)

Here, then, we have half a dozen more MSS of the ninth century and three later ones which it seems impossible to co-ordinate with any of the preceding MSS, or with one another. We know, indeed, that displacements are sometimes due to accidental transpositions of quaternions, and that sometimes a selection is first made and then those omitted added as an afterthought (so perhaps in the case of B, above). But any attempt to explain the order of contents of these MSS would be mere guesswork. Until we have studied the text which they each preserve, we must treat them as independent witnesses.

We can not only be reconciled to this necessity but recognize its inevitability if we add to our survey the order of contents of MSS no

---

¹ Beginning of ninth century, in France. At one time, at least, probably at Fleury (cf. Catalogue, Dom Wilmart).

² First half of ninth century, Western France. First quaternion begins with X, but a fragment of I is bound in before it.

³ Early ninth century, precise origin uncertain. Possibly at one time at Murbach, but not written there (B. Bischoff). At V is a new beginning, with different hand, and no more numbering of quaternions.

⁴ First half of ninth century, Northern France. First quaternion missing, two items supplied from allied MSS.

⁵ Middle or later ninth century, Tours? Beginning of I and beginning of X both missing.

⁶ About 900; almost certainly St. Gall.

⁷ Eleventh century; belonged to Cathedral in Bamberg. Order of Ho, except that XI, XII, VII are postponed.

⁸ Twelfth century; belonged to Abbey of Bonneval (O.S.B.), near Chartres. In great part similar to first half of Paris, Lat. 1654 (from Abbey of St. Maur Fossat), the second part of which is identical with Chartres 36 (cf. Bec, below).

⁹ Twelfth century. Order not unlike that of the MS listed in the ninth century Murbach Catalogue. Has a number of peculiar readings of the lost Verona MS, but its order is quite different.

longer extant, as revealed by early writings or in ancient monastery catalogues. Here we find but little that connects with our surviving MSS, and as such testimonies are rare compared with the number of MSS of Cyprian which were once in existence, we may perhaps resign ourselves to remaining in the dark as to the lines of tradition which lie behind the MSS at our disposal.

Ancient lists of treatises

Pontius[1]	I IV VI V VII X VIII XI XII XIII (IX)[2]
Cheltenham List[3]	I IV VI XI X V XIII VIII XII (IX) VII (III) . . .
Augustine[4]	X IV XIII VII VI XII V VIII (II) XI
Reichenau Catal.[5]	I X IV XII VII XIII VI VIII XI (IX) V (63, 58 II) . . .
Murbach Catal.[6]	I IV X VIII XI XII XIII V VII VI (IX 58 II III) . . .
Latini's Veronensis[7]	I IV XI XIII V VIII X XII VI (IX) VII III . . .
Latini's Beneventanus[8]	V XI VIII XII (63 30?) VI· IV XIII (App. vii IX III) . . .
Bec Catal.[9]	(Epp. no. xvi) I X (IX) XIII XII VIII IV V VI (. . . III)
Erfurt Catal.[10]	I (13) IV (App. ii) VI V (II) XII XIII VIII X (IX) VII (63, 11, App. iv, 58) XI
Pontigny Catal.[11]	I IV VI V VII VIII XI XII XIII X (IX App. iii III) . . .

One could add to the list by including evidence later than the twelfth century, since some of it might refer to very old MSS not previously recorded. But both here and in what follows, evidence even from the

---

[1] *Vita C. Cypriani*, 7 (*C.S.E.L.* III. xcvii).

[2] With Mengis and Turner, against von Soden and H. Koch, who replace IX by some of the letters. Ho differs from this order only by having X two places later.

[3] Phillipps 12266 (now London, Robinson collection), tenth century; and St. Gall 133, ninth century. The list is dated A.D. 359.

[4] Serm. 26 (Guelf), cf. G. Morin, *Miscellanea Agostiniana*, i. 530–1.

[5] Of A.D. 822.   [6] Of A.D. 840. Cf. order of the Berne MS above.

[7] Sixth century, if Latini's conviction that it was 1,000 years old can be relied on. In the letters, some attempt had been made to group them according to subject-matter or destination (von Soden).

[8] 'Mirae vetustatis'. 30 is suggested by von Soden for a missing item. There were some lacunae in the model of this MS, but its order seems to have been kept.

[9] Twelfth century (cf. *214* above).

[10] 1410–12. Of the Collegium Amplonianum. Probably F 90 in that library, of the fourteenth century (cf. K above).

[11] Twelfth century. This order is the same as that of D (Oxford, Laud Misc. 451) and of the eleventh-century MS from Moissac (our *122*; now Paris, Lat. 1656A). The latter contains only the first volume (i.e. up to III) and is followed by the Apologeticum of Tertullian. This same combination is also found in the Cluny MS, mentioned in their 1158–61 Catalogue. D, *122*, and Cluny all have Prudentius's poem on Cyprian's martyrdom preceding the treatises.

thirteenth century has been omitted, save in the case of England because of a peculiarly interesting document of that period.

The variety in the order of contents helps to remind us of the six centuries which separate our oldest more or less complete MSS from the days of Cyprian himself. Our surviving MSS depend on unknown intermediaries, with unknown orders of contents save for a tiny handful. How many they were, and which of them contributed to our surviving collections, who can say? As it is, even a rapid perusal of the works of Becker, Lehmann, Lesne, and Ruf suggests the enormous number of copies which once existed, if we may judge from the not inconsiderable number which chance and industry have rescued from complete oblivion.

For, to complete our survey, we must add the evidence which we have of MSS of Cyprian of which we do *not* know the contents. In some cases we have fragments which can be dated approximately, and of which we may know where they were at some time or other, but little or nothing more. We have examples of collections of two or three treatises and perhaps a letter or two. And when we pass to the surviving catalogues of ancient libraries, they rarely give the full contents, most having simply *Item epistole S. Cypriani*. But catalogues do tell us that at the time of writing there was a copy of some works by Cyprian in the library they are describing. Similarly, a writer who quotes Cyprian most likely had at his disposal the works which he quotes.

For France, we have fragments of the fifth and eighth centuries, which were long at FLEURY. So too a collection of four treatises (Paris, Lat. 13047) of the eighth century at CORBIE. We know that Florus annotated our S (of about 500), at LYONS in the ninth century. P of the ninth comes from ST-DENYS, and its brother k of the twelfth is still at Metz.

From catalogues and writers we know of the presence of Cyprians:

in the *ninth century*, at St-Wandrille, St-Germer de Flay, Ferrières, Rheims;

in the *eleventh century*, at Chartres, Massay, Cluny, St-Epvre in Toul, Lobbes;

in the *twelfth century*, at Maillezais, Angers [= ours of the 9th cent.?] Bec, Mont-Saint-Michel, Tournai, St-Amand, Arras, Stavelot, Cluny (two more), Moissac [= our *122* of the 11th cent.]. Also, 'before 1200', at Cysoing and Angoulême.

For Germany and Switzerland, our catalogues tell us of Cyprians:

in the *ninth century* at Würzburg [= our W of the early 9th] and at St. Gallen [= our G?];

in the *twelfth century* at Bamberg [= our B of the 11th], and at Hirschau.

For Italy we have the fragmentary *fifth-century* MSS at Turin (G V 37, from Africa?, *C.L.A.* iv. 464, cf. 444) and at Brescia (H VI 11, *C.L.A.* iii. 283); also the Pomposa Catalogue of 1093.

Of the existence of copies of Cyprian's works in England in the Middle Ages, we have as evidence first of all the seven MSS still in the country, which are traceable to the B.M. fragments (**E**). One of these (Camb. Pemb. 154) from BUILDWAS, is mentioned in the Franciscan compilation of patristic and other works in England made at the end of the thirteenth century: *Registrum librorum angliae.*[1] This became better known as worked up by John Boston of Bury St. Edmunds under the name of *Catalogus scriptorum ecclesiae.* But in the case of Cyprian he only gives the contents of the copy in his own library (as is shown by his carefully noting the first and last words in each piece) and he ignores all the rest. The order of contents, if it really is the order found in his BURY MS, is:

App. xii, I VI App. vi, V VII VIII XI XII XIII X IX III IV App. iii, 55, 73 63 47 App. vii

From the earlier work, the *Registrum*, we can only be sure of the order of the bulk of the treatises at the Augustinian monastery of HEXHAM, and it suggests that this MS can be classed with **E**. After *Epistole* (which is sometimes all that is reported for a monastery), we have IV VI V VII VIII XI X XII XIII, which is the Ho order, and so that of **E**.

Of other monasteries, we have the contents (but not their order) of the Cyprians at the Cistercian houses at FORDE (Devon) and MARGAM (Glam.); and also at Christ Church, CANTERBURY. The rest of our indications are vague, either ascribing merely *epistole* or one or two treatises to the place in question. It is clear that these are merely summary indications, since, for example, we still have the SALISBURY Cyprian (No. 9 in its catalogue), which contains five treatises (it comes from G)—and yet the *Registrum* only records two of them there.[2] With these reservations, we can add to our list:

Bodmin, Kelso, Bordesley, St. Mary's Winton, Woburn, St. Albans, Buildwas, St. Mary's York, Cirencester, Salisbury,

---

[1] Oxford, Bod., Tanner 165, fols. 103–20; cf. Cambridge, Peterhouse 169, fols. 54ᵛ–61.
[2] To give but one other example, a number of surviving Exeter MSS, known to have been there at the time of the compilation of the *Registrum*, are not mentioned in it.

Dunfermline, Merevale, Rochford, Bradenstoke, St. Andrews, Crowland, Clifford, and Wenlock.[1]

Of the 500 or more monastic libraries in England, the Franciscans visited less than 100. Furthermore, their inventory of these was demonstrably incomplete, and Cyprian comes rather low in their scale of interest. Yet here we have over twenty actually recorded. Were some of these (and those not recorded) perhaps very old? And what models had they copied? Several no doubt went back to the MS of the B.M. fragments; but we know that Bede's Cyprian was of a different family, and we cannot say what kind of Cyprian was in Aldhelm's hands when he wrote his *De laudibus virginitatis*. Our knowledge of the MSS of those centuries is too fragmentary to hope to trace the ancestry of those which followed them and have survived.

Our study of the 'External Evidence' has only given us a few fixed points; it has enabled us to group a few of our MSS together. It is time we turned our attention to the 'Internal Evidence'.

---

[1] The order is that given in the *Registrum*, for all the details of which I am deeply indebted to Professor R. A. B. Mynors.

PART II

INTERNAL EVIDENCE: THE TEXT OF THE
DE ECCLESIAE CATHOLICAE UNITATE

T H E expression 'external evidence' has been taken in a very wide sense, so as to include even lacunae which occur in the MSS. The 'internal evidence', on the other hand, which will now occupy our attention, is taken in a very precise sense, viz. the MS witness to *the text* of Cyprian's treatises. To make the meaning quite clear: this will include (where available) quotations made by early and medieval writers, because these, even when not quoting verbatim, may provide evidence of the text in the MS which they used at the time, quite as much as do the MSS of Cyprian themselves. Even though the extant MSS of these authors should date several centuries after their originals, they are at least as good evidence as Cyprianic MSS of the same date. They may even be better; for a scribe copying a Papal letter, for instance, which contained a quotation from Cyprian, was less likely to 'correct' it by comparing it with a Cyprianic MS, than one who was actually at work on another Cyprianic MS. For this reason, though we shall rarely have occasion to use the evidence of such authors, it has here been included as part of the 'internal evidence', though from other points of view, it would usually be regarded as 'external'. Suffice that it should be evidence of the *text*.

It would be foolish to pretend that in the classification of MSS these two types of evidence can be kept separate. They act and react on each other. Thus in the first part of this study, the internal evidence was playing an important if mostly hidden part. The basis of the first rough classification tabulated at the end of the Introduction, was not only the order of contents, and the various ways in which PT 'contaminated' TR in *De unitate*, chap. 4, but also the textual readings in that chapter and in chap. 19. Inevitably, too, some of the results of a rough collation of the

MSS affected the choice of the MSS treated there in any detail. Similarly, in the present part, advantage will be taken of anything that has been established from the 'external' evidence, and surmises made there will be tested by the textual evidence.

As was indicated in the Introduction, our aim here is to provide a basis for the selection of those MSS which, in combination, should enable an editor to produce a reliable text of Cyprian's treatises. The method is to study one of these treatises closely, to establish its text as accurately as possible, and from the critical apparatus to deduce which of the MSS used seem to promise the best results. The treatise chosen as the *corpus vile* is the *De ecclesiae catholicae unitate*, and it is reasonable to assume that the results will be applicable to all the treatises so called, with the certain exception of the *Testimonia* (III), and the possible exception of the *Ad Fortunatum* (IX).[1] The *Quod idola dii non sint* (II) can be treated as spurious: both the evidence of its place in the MSS and especially its contents seem decisive against it. The mind that was responsible for it was not the mind of Cyprian.[2] III and IX are almost entirely made up of Scripture texts and, if for no other reason, call for special treatment. If IX generally appears with the other treatises, III gives the appearance of being tacked on, either at the end of the first volume, or at the beginning of the second, so that at least in many cases it will not have shared the same experiences as the *De unitate*, and conclusions derived from the text of the latter cannot safely be applied to it. However, the results of the present study may well provide a first orientation for these two treatises too, and (to a much lesser extent) even for the letters, or at least a good number of them.

[1] Cf. p. 138, n. 1, where it is suggested how the results can be used for the *Ad Fortunatum* too.

[2] Its authenticity is still maintained in some distinguished quarters. H. Koch devoted 78 pages to its defence in his *Cyprianische Untersuchungen* (1926), yet he did not even mention its non-Cyprianic use of *altare* for a heathen altar, and of *vulgus* for the 'common herd', crucial facts already pointed out by Watson in 1896 (*Studia Biblica*, iv. 193, n. 2).

CHAPTER VII

The Alternative Version of Chapter 4 (PT) and the Tradition of its MSS

At the outset we are confronted with a special problem which will have
to be borne in mind throughout. It is a complex many-sided problem. A
previous study of *De unitate*, chap. 4, led to the conclusion that Cyprian
revised this chapter (and also chap. 19), and that there were therefore
two editions of this treatise. Whether this was so or not (and no conclu-
sive argument has yet been adduced against it), the MSS present us with
two versions of this chapter, one the more common, TR (= *Textus
receptus*), the other, rarely but solidly evidenced, PT (= 'Primacy' Text).[1]
This rarer text is preserved wholly—or practically so—in four ways, in
as many 'families'. Family 1, represented by one MS alone, H, contains
PT without a trace of TR. Family 3 contains both texts in immediate
succession: PT+TR, its chief representatives being the sister MSS, M
and Q. Family 4 also presents both texts one after the other, but the last
two sentences of PT are transferred to the middle of TR, where they
replace the two sentences to which they are parallel. So the Vatican MS
T and its Oxford sister U. Lastly, in Family 7—presenting the so-called
'interpolations'—the basic text is PT, but into it have been inserted two
passages and a word or two more from TR. So h, and many MSS after it.
Thus we have PT preserved for us in four different shapes, all but one
being accompanied by the whole or by part of TR.

So much for chap. 4. What of the rest of the treatise? Whether
Cyprian himself revised other parts of it or not, in so far as the version
containing PT was transmitted independently of the version with TR, it
should reveal variations of text that are equally independent. If one
could determine which these are, it would help to classify our MSS at
least as 'PT MSS' or 'TR MSS', and the PT MSS could be treated
separately. What evidence is there of their independent transmission?

We can, and must at least for the present, set aside Family 3 (MQ).
The reason is that the other three families all agree in their order of the
treatises—an order not found in any of the other MSS—and even a

[1] Cf. above, p. 8.

superficial collation shows them to have a number of common readings peculiar to themselves. M and Q have a different order and only share a few of these readings.

But the other three families (A1, A4, A7, of which H, T, and h may be taken as representative) do not speak with one voice, and their differences need careful attention. For, apart from Family A1, the presence of TR or of parts of it in chap. 4 shows that the writers who made the combination in chap. 4 had at their disposal MSS which, containing as they did TR, belonged to a different tradition of transmission. What was to prevent their borrowing from that tradition readings in other chapters too which appeared better than their own? We have therefore to face the possibility of 'contamination' even in MSS which preserve the PT order of contents. This will render it more difficult to decide, in many cases, whether a reading belongs to the PT tradition or not.

What is clear from the first is that H and T are very close together, and certain passages suggest that (with three centuries between them) they were yet copying the very same codex of the PT tradition (both are MSS written in France). They have a great number of peculiar readings, good and bad, in common. On the other hand, h, which has the 'conflated' chap. 4, while it has many of these same readings, replaces the others by the standard readings of TR or by the reading of one of its families. 'Replaces' may be the wrong word. Might it not be that the peculiarities of H and T not shared by h, are simply aberrations due to the MS on which H and T depended, and that h is simply following a purer PT tradition? In that case we could only consider as peculiar to that tradition what is found in all three, H, T, and h, and nowhere else. It would be playing for safety, of course, for, on the one hand, we cannot exclude the possibility that h *was* replacing a genuine reading of the PT tradition by what he read in his subsidiary TR MS, nor, on the other, that a genuine reading of the PT tradition was preserved by h alone of the three, and was borrowed from it (or rather from one of its ancestors) by one of the TR families. A couple of illustrations will perhaps make the problem clearer.

We have, for instance, a reading in 233. 9 which is common to HTh and also one family of **M**. The context is our being ready for the Lord's coming with our lamps burning. The standard text reads: 'Luceat in bonis operibus nostrum lumen et fulgeat, ut ipsum nos ad lucem claritatis aeternae de hac saeculi nocte perducat.' The variant reading is slight and might be explained in more ways than one. The fact remains that both the PT MSS and **M** read *ipse* in place of *ipsum*. This makes Christ himself our light—a favourite idea of Cyprian's (cf. *Dom. orat.* 35: '. . . filiis lucis et in noctibus dies est. Quando enim sine lumine est cui lumen in corde est? Aut quando sol ei et dies non est cui *sol et dies Christus est*?' So too *De zel. et liv.* 10: 'si homo lucis esse coepisti, quae sunt Christi gere, quia *lux et dies Christus est*'). If it is not a mere coincidence, are we to exclude *ipse* from among the PT readings simply because it also occurs in **M**? Does its presence in **M** mean that it was the original reading in both the PT and the TR originals, and that **M** has preserved it alone among all the TR MSS? Or was it simply that **M** borrowed it from the PT tradition? At this stage, no sure answer can be given to these questions, but they may suffice to present one aspect of our problem.

Another aspect can be illustrated by 217. 4, a passage that will be treated more fully below (pp. 70-72). Hartel reads: 'Cum dictum sit ad Rhaab, in qua praeformabatur ecclesia . . . .' This is also the reading of H and T, but h has, unexpectedly, *ei* in place of *ad Rhaab*. Reasons will be given later for preferring *ei* as the original reading, but what interests us for the moment is not only the fact that h here differs from HT, but that two families of the TR MSS agree with h, viz. **M** once more, and **D**. Did h, **M**, and **D** all independently preserve a correct reading from the original MSS, or was there some borrowing? We have just seen **M** and h together: did h perhaps borrow from **M**, or did **M** borrow from h? And where does **D** come in? **D** has many readings in common with the PT MSS: in which direction did the borrowing, if any, take place?

The questions which can be raised about individual readings must not be allowed to obscure certain outstanding facts. The first is the position of h with regard to the trio HTh. If there is a distinct tradition of PT MSS, it will show a number of characteristic readings, by which h can be tested. With this in view a rough collation was made and it produced some 48 readings common to all three; half of these were at once eliminated as being also found in more than one family of TR. Eighteen readings were common to H and T and not found elsewhere or at most in one other family. That gave us 42 practically certain readings representative of the PT tradition. Of these 42, h contained 28, so that in only 14 cases did it depart from that tradition. So that h followed the PT tradition in two cases out of three, and deserved to retain its place as one of its representatives, whether it preserved a purer form of it than either H or T, or had been 'corrected' according to the MS from which it derived its bits of TR in chap. 4.

The second outstanding fact is the position of M and Q with regard to HTh. Of the 42 readings regarded as belonging to the PT tradition, only five were found in MQ. These could be simply explained as borrowings from the PT MS from which it incorporated PT. In other words, as was originally surmised (chiefly from the different order of its treatises), M and Q do not belong to the PT tradition at all, and may be treated as TR MSS.

These rough calculations served as reassuring pointers in the work to follow and verified the existence of a group of MSS which fulfil a double function (**H**). On the one hand, they may enable us to establish a text distinct from the other MSS in other places besides chaps. 4 and 19—yielding a number of readings which have at least a chance of representing Cyprian's first edition of the treatise.[1] On the other hand, their witness for the rest of the text will be at least on a par with that of the MSS of the TR tradition, and their readings can join the pool from which the final text will have to be selected.

[1] See Appendix I.

CHAPTER VIII

Crucial Passages

T HE rough collations of a number of MSS just referred to revealed the existence of many passages where the MSS divided into two or more groups. The closer study of these passages was suggested by the question: 'Do the MSS group themselves consistently, so that any one of a group can be taken as representative of the group, or do the groups cut across one another, so that some other method of elimination must be looked for?' It was soon clear that the grouping was not consistent, yet some at least of the 'crucial passages' left little or no doubt which was the true reading among the variants. The more true readings a MS showed, the greater would be its value as a witness throughout. This consideration played an important part in the selection of the MSS reserved for detailed collation.

The passages dealt with below are, with the exception of the first, in the order in which they appear in the course of the treatise. The exception is made for '*indictoaudientes*', because there can be no doubt that this is the true reading, and also because both more MSS were consulted on this passage than on any other, and there are more variants in the MSS here than anywhere else. In this instance, each MS is given its catalogue reference, to which are prefixed its century and its siglum [both a letter (if it has one) and a number (in accordance with von Soden's method)]. With each is also indicated the 'family group' to which it belongs, according to the table given above, pp. 14–15.

Thereafter only sigla and/or 'family groups' are given, a certain variety of method being followed, to break the monotony or to emphasize some aspect of the grouping of the MSS. Considerable use has been made of the portmanteau sigla for the same reason. Thus $E_{\frac{1}{2}}$ means that the 'English' group is divided in its witness, and $D-1$ (or $D-2$) means that the large group [2Ca], beginning with D and including the 'Cistercian' MSS, all have the reading in question except one (or two). However, where such a group is referred to, only a few of its typical members may have actually been consulted, which will be understandable under the circumstances.

I. 224. 20

'*Parentibus indictoaudientes*'

A. That this is the original reading can be taken as certain (cf. *T.u.U.* 63: *Studia patristica*, i. 249–52). It occurs—at least first hand—in five of our ninth-century MSS, and survives in three of the eleventh century and in four of the fifteenth. According to L. Latini, it was also in the Verona MS. The fact that it was the original reading does not necessarily make a group of them; true, that reading goes back to the original source, but a MS may belong to a subordinate group, recognizable by a number of common traditions, without losing *this* original reading as the others of the group did. Hence any of these MSS might belong to any of the groups we know, and so not form a group among themselves. Whether any of them go together or not must depend on other considerations. Here they are listed by centuries, and their 'family group' indicated:

	R (50)	Vat. Reg. lat. 116 (*m.* 1)	2 X a
	W (44)	Würzb. Theol. fol. 145 (*m.* 1)	2 B a
9	Y (41)	Mun. Lat. 4597	2 B a
	J (58)	Angers, 148	5 X f
	O (65)	Oxf. Bod., Add. C 15 (*m.* 1)	5 X b
	B (100)	Bamberg, Patr. 63	6 X a
11	m (115)	Mantua, B III 18 (*m.* 1, probably)	2 B c
	p (111)	Vat. Lat. 202	2 B c
	503	Mun. Lat. 18174	2 B a
15	μ (504)	Mun. Lat. 18203 (*m.* 1)	2 B b
	536	Turin, E III 5	2 B b
	559	Rome, Vallicelliana, D 21	2 B b

We can say for certain that W, Y, and 503 go together, and so, too, do μ, 536, and 559.

B. The simplest 'correction' was to insert *non* between *indicto* and *audientes*, as we find actually done by the second hand in W. This was, however, so 'obvious', that again we cannot ascribe it to a common source. One can show, for instance, that the other MSS which have it do not form a group with W, the oldest example which we have. *Non* is found inserted thus in the following:

	W (44)	(*m.* 2)	2 B a
9	G (47)	St. Gallen, 89	2 B b
	K (64)	Leyden, Voss. lat. fol. 40 (*m.* 1)	5 X e
	O (65)	(*m.* 2)	5 X b
	b (208)	Berne, Bongarsiana 235	5 X a
12	214	Vat. Reg. lat. 275	5 X c
	229	Paris, N. a. l. 1792	5 C a
13	350	B.M. Add. 21074 (*m.* 1)	5 X c

Only *214* and 350 can be shown to be connected.

C. Another variation which prevents grouping is that where the Vulgate reading has coalesced with the original, thus: *indicto non obedientes*, or (to keep closer to the original) *indicto non obaudientes*. Each is as old as the other:

	M (40)	Mun. Lat. 208 (obaud-)	3 D
9	Q (60)	Troyes, 581 (obaud-)	3 D
	R (50)	(m. 2)	2 X a
	K (64)	(m. 2) (obaud-)	5 X e
	a (202)	Admont, 587	2 X c
	206	Admont, 136	2 X c
	207	Admont, 381	2 X c
12	205	Vienna, Lat. 850	2 X c
	234	Troyes, 37 (obaud-)	3 C
	253	Lambeth, 106	5 B
	255	Oxford, Bod. 210 (obaud-)	5 B
	306	Vienna, Lat. 789	2 X c
13	350	(m. 2)	5 X c
	354	Oxford, New Coll. 130 (obaud-)	5 B
14	435	Carpentras, 31 (obaud-)	3 C
	450	B.M. Add. 21075	5 X e
15	Ho (583)	Holkham, Lat. 121 (vel non obed-)	2 B d

Of these, MQ are well known as sister MSS; the affinities of the 2Xc MSS are no less patent; they are all in Admont and Vienna, and are close to, if not directly dependent on, the lost Lorsch first volume, corresponding to L.

What deserves special notice is that both K and 350 have been corrected from *non audientes* to *non obaudientes* or *non obedientes*, showing that this reading might be reached in two stages. We can notice that, on the one hand, 450 is of the same stock as K (recognizably, though K, at least now, is defective), but that 350 (which is of a different stock) came to the B.M. together with it. Perhaps more important, because of their probable dependence on a MS of about A.D. 400 [of which we have fragments in B.M. 40165A 1], are *253*, *255*, and *354*. Two MSS of the same century, also in England, and of the same stock are 252 and 250. The former (B.M. Royal 6 B XV), after writing *parentibus* left a space till the end of the line—obviously puzzled by *indictoaudientes*, and began the next line with *ingrati*. The latter (B.M. Arundel 217), which probably depended on it, copied *parentibus ingrati* without any suggestion of an omission.

But by far the most important conclusion from this lot of MSS is that neither those in the preceding section, nor *a fortiori* those in the first, depend on any of them. For from *indicto non obaudientes*, no one is going to produce *indicto non audientes*, still less *indicto audientes*. Nor indeed *indicto inaudientes*, the reading we shall next deal with; so that M and Q, as well as their common ancestor, cannot be regarded as the source of any of them.

D. *Indicto inaudientes* is represented in three of our family groups, but in this case the reading does suggest that they must be grouped together, and will confirm some of our previous findings. For this 'correction' of *indicto audientes* is not at all an obvious one, likely to have occurred to anyone. Like the two preceding corrections it introduces a negative, but does so by prefixing *in-* to *audientes*. *Inaudire*, however, means 'to get to hear' something; it is a rare word, but nothing like so rare as *inaudiens*, with a negative sense, which is only found in Hilary, once certainly and a second time probably. *Inaudientia*, its derivative, is also found once in Hilary and once in Cyprian (ep. 34. 2).[1] And that is all. The creation of *inaudientes* here, then, is a 'learned' correction, not likely to occur again.

We find it in the following MSS:

9	T (*51*)	Vat. Reg. lat. 118	4 A
	U 67	Oxford, Laud Misc. 105	4 A
11	h (*150*)	Leyden, Voss. lat. oct. 7	7 A
12	H (*228*)	Paris, Lat. 15282	1 A
	270	Madrid, Bibl. Nac. 199	7 A
15	501	Berlin, Hamilton 199	7 A

Here we have examples of our three families, 1, 4, 7, which on the basis of the order of the treatises and of the presence of PT we already concluded went back to one archetype, the original of which was Cyprian's first edition of the *De unitate*. That archetype, then, will have read *indicto inaudientes*, which is found nowhere else, and if we did not know of the existence of *indictoaudiens* elsewhere, we should have had to resign ourselves to accepting it as Cyprian's own first version. But as *indictum* was not used in that sense in his time, and as Cyprian actually has *indictoaudiens* elsewhere (*Test.* 2. 27), it is clear that Cyprian wrote *indictoaudientes* in both versions. Thus we can get behind the archetype, to which alone our MSS would of themselves lead us.

E. *Indicto inobedientes* is almost as obvious as *indicto non obedientes*, and so could scarcely form a group. Actually it is rare.

---

[1] Cf. *T.L.L.* vii. 1. 386. Of course *inauditus* is quite common, meaning 'unheard of'.

9 P (55)	Paris, Lat. 1647A	2 (C) a
13 *370*	Escorial, S.I. 11	2 (C) b
15 μ (504)	Mun. Lat. 18203 (*m.* 2)	2 B b

Of these *370* is a copy of P and so can be neglected. μ's second hand does not help either. But cf. below, G.

F. There seems to be a certain relationship between the following peculiar variations:

(*a*) *arentibus indito audientibus ingrati*

| 11 101 | Bamberg, Patr. 64 | 2 C a |
| 13 305 | Vienna, Lat. 810 | 2 C a |

(*b*) *arentibus inaudientibus ingrati*

| 9 D (66) | Oxford, Laud Misc. 451 (*m.* 1) | 2 C a |

Here a second hand corrected it to:

(*c*) *parentibus inaudientes, ingrati*

In a MS related to the last, the first hand read:

(*d*) *parentibus obedientes, audientibus ingrati*

| 12 *201* | Berlin, Theol. lat. fol. 700 (*m.* 1) | 2 C a |

This was duly corrected (?) by turning *obedientes* into *inobedientes*.

And among the Cistercian MSS which are in this tradition too, but had other MSS at their disposal, we find

(*e*) *parentibus indicto audientibus ingrati*

| 12 {233 | Dijon, 124 | 2 C a |
| {g (*219*) | Paris, Lat. 1650 | 2 C a |

which reading, besides having the merit of retaining *indicto*, achieves sense by the minimum emendation, though the sense is not St. Paul's nor Cyprian's.

All these MSS are connected, as is suggested by their belonging to 2Ca, and as is clear from innumerable other details. But none of the other MSS depend on these.

G. We now pass to the rest of the MSS, those which found *indicto* an insuperable stumbling block, and threw it out altogether.

(*a*) *parentibus inobedientes*

9 59	Tours, 256	5 (C) b
11 {110	Vat. Reg. lat. 117	5 (C) b
{k (*126*)	Metz, 224	5 (C) a

12	216	Turin, D IV 37	5 (C) b
	225	Paris, Lat. 1654	6 X b
15	505	Munich, Lat. 21240	5 (C) b
	516	Vat., Urb. lat. 63	6 X c
	566	Rheims, 370	5 X g
	577	Oxford, New Coll. 132	2 C b

Here we have five which are of the same stock as P, and show that they derive from E, above, which read *parentibus indicto inobedientes*. Worthy of special notice is *126*, which was copying the same MS as P had copied, but 'improved on it' here, besides incorporating the first two sentences of PT in chap. 4. Some of the peculiarities of P, *126*, 370 are shared by 225, but not all; which suggests an older ancestor of theirs, or else partial corrections. *516*'s order (in the neighbourhood of the *De ecc. cath. unit.*) is the same as that of 225; it might, therefore, have been moved up to 6Xb [as also its companion 534]. As for 577, its family group and various other data which we shall see presently, show that it acquired this reading 'on its own' and not because of the other MSS here.

(*b*) *parentibus ingrati*

12	250	B.M., Arundel 217	5 B
	e (252)	B.M., Royal 6 B XV (but a space left between the two words)	5 B

These two MSS must be compared with *253*, *255*, *354* to which they are closely allied (cf. above, under C). 250 would seem to depend on e, and the blank left in the latter is too small for *indicto non obaudientes* which the others read. Between them they suggest *indicto audientes* in their common source.

[59 MSS listed above—8 of which present a second reading.]

II. 210. 3–4

The Fall was due to the cunning of the devil, who 'verbis mendacibus blandiens rudes animas incauta credulitate decepit'. There is, however, a fairly common reading: *crudelitate* instead of *credulitate*. The general sense is not affected, though the precise angle from which the temptation is considered is altered. Did he deceive them because of their 'unsuspecting credulity'? That fits *rudes* well enough: inexperienced as yet, not yet 'knowing good and evil', they were ready to believe whatever was told them. At the same time, the construction is a little harsh: *incauta credulitate* has to be made to refer to the *rudes animas* and yet by its position should be taken with *decepit*.

On the other hand, *incauta crudelitate* presents difficulties of a different kind. It is really Adam and Eve who were *incauti*, and only in poetry could the epithet be transferred to the cruelty with which the devil attacked them. But what is perhaps decisive against this reading is that not only is the idea of 'cruelty' alien to the context here, but it is not one which is usually, if ever, associated with the deception which the devil practised on our first parents.

The evidence of the MSS is as follows:

credulitate: m, 577; h, T, *67*; Y *m.* 2, G *m.* 2, P *m.* 2, k *m.* 2; **D**(−1), J, O *m.* 2, **E**$\frac{1}{2}$,K *m.* 2, *214*, 225, Ho
(*incredulitate*: K *m.* 1)
crudelitate: p; H; M *m.* 2, Q; W, **L**, P *m.* 1, k *m.* 1, 110; *201*, S, b, R *m.* 1, **E**$\frac{1}{2}$, J, O *m.* 1, B, *229*
(*credelitate*: Y *m.* 1, G *m.* 1)
(*crudelitas*: R *m.* 2)
(*cruditate*: M *m.* 1)

It is interesting to note how families are divided internally on this point. **M, H, W, D, E** have each at least one member in either camp. In two instances, at least, *crudelitate* has been changed into *credulitate* in the same MS: it is clear that we are not the first to be puzzled about the true reading.

If on general grounds we can exclude *crudelitate*, is *credulitate*, too, necessarily ruled out? In late Latin an ablative of 'attendant circumstances' could be fused with 'abl. of cause' and 'abl. of means', so that *incauta credulitate* can after all go quite well with *decepit*: 'he took advantage of their unsuspecting credulity to deceive them.'

III. 210. 24–25

'Ceterum credere se in Christo quomodo dicit qui . . . .' So Hartel reads, following S, G, M, V, R, but noting *Christum* in the apparatus as the reading of Wv.[1] He would seem to be on safe ground. But since many other MSS read *Christum* too, the question may be raised whether Cyprian was accustomed to write *credere in Christo* or *credere in Chrisstum* (*Deum*). Consulting Hartel's index and apparatus, we find the accu-

---

[1] Hartel's 'v' stands for *editiones vel omnes vel aliquot*. His 'O' (referred to immediately) is the homiliary of Fleury (mid-8th cent.): Orleans, 154 (131)+Paris, Nouv. acq. lat. 1598, 1599 (*C.L.A.* vi. 802). Of Cyprian it contains only VIII and 63, so that there should be no danger of confusing it with Oxford, Bod., Add. C 15, for which the siglum O is used in the present study.

sative eight times (with no variants) and the ablative only four times. But one of these latter is *credidit in nomine eius* (272. 17) which is not quite parallel; the reading of another is very doubtful (379. 25) and depends on an unlikely punctuation; in the third, we find that his apparatus gives OWv with *in Christum credimus* (310. 18), and the fourth is our present passage. So that, even on Hartel's showing, the evidence favours a consistent use of the accusative after *credere in*. This, then, should be adopted here—with all allowance made for carelessness in copying $\overline{\text{xpm}}$ as $\overline{\text{xpo}}$.

in Christum: **M**, h, H, T, *67*; W, Y, μ, **L**; 110, *216*; **D**(−1); B *214*, 225
in Christo: G; MQ; P, k, 101, **E**, S, b, R, J, *59*, O, K, Ho, V

IV. 212. 4

Before quoting the famous Petrine passage in chap. 4, Cyprian tells his hearers that they are not faithful to the *magisterii caelestis doctrina*. So Hartel. It is a possible reading and there may be an exact parallel somewhere. For Cyprian can say: '*Dominus hoc magisterio suo docuit dicens*' (ep. 13. 2, 505. 16) and '*ut . . . (presbyteri) . . . oves . . . divino magisterio instruerent*' (ep. 17. 2, 522. 15). But more natural and with overwhelming MS evidence is the reading *magistri caelestis doctrina*. It brings Christ into the foreground, as we should expect when it is Christ's action and not merely his words that are the *caput* and *origo* of the Church's unity.

It is only necessary to enumerate those MSS which read *magisterii*. They are: V, S, b, M, Q; J and **E**. All the others read *magistri*, which should therefore be adopted in the text.

V. 213. 16 (cf. VIII below, pp. 69–70)

VI. 214. 13

An unusual reading found in a number of good MSS cannot help arresting one's attention. Thus in chap. 5 '[ecclesia Domini . . .] profluentes largiter rivos latius pandit', the majority of MSS are about equally divided in reading *pandit* or *expandit* for the last word. But there is also a minority, of good alloy, which here read *spandit*, which in about half of them has been 'corrected' to one or other of the commoner readings. Even if there were no other evidence for the existence of a form *spandere* (for *expandere*), its presence here, in MSS which seem quite independent of each other, would justify its inclusion in lexica. Here are the data:

spandit: **M**; h, T *m.* 1, *67*; W *m.* 1, G *m.* 1; b, *59 m.* 1, O *m.* 1, B
pandit: W *m.* 2, Y, G *m.* 2, μ; Q *m.* 1; **L**; P, k, **E**$\frac{1}{2}$, S, J, *59 m.* 2, O *m.* 2, Ho (?)
pendit: M *m.* 1
expandit: H, T *m.* 2, M *m.* 2, Q *m.* 2; 110, *216*; **D**, **E**$\frac{1}{2}$, R, K, *214*, 225, *229*

So rare a form is unlikely to have been accidentally introduced in different families, or deliberately inserted; whereas its replacement by one or other of the two common words is easily explicable.

Besides, this form of *expandere* is not entirely untestified. The evidence is collected in *T.L.L.* v. 2 (s.v. *expando*), 1597, 49–51. Besides *Visio Pauli*, 13 [8th-cent. MS], which is also referred to by Souter and by Blaise-Chirat, and Dioscorides, 1. 85 (also in Souter) it includes the elder Pliny (*nat. hist.* 9. 103), inasmuch as two of his most important MSS [R (9th cent.) and d (13th cent.) according to Sillig] describing the shape of sea-shells, read: '*in obliquo, in rectum spansa.*' That *expansa* should have been adopted for the text instead, is not surprising.

For the above reasons it seems necessary to restore *spandit* and to assign a good mark to those MSS which have preserved it.

VII. 214. 23–24

'Habere non potest Deum patrem, qui ecclesiam non habet matrem.' This much-quoted dictum presents us with a tiny variation which may turn out to be a pointer to greater things. By far the greater number of MSS insert *iam* after *habere*. Was this perhaps original? If not, who would have thought of putting it in? The sentence is excellent as it stands and does not call for correction. For the same reason, the accidental omission of *iam* could easily escape notice.

However, the presence of *iam* does make a difference to the sense, and fits more exactly the context of Cyprian's thought. He is preoccupied with schismatic movements, not with the fate of those who have never known the Church. It is those who are or were in the Church that he is addressing, and [with the reading *iam*] he is telling them that they can *no longer* expect to have God as their Father, if they do not look to the Church as their Mother. So that it is the reading with *iam* that, if anything, is the more likely.

However that may be, this variant enables us to divide the MSS into *iam* MSS and non-*iam* MSS, and this gives us some interesting results.

It was, of course, possible for *iam* to be borrowed and inserted into a non-*iam* MS, but not likely at all that *iam* should be dropped because absent from a non-*iam* MS used for comparison. Its loss might, however, be accidental.

iam MSS: **H, D, M,** Ho, *577*, the large family 5(C)b (with the excep- tion of *59*), M, Q, **L**; J; the family 6X

non-*iam* MSS: **W,** μ, *559*; G; P, k; **E,** R, *59*, K, O, *214*

We should have expected 5(C)b to follow Pk, as they normally do, but they may have picked up *iam* elsewhere. What is perhaps more significant is that **L** does not go with **W,** μ, &c., for this may confirm our surmise (pp. 43–44) that though L's *letters* go with theirs, its treatises and theirs belong to different traditions.

R, J, *59*, K, and O are all ninth-century MSS which are difficult to place. Their being together here does not necessarily imply interdependence.

VIII. 215. 14–15 (and V. 213. 16)

Christ's robe, for which they cast lots at the foot of the cross, is referred to thus: 'integra vestis accipitur, et incorrupta adque individua tunica possidetur.' But did Cyprian write *individua*? The number of MSS which read *indivisa* makes one hesitate. In fact **H** and MQ, **L, D, E,** and a number of other outstanding MSS (including V) have it.

The sense required is 'undivided', not 'indivisible', which is the ordinary sense of *individua*; the meaning 'undivided' is, by comparison, rare.[1] Hence, if Cyprian had written *indivisa*, it is most unlikely that anyone should have corrected it to *individua*, but *individua*, whose associations (e.g. with *Trinitas*) came to exclude the very possibility of division, will have appeared to be an obvious misreading of *indivisa*, which was therefore 'restored'. Only the following MSS have been noticed to retain the *lectio difficilior*:

individua: WY, Pk, *110*, *216*, *370*, B, *578*, 225, Ho.

[It was, however, excluded from the final text when the close connexions between the chief MSS here had been made apparent. A misreading in some early MS would explain it. The unanimity of all the rest of our MSS must be allowed the advantage.]

An earlier passage (213. 16) also leaves us in doubt whether to read

---

[1] For the meaning of *individuus* cf. *T.L.L.* vii. 1208–10 (especially the end of the article, where our passage is quoted).

individuum or *indivisum*. It comes in the textus receptus of chap. 4, where Cyprian says that the bishops have a special duty to hold to and defend the Church's gifts and prerogatives, 'ut episcopatum quoque ipsum unum adque indivisum probemus'. Here again 'undivided' must be the sense, but then how explain the alternative reading *individuum compro-bemus*? In its favour, besides the argument used in the previous passage, is the fact that this makes a very good clausula, whereas *indivisum probemus* is formless. The new reading is found throughout the two allied groups 2Bc (**M**) and 2Cb, and what may be vestiges of it in the following MSS:

324 5 (C) b: *individuum probemus*
548 and 555 5 (C) b: *indivisum unum probemus*
569 and 641 2 X d: *indivisum esse probemus*

However, the witness of all the other groups should perhaps prevail here.

IX. 217. 4

'Cum dictum sit *ad Rhaab*, in qua praeformabatur ecclesia: "Patrem tuum . . .".' In this passage, to which reference has already been made (p. 58), we need not delay over the varied spellings of the name of this benevolent *meretrix*: Rhaab, Rahab, Rachab, Raab, &c., which may be mere vagaries of the copyists and are unlikely to give us any clue. But in a very few MSS, instead of *ad Rhaab*, we read *ei*. Where did this come from? Not from *ad Rhaab*, however badly it may have been written. But does it even make sense? We look at the text again, and see that indeed it does: 'Since it was said to that woman in whom the Church was pre-figured' or simply 'to one who was a type of the Church'. It may be worth consideration. The reading *ei* is found in the following MSS:

9	D	Oxford, Laud Misc. 451	2 C a
	101	Bamberg, Patr. 64	2 C a
11	p }M	Vatican, Lat. 202	2 B c
	m }	Mantua, B III 18	2 B c
	h	Leyden, Voss. lat. oct. 7	7 A
	201	Berlin, Theol. lat. fol. 700	2 C a
12	233	Dijon, 124	2 C a
	270	Madrid, 199	7 A
13	305	Vienna, Lat. 810	2 C a
	355	Cambridge, Pemb. 161	7 A

To these may be added:

15	577	Oxford, New Coll. 132	2 C b
		which reads *ad eam* (exactly as in Jos. 2. 17)	

The five MSS of 2Ca, headed by D, form a unity and are at the back of the Cistercian MSS. If the reading is not in H or T, it is in h and its two successors to the conflated text in 7A (and probably in the rest of the family). What is more, it is in **M**, MSS which seem to be gaining in prestige.

Now it is highly improbable, to say the least, that a copyist or revisor should spontaneously have replaced *ad Rhaab* by *ei*. And if he were confronted with both readings, it is inevitable that he should have preferred the personal name to the pronoun. Thus, in h, which undoubtedly derives from a manuscript with the PT order but may depend for many of its readings on some other family, the presence of *ei* shows that this was both in its direct ancestor and in that from which it borrowed. For had *ad Rhaab* been in either of them, it would have prevailed against the other. Thus we seem to have three ancient traditions, independently testifying to *ei*: the pre-Cistercian, that of h, and that of **M**.

That may seem little against the overwhelming majority of the MSS, yet the possibility must be envisaged that *ei* was the original reading. If so, there is no difficulty in explaining *ad Rhaab*. Anyone knowing his bible would recognize who was meant by *ei*, and what learned student could resist the temptation of putting the harlot's name in the margin? Its incorporation in place of *ei* would follow as a matter of course at the next transcription. And this is the sort of 'correction' which could be made independently by any number of copyists.

Of course, Cyprian, the creator of the original, could have used either. But in this case he had a good reason for avoiding the name of her 'who was a type of the Church'. No doubt Origen spoke freely about the harlots of the O.T. and had no misgivings about finding in them types of the Church—especially as representing the now repentant Gentiles (cf. *in lib. Jesu Nave*, Hom. 3. 3–5 [Baehrens, *G.C.S.* VII. ii. 304–7] where precisely Raab is the occasion of this treatment. This is on Jos. 2. 8. Similarly on Jos. 6. 22–25, Hom. 7. 5 [ibid. 331–2]). But Cyprian had a different object in view. He wanted simply to illustrate the unity of the Church by means of the passage where she was told to gather all her people into the one house. No need to recall what she was by mentioning her by name: to say 'someone who prefigured the Church' was enough. Anything that reminded his hearers that it was a harlot that did so, would have been inopportune, since he had only just now insisted on the purity of the spouse of Christ: 'Adulterari non potest sponsa Christi, incorrupta est et pudica: unam domum novit, &c.' (chap. 6. 214. 17 ff.).

One might argue that this could have occurred equally to some later copyist, and this would explain the presence of *ei* in these few MSS. But whereas the change from *ei* to *ad Rhaab* might occur to anyone, it is unlikely that precisely *ei* should have been chosen to replace *ad Rhaab* in three, apparently independent, traditions. For these reasons, one is led to prefer *ei* as the original reading—a reading kept by Cyprian himself even when he revised his *De unitate*.

X. 217. 2–10

In chap. 8 there is a long sentence which gets into trouble towards the end. It is a rhetorical question: 'Do you think that a man can survive if he leaves the Church . . . when scripture says (*cum dictum sit*) . . . *and likewise the sacred meaning of the Pasch consists* essentially in the fact that . . .?' How is this last part linked to the first? As it stands in Hartel (which is most probably right) we read: 'item sacramentum Paschae nihil aliud in Exodi lege contineat quam . . .' where *contineat* is governed by the *cum* of *cum dictum sit*. *Cum* is a long way off, no doubt, and one is a little surprised by the subjunctive *contineat* if one has made a pause after the quotation. But the construction cannot be said to be impossible and the text can be allowed to stand.

On the other hand, an analysis of the chief MSS of the Primacy Test suggests that they represent a different original. They all make much of the word *Item*, and in spite of it add *quoque* to *sacramentum*, and then read *continet*, which confirms the impression of a quite independent sentence, divorced from the distant *cum*. However, *ITEM sacramentum quoque* can hardly be original.

Our oldest MS, T, presents the passage as follows. It so happened that the original scribe was here beginning a new line, and he set off with *Sacramentum quoque paschae*, giving the first word a big capital S. Thereafter he (or whoever put in the uncial titles of the treatises) prefixed ITEM to Sacramentum, using uncials no doubt to overpower the capital S, and to show that, though in the margin, *Item* indeed began the sentence. This insertion can easily be explained if, as is likely, this is the MS in which the double version was created in the shape of our family 4, for *item* does precede *sacramentum* in the MSS of the *Textus receptus*, and the scribe, or rubricator, or revisor, would naturally have the two codices, which were being drawn on, at his disposal. The Oxford MS, 67 (Bod., Laud Misc. 105), which seems after all to be a copy of this one, also reads 'Item sacramentum quoque paschae'.

H, the unique representative of the pure PT text, seems to depend, for this passage, directly or indirectly on T. Taking the uncial ITEM as indicating the beginning of a new section of the treatise, Wittelo's assistant, who was responsible for it, made elaborate provision for this. He manœuvred so as to begin a line there, and his ornamental 'I' is the height of nearly four lines—looking almost as important as the initial letter of the whole treatise. He also wrote *quoque*, but this has been lined through (by him too?) as superfluous.[1]

Lastly, the MSS which have the conflated text (family 7) all read simply '*Sacramentum quoque . . . continet*', and this must have been the original reading of the MS of this version. *Item* is an intrusion from the other, and either it or *quoque* is superfluous. And as *continet* is found in all these MSS, *sacramentum* does begin a new sentence which is independent of the *cum* earlier on.

This text, however, now raises a doubt about that of the TR MSS. Did Cyprian 'revise' it in the second edition so that the two sentences should combine under the *cum* in the first? Or was it a piece of editing devised later on? There would be no reason for suggesting the latter were it not for J, our Angers MS, which has considerable authority. Its evidence, however, is ambiguous. For whereas it begins the sentence without *Item*, it omits *quoque* too and its first hand wrote *contineat*. So that even though the second hand makes it a separate sentence—by correcting to *continet*, as it had to, since there were no connectives—this MS tells as much for as against either of the two versions. Until confirmation appears elsewhere, its evidence can give us no real help.

XI. 217. 14, &c.

Unanimis or *unianimis*? The latter form of the word will appear unfamiliar to most, but Souter assures us that it is found 'saec. iii on, in the oldest and best MSS'. Including its cognates (*-itas*, *-iter*), the word occurs some sixteen or seventeen times in the *De ecclesiae catholicae unitate*, and the form *unanimis* predominates in the MSS. Most of them present this form alone, which is not surprising as the other had gone out of use completely by the time our MSS were transcribed. All the more valuable are the instances where *unianimis* has survived, and if it is

---

[1] Cf. '*De un.* MSS', pp. xi ff. An alternative, and perhaps preferable, explanation of the facts would be that T and H both used the same old MS, on which ITEM had already been inserted from the *Textus receptus*. If it was prominent there, it would explain both the uncials in T and the large capital in H, as well as the presence of *Item* in 67.

true that an old reading can be preserved in an otherwise defective MS, and that a MS may 'correct' an old reading without ceasing to be a 'good' one in other respects, yet such a preservation can be reckoned as a good mark for any MS, and it is these which we are looking for.

Below is given the incidence of the form *unianim-* so far as it has been noticed. MSS not mentioned may be taken as having *unanim-* throughout.

Y: 2; T: 3; R: 5; K: 4; *59*: 15; D: 6; *67*: 3; B: 2; H: 8; *253*: 1; 252 and 255: 2; G: 4; (Pelagius II: 2/2)

For completeness, the following variations occurring in some of the above MSS may be recorded:

217. 14 (*unanimitatis*): J has *unitas* corrected to *unitatis*, which is also found in *59* and **L**
217. 24 (*unanimitatis*): B (*m.* 1) reads *una animitatis*
220. 9 (*unanimitatem*): R; T (*m.* 1), *67* and H (*m.* 1) read *una animitatem*

From the above, we notice that to a varying degree, the form *unianim-* has survived in nine of our ninth-century MSS, the most consistent being *59*, whereas all the others have *unanim-* more often than not.

H deserves a little note to itself. The first three occurrences were all given as *unianim-*; the fourth reads *unanim-*, but the *a* is a transformed *i*, which shows that he had copied *uni* before he realized that this 'badly spelt' word had occurred again, and that he ought to correct it. For the fifth he originally wrote *una animitatem* (cf. above), but the sixth shows the same change as the fourth, and he only gets it 'right' at the seventh and eighth. He slips up again at the ninth and corrects himself, and so gets the tenth 'right', and the eleventh, twelfth, and thirteenth. The fourteenth caught him out and he scratched out the top of the *i* before turning it into an *a*. The next two follow immediately and so he naturally got them 'right', but a few lines later he had again to correct himself in the last passage of all. Nothing could show more clearly that the MS which H was copying always had *unianim-*.

The above enumeration excludes *unanimi consensione* which comes in the Primacy Text itself. It is never written *unianimi* in the MSS (not even in H), but this need not tell against it any more than the vast majority of the readings with *unanim-* discredit the MSS which bear them. Pelagius II, however, does read *unianimi consensione* here (ninth century MS.).

At the same time, it is unlikely that Cyprian spelt the word in two ways, and it is beyond the bounds of probability that so many of the oldest MSS should have replaced an original *unanim-* by the archaic *unianim-*, and that not consistently. It seems clear, then, that *unianim-* must be restored everywhere, and that *ceteris paribus* the MSS which have preserved it at all should have special consideration.

XII. 218. 18

Christ allows schism and heresy in order to test our loyalty. Cyprian describes the process: '(ut) dum corda et mentes nostras veritatis discrimen examinat...'(chap. 10. 218. 17–18). Someone, thinking of Christ as still being the subject, wrote *discrimine* instead, influenced perhaps by the first letter of *examinat*. This would be possible, in fact almost necessary, if Christ were the subject of the main sentence which follows. But this reads: '(ut) dum . . . examinat, probatorum fides integra manifesta luce clarescat', so that *discrimine* must be reckoned a black mark against the following:

discrimine: h, H, T, 67, b, O

XIII. 219. 21–22

In chap. 11 Cyprian is deriding the baptism of heretics: 'Non abluuntur illic homines sed potius sordidantur, nec purgantur delicta sed immo cumulantur.' So read the great majority of the MSS. But some of considerable importance change the last word to *maculantur*. The sense is against it, though with the thought of the men who *sordidantur*, a scribe might easily misread *cumulantur* and substitute *maculantur* for it.[1] It is not, however, the sort of mistake likely to be made accidentally more than once; we can, therefore, expect to find a relationship between the MSS which present us with it. These are:

maculantur: **W** μ; M, Q, P, k, *370*; **D**$\frac{1}{2}$ (viz. D, 101, 305); B

and it means a black mark against them.

XIV. 220. 7

Unnecessary tinkering with the text must also count against a MS, though the following may in some cases be due merely to accidental carelessness. Cyprian is inveighing against those who quoted a truncated

---

[1] Especially if, a few pages earlier, he had been copying the *De habitu virginum*, and remembered the passage about the virgins at the public baths: 'Sordidat lavatio ista, non abluit, nec emundat membra sed maculat' (*De hab. virg.* 19).

text: 'partis memores et partem subdole comprimentes'. For this we have no less than four variations:

partim . . . partim:	P (*m.* 2); **D**; b, *59*, K, *214*, *229*	
partis . . . partim:	**W**, P (*m.* 1)	
partim . . . partem:	G, H (*m.* 2)	
partem . . . partem:	B	

Between them, they really confirm the received text found in the other MSS.

XV. 221. 8

Cyprian says that Christ stood by the three youths in the fiery furnace and 'flammis ambientibus medios spiritu roris animavit'. Strange to say, about half the MSS for *medios*, read *medio*, which presumably is to be taken with *spiritu*. μ tries to get out of the difficulty by reading *in medio*; a has *medio*, with *fornaci* above the line, and the rest of **L** read *medio fornacis* from the Vulgate, while J omits *spiritu*, thus leaving us with *medio roris*. The MSS with *medio* are the following:

medio: h; G; **L**; 110; **D** (except 233), b, R, J, *59*, O, K, B, *214*, *229*

XVI. 222. 24–223. 2

We now have to deal with a passage which has given rise to many variations, but of whose original form there can be no reasonable doubt. It will be simplest to print out Hartel's text, indicating the places where we find insertions made in the various MSS. 'Ad regnum caelorum non potest pervenire discordia, ∧ ad praemium Christi qui dixit: "Hoc est mandatum meum ut diligatis invicem, quemadmodum dilexi vos", ∧ pertinere non poterit ∧ qui dilectionem Christi perfida dissensione violavit.' This text of Hartel's is undoubtedly correct, and yet it is represented by only four MSS: G (2Bb); m, p (2Bc); 577 (2Cb). Nearly all the others have inserted *nec* after *discordia*, and *ad praemium Christi* (or the like) either before or after *pertinere non poterit*. This can be explained by the asyndeton at *discordia*, and by the long wait for the main verb *pertinere non poterit*, whose connexion with *ad praemium Christi* at the beginning of the sentence is obscured by the quotation of Christ's words intervening. The ancients had not the help of punctuation and inverted commas to control the run of the sentence. But not only the variations of the second (main) insertion (*ad praemium Christi, ad Christum, ad Deum, ad regnum Dei, ad Christi praemium*) but especially the variations in its position, show it to be due to a marginal note which has come to be inserted in the text.

This explanation is reinforced by the fact that some of the MSS (9) have not yet added *nec*; i.e. they took the construction correctly, but in order to help the reader, repeated *ad praemium Christi* in the margin to show what *pertinere* went with. It was natural to transfer this to the text, but once this was done it became necessary to precede the whole by *nec*. Thus M, which, like its sister manuscript Q, reads 'pertinere non poterit ad praemium Christi', has had *nec* added earlier on in the margin by a second hand. [Instead of *nec* we find *non* in five allied MSS (those deriving from the lost Lorsch MS), and *et* once (in O).]

But however these readings came about, they provide us with a good basis for grouping our MSS.

(1) MSS with *ad praemium Christi* after *poterit*:

    (a) Without *nec*: Y, W, 503, µ (*m.* 1), 536, *559*; Ho; M (*m.* 1), Q; B, 578.

    (b) With *nec* (after *discordia*): µ (*m.* 2); **E**; P, k (and practically all in the (C) groups); M (*marg.*); J (with *pervenire* for *pertinere*); 566; 225; *516*.

(2) MSS with *ad Christi praemium*:

    (a) Before *pertinere* (and without *nec*): m (*m.* 2); 435.

    (b) After *poterit* (and with *nec*): b.

    (c) After *poterit* (with *et*; and with *pervenire* for *pertinere*): O.

(3) MSS with *nec*, and with *ad Christum*:

    (a) Before *pertinere*: H, T, h, 270, 501; **D** (i.e. D and all the 'Cistercians'; but *219* and 233 read *pervenire*. So too does *214*); 59.

    (b) After *potest* (for *poterit*): K, 450.

(4) MSS with *non* and *ad regnum Dei*, before *pertinere*: **L**.

(5) MS with *nec* and *ad Deum*, before *pertinere*: R.

(6) MSS with *no insertions*: G; m (*m.* 1), p; *577*.

Given that the last, (6), represents the original, the main insertions seal off their respective MSS from one another (except, possibly, not (2) from (1)). We find all those which we derived from Ur-Ho in (1), indeed nearly all of them in (1) (*a*). P and its (C) groups are together in (1) (*b*), secondary, that is, to (1) (*a*), as we might expect in a rearrangement of the Ur-Ho order (cf. p. 33).

In (3) (*a*) are all the PT MSS (**H**), together, as we have learnt to expect, but M and Q are in (1)(*a*)—a fresh confirmation that the PT MSS are not derived from them. In the same class are D and the 'Cistercians', so often allied with **H**.

In (4) we have confirmation that, in the treatises, **L** came from a tradition different from that of Ur-Ho (cf. pp. 43–44). If, as other indications suggest, they are, nevertheless, in some way connected, this must have been at a stage before *any* insertions had been made, the stage represented today only by G; m, p; 577.

XVII. 223. 4–5

In a passage that follows closely on the last, Cyprian quotes a text from St. John in an unusual form. Furthermore, some of the MSS suggest that the original did not give the whole text. So that we here have a double problem, complicated by the outside influence of the Vulgate text. This, in full, reads: 'Qui manet in caritate, in Deo manet et Deus in eo' (I Jn. 4. 16). No Cyprianic manuscript reads *caritate*, and only one *eo*; we can be certain that Cyprian used *dilectione*, and also *illo* (if he used the last phrase here at all). Neglecting this last point for the moment, we find that the vast majority of MSS read: 'Qui manet in Deo, in dilectione manet', and seen against the background of the Greek, of the Vulgate, and of Cyprian's own use elsewhere, it can only be explained as being in the original. No one would have deliberately altered the standard text in this way if it had stood in Cyprian's own work: the inversion is Cyprian's own—whether this was through a lapse of memory, or influenced by the current of his thought, or because of both, we need not decide.

For *et Deus in eo*, most MSS read *et Deus in illo manet*. But four MSS at least omit *manet* (with the Vulgate); the 'Cistercian' group reads *Dominus* for *Deus*, and two important groups omit the sentence altogether. These are the Lorsch tradition, L (2Xc) and the group 2Bb, including G. As the temptation to complete a quotation would always be strong, and there is, therefore, no difficulty in explaining the sentence as an addition,[1] we are forced at least to put a question mark against this sentence. But if *manet* did end it, its omission might have occurred by homoeoteleuton.

    (i) *qui manet in dilectione, in Deo manet et Deus in illo manet*: T, 67; **E**-e; O; also **D**, but with *Dominus* for *Deus*.

    (ii) *qui manet in Deo, in dilectione manet et Deus in illo manet*: H, h,

---

[1] But if it is an addition, it must have been made very early, for the Vulgate does not include the last '*manet*'.

270, 355; W, Y, 503; **M**, 577; Ho; P, k, *370*; e; M, Q; R, J, O,
59, B, K (omits last *manet*); 566, b.
(iii) *qui manet in Deo in dilectione manet* [. . .]: G; μ, *559*, 536; **L**.
(iv) *qui in dilectione manet manet in Deo, et Deus in illo manet*:[1] 110,
505; 225; *516*.

Here we have several instances of MSS differing from their usual
companions. Thus e, against all the others in its family (**E**), reads the un-
scriptural but best attested text (ii), and thereby enhances its authority.

On the other hand, T and *67* have for once left the **H** group (here represented by H and h with 270, 355 in (ii)), possibly owing to contamination from the **D** family to which their letters belong.

And whereas G, μ, *559* (2Bb) usually go with W and Y (2Ba), and in
the *iam* problem (above VII) did not go with **L**, here (in (iii)) we find
them joining **L** against all the others, W and Y included. Such examples
of contrary textual indications make one aware of the presence of contamination, without the possibility of locating it.

In favour of (iii), this much can be said. If, according to the prepon-
derance of the MSS, Cyprian indeed wrote 'Qui manet in Deo in dilectione manet', the general context is in favour of his having stopped there.
For thus his thought is simple and clear. Lack of charity, he says, means
lack of God. For as St. John says: 'God is love and he who abides in God,
abides in love.' Hence, he concludes, a man cannot be abiding in God
who is at variance with the rest of the Church (i.e. his not abiding in love
proves that he is not abiding in God). The simplicity of his argument
might have lost some of its force by the introduction of the idea that God
also 'abides in him'. This is not part of his effective thought here, and the
possibility of its absence in the original must be borne in mind when we
come to estimate the pattern of the MS tradition.

XVIII. 223. 25

A good example of the Vulgate affecting Cyprian's texts is found
in chap. 15. He quotes Our Lord's reply to those who rely on their

---

[1] This last is so characteristic that 225 and *516* (with their companions in 6Xb and
6Xc) might safely have been incorporated with 5(C)b—110, &c. The origin of this
reading is not far to seek. The discrepancy from the Vulgate which the form (ii) shows
was 'corrected' in the usual way: 'Qui manet in Deo in dilectione manet. . . .' If the
first mark was a little too far back (as indicated here), the next copyist would transfer
manet in Deo beyond the second *manet*; thus recovering St. John's statement if not the
order of words in the Vulgate: 'Qui . . . in dilectione manet, manet in Deo.' So that
for all its strangeness, this reading confirms the form (ii), and gives us a further reason
for linking the MSS which have it with the other (C) groups which have this form.

charismatic exploits: 'I never knew you: depart from me, ye who work iniquity' (Matt. 7. 23).

For the last word, the MSS vary between *iniquitatem* and *iniustitiam*. Which it should be, is clear from the following words: 'Iustitia opus est ut promereri quis possit Deum iudicem.' And if *iniquitatem* so often replaces *iniustitiam* it is not only because the Vulgate of Matthew reads it here, but chiefly because that is the reading in the Psalm (6. 9) which Our Lord is quoting. In the Middle Ages every cleric knew the Psalms by heart: Cyprian's copyists would all feel the itch to correct this 'false' quotation. However, the majority resisted it.

iniustitiam: **H, D, M**, 577; **E, L**; M, Q; R, 59, O
iniquitatem: **W**, μ, *559*; G; Ho; **P** (and the rest of the (C) groups); J, K, B, b, *214*, 225

Here we find *iniustitiam* not only in nearly all the *iam* MSS (cf. VII) but also in the English group (**E**) which had no *iam*. This adds to the credit of those which have both *iam* and *iniustitiam*. **W** and **P** have neither.

XIX. 224. 13–16

Asyndeton misunderstood can provoke the insertion of *et*, and if the first word is *exsurgere*, change it into *et surgere*. On the other hand, the run of the sentences may be such as to exclude asyndeton, and this would seem to be the case in our next example. Is this a likely asyndeton: 'Malum hoc . . . iam pridem coeperat, sed nunc crevit eiusdem mali infesta clades. Exsurgere ac pullulare plus coepit haereticae perversitatis et schismatum venenata pernicies, quia &c'? The *plus coepit* is harsh in a completely independent sentence, but it is quite in place if linked up with *iam pridem coeperat*, and *sed nunc crevit*. Hence the more common reading '. . . clades, et surgere ac pullulare . . .' is to be preferred.

Exsurgere: h, H, T, *67*; **L**; **E**; b, *59*, O, K

XX. 224. 16

The preceding quotation continues 'quia et sic in occasu mundi oportebat', which is proved by St. Paul. The reading *in occasum mundi* is either simply a slip, or else a 'learned' correction, as if the spread of heresy was intended to bring on the end of the world. But such an idea is foreign to the context: St. Paul simply says that sin will be prevalent *in novissimis diebus*. However, the following MSS read *in occasum*:

in occasum: P (not, however, k); **D, E**, b, K, *214*, *229*, O (*m.* 1), J, **L**.

[For 224. 20 *parentibus indictoaudientes*, cf. above, I, pp. 61–65.]

XXI. 225. 14–16

A complicated line of thought may lead to unnecessary corrections if the thought is not properly understood. Thus at the beginning of chap. 17 Cyprian is telling his flock not to be dismayed at defections, for these had been predicted. Then he adds that their own resistance to these defections had been predicted too—a further reason for encouragement. This addition to his thought is expressed in a new sentence beginning '*Ut . . . ita*.' But trouble is bound to follow if this is taken not as a new sentence, but as the purpose (or consequence) of the preceding one: '*ut . . . caveant*'. Most of the MSS read correctly as follows: 'Non tamen nos moveat aut turbet multorum nimia et abrupta perfidia, sed potius fidem nostram praenuntiatae rei veritate corroboret. *Ut quidam tales* esse coeperunt quia haec ante praedicta sunt, ita ceteri fratres ab eiusmodi caveant quia et haec ante praedicta sunt.' Some, therefore, have inserted *quoniam* after *ut*, others have changed *ut* into *et*, because of the indicative following. A corrector of M has even changed *Ut* into *utinam*! The variations can be listed as follows:

ut quoniam quidam:	h, H, T, 67; J, K
ut quidem:	O
Et quidem tales:	**M** [but m (*m.* 2) corrects to *Ut*]; **P**
Et quidam fallaces:	**D**
Ut quidam tales fallaces:	B, 578

XXII and XXIII. 225. 14–15; 231. 11–12

Reference has already been made to a pre-Cistercian tradition which persists in a well-defined group, **D**. It can be illustrated by two very obvious mistakes which they and they alone perpetrate. The first occurs in the passage just dealt with, where Cyprian is warning his people that the emergence of disloyal agitators must not surprise them: it is an eventuality long since prophesied. 'Ut quidam *tales* esse coeperunt, quia haec ante praedicta sunt, ita ceteri fratres ab eiusmodi caveant quia et haec ante praedicta sunt' (chap. 17).

Instead of *tales*, this group reads *fallaces*, which, if it were original, would scarcely have been uniformly replaced by *tales* everywhere else [B reads *tales fallaces*].

The second text is the conclusion of an appeal not to be led away by the malcontents into schism. 'Quicquid a matrice discesserit, seorsum vivere et spirare non poterit: substantiam salutis *amittit*' (chap. 23). Here, at one stage, the last word was taken to be *admittit*; which could also be written not only as *ammittit* (which P originally wrote here), but also as *amittit*.[1] The reading *admittit* demanded a negative, and so we find in this group: '. . . NEC *substantiam salutis* ADMITTIT.' In fact, one of the group, 234, actually reads *amittit* in spite of the introduced negative. MSS concerned in these two errors are:

D, 101, *201*, *219*, *229*, 233, 234, 305

These two texts (and they are only the clearest) show that all these MSS go back to a common source, and that if they share some other peculiarities (as we saw they do *ei*) with other MSS, there must either have been borrowing (which in that instance is unlikely), or else there is a common source older than that (or those) which introduced these mistakes.

XXIV. 225. 24

In Chap. 17 there is the same false correction in so many MSS that we are left in doubt whether it is due to a single mistake perpetuated in them, or whether it was made independently by several. Hartel reads 'Aversandus est talis adque fugiendus quisque fuerit ab ecclesia separatus.' The first word often stands as *adversandus*. There is no doubt that this is wrong. It is true that *T.L.L.* quotes five instances in which *adversor* is followed by an accusative (though in three of them the verb may be *aversor*), but otherwise in its wide use it always takes a dative. And there is no single case of its being used with a passive sense, as is required here. On the other hand, *aversor* is a much less common word, it takes the accusative regularly, and *T.L.L.* gives three instances of the gerundive with passive meaning. Besides two in Augustine, one comes already from Seneca (ep. 66. 6): '*alia optanda . . . alia aversanda.*' In fact there is a very rare active form too. So that *aversandus est* can hold its own.

Can we explain *adversandus*? At least *aversor* was uncommon, and something with *adversus* in it may have seemed required, and in certain periods grammar was not too good. We can quote at least one parallel for this mistake or: in Tit. 1. 14 we read '*aversantium se a veritate*', but two of the chief MSS give us *adversantium* instead. These are M and N, viz. Munich, Lat. 6229, saec. viii, and Colmar, (Bibl. publ.) saec. ix (see Wordsworth and White in loc.).

---

[1] For this last form, cf. Schwartz's edition of the Councils, *A.C.O.* IV. ii, p. xxi, where he says that at times '*geminatio* [*consonorum*] *omittitur*'. There is a pertinent example in the ninth-century MS (Paris 1682), where in the third letter of Pelagius II to the bishops of Istria, we read: '*qui . . . s. Chalcedonensi concilio amissus . . .*' (op. cit., p. 129, l. 27). Cf. also the critical apparatus of 227. 9, '*quod admisisse lapsi videntur*'.

Aversandus: p; T, *67 (m.* 2), h; **W**, G, μ (*m.* 2), Q (*m.* 2); **L** (−1), **P**; **D** (½); **E** (½, e); R, J, O (*m.* 2), K, B, 225, Ho

Adversandus: m, 577; H, *67* (*m.* 1); μ (*m.* 1), M, Q (*m.* 1); 205; D, 101, *229*, 305; **E** (½); b, O (*m.* 1), *59, 214, 578*

We can notice that several of the 'groups' or 'families' split on this issue and that in some cases the false reading is corrected in the MSS themselves. We note again that e has the correct reading among the hesitations of **E**, and that of the ninth-century MSS, which are difficult to place, *59* and O (*m.* 1) fail us, whereas R, J, and K are correct.

XXV. 226. 13

Moses no doubt offered sacrifice more than once, and yet the title of 'priest' was reserved to his brother Aaron. The opposition to them in the desert is referred to by Cyprian as being '*contra Mosen et Aaron sacerdotem*' (chap. 18: 226. 12–13). A few MSS read *sacerdotes*, perhaps because of Ps. 98 (99). 6.

sacerdotes: h; **W**; **E**; R, *214, 229*

XXVI. 229. 23–24

'Et tamen Dominum Iudas postmodum tradidit' (*or* prodidit?) (chap. 22). As we have at times found that the MSS which secured a good mark were few, in the present instance it is only a few which incur a bad mark. Our starting-point may be taken from a MS note of C. H. Turner, which he perhaps failed to publish: '*Prodere* and *proditor* of Judas was perhaps the earliest use in ecclesiastical Latin for "the traitor". I do not know whether data have ever been collected, but I have noted the following.' He then quotes the evidence of Hartel's apparatus here, and the passage in ep. 59. 2. With these he compares *k* at Mark 14. 10 (elsewhere in *k*, 'tradere'); ps.-Cyprian, *ad Novatianum*, 14; Irenaeus, *adv. haer.* i. 28. 9 [31. 1], and ii. 32. 3 [20. 5]; ps.-Tert. *adv. omn. haer.* 2; and Jerome's Vulgate Lk. 6. 16.

Concerned as we are only with Cyprian's *De ecclesiae catholicae unitate*, we can amplify the meagre data provided by Hartel, so that the evidence in our passage is quite overwhelming. *Tradidit*, which is the reading adopted by Hartel, is found in only a tiny handful of MSS, so that only these need be indicated here. All the others read *prodidit* [G: *prodit*], which therefore on every ground should be restored to the text.

tradidit: W, Y, 503; B, 578; K; *229*; μ (*m.* 1?), *536, 559*

The first three go together, as do the last three, and there are many indications that the two groups come from a common source. We can notice also *229* which, as at times elsewhere, departs from the Cistercian group to which it fundamentally belongs.

So that C. H. Turner's flair for detail is once more justified.

XXVII. 230. 22–23

Usually when a word appears in some MSS in one place, in others in another, and in some not at all, one can conclude that it is a marginal note which has been variously inserted, and that it did not belong to the original text. But it may happen that a word was accidentally omitted and, having been replaced over the line (or in the margin), may be either restored to its original position or misplaced. The difficulty of deciding may be very great.

In chap. 23 Hartel prints: 'Contestantis apostoli vox est: praecipimus vobis in nomine Domini Iesu Christi . . .', and in his apparatus gives the readings *vobis inquit* RGv, *inquit vobis* M, leaving us to imply that W (and possibly V)—the only other MSS which he is using—omit *inquit*. There is the whole problem in a nutshell. Should *inquit* be restored, and if so should it go before or after *vobis*?

The MSS are divided as follows:

(1) *Praecipimus inquit vobis*: H; 536; M, Q; 110; *201*, 233; **E**; b, *59*, *214*, *229*, Ho
(2) *Praecipimus vobis inquit*: **M**; G, **L**; P (*m.* 2), *216*, D, 101, R, J, O, B, 225
(3) [Omit *inquit*]: h, T, *67*; Y, W, μ; P (*m.* 1), k; K

Cyprian's ordinary practice is to insert *inquit* whenever a definite speaker is referred to and *dico* in some form has not been used. But there are exceptions. When he uses *inquit* he generally puts it as early as possible. This would favour (1) above, but the weight of the MSS is rather in favour of (2). The only conclusion one can draw with any confidence is that (3) is not original, since it is unlikely that anyone should insert *inquit* quite gratuitously.

Therefore our pursuit of this promising indication has provided little to help us either in establishing the text or in grouping the MSS.

XXVIII. 231. 7

'Unus Deus est et Christus unus, et una ecclesia, &c.' (chap. 23). Here the consensus of MSS is overwhelming, but the variants deserve a moment's attention.

Unus Deus est et Christus unus:	The vast majority of MSS
Unus Deus est et Christus unus est:	O (*est* replacing *et* which follows)
Unus Deus est unus et Christus:	M, Q
Unus Deus est et unus Christus:	K, **L**
Unus Deus et Christus unus:	*214*
Unus est Deus et Christus unus:	**E**
Deus unus est et Christus unus est:	H, T, 67, h

Some of the variants are better than others, and there is nothing to determine their origin, or their relationship to one another, if any. The last group, made up of the Primacy Text MSS, may well go back to Cyprian's first version of the treatise, and the 'consensus' to his second version. If so, the latter is definitely an improvement of the sentence, such as a stylist like Cyprian would make in his own text.

XXIX. 231. 7–9

'Unus Deus est et Christus unus et una ecclesia eius et fides una et plebs una in solidam corporis unitatem concordiae glutino copulata' (chap. 23). So Hartel in his text. In his critical apparatus: *plebs una* VW, *plebs* WGRv, which leaves us wondering what W really reads. Actually the first W must be a misprint for M. Anyhow, even from this we see that *una* is omitted in several good MSS. And there is much to be said for the omission. After '*unus . . . unus . . . una . . . una*', Cyprian would need a little variation. Instead of a third *una* he expands the idea: 'plebs in solidam corporis unitatem concordiae glutino copulata.' *Una* is clearly out of place here. But a copyist who finds *unus(-a)* so repeated, is likely enough to continue the series and write *plebs una*.

Whatever the explanation, the MSS support the omission. But the exceptions have some interest. All the PT MSS have *una* (1A, 4A, 7A), as do M and Q (3D). Also b (5Xa), and apparently V, of which b has retained many vestiges.

What stands out is that, apart from the PT MSS (and we can recognize their influence on MQ), all the major groups agree in omitting *una*. After the considerations outlined above, there can be no reasonable doubt that this gives us the true reading—at least of Cyprian's own revised edition.

[For 231. 11–12 *substantiam salutis amittit*, cf. above, XXIII, pp. 81–82.]

XXX. 232. 20–26

The last half-dozen lines of chap. 26 are a happy hunting ground for variations. Mistakes of punctuation have led to corrections of all sorts:

to list them all here would serve little purpose. We will confine ourselves to the last words, given in Hartel as: *si caveret, et evaderet*. The only serious rival to this is *si caveret, evaderet*, and it is obvious that either might give rise to the other, by the duplication or the suppression of an *-et*. The evidence collected is as follows:

Si caveret, et evaderet:	H, T (*m.* 1); G, L, **E**, R, K, B
Si autem caveret, et evaderet:	M, Q
et evaderet:	O, b
evaderet:	Ho
Si caveret, evaderet:	T (*m.* 2), h, *67*; W (*m.* 2), Y, μ; P, k, 110, *216*, **D**, J, *59*, *225*
Si caveres, evaderes:	**M**

The reading of the **M** MSS, wrong as it is, may be important. It could scarcely be a variant of the first group; had *et* been in their source, it would have remained. They therefore depend on the group without *et*. But they are outstandingly good MSS, as we have seen, and for that reason one is tempted to adopt the reading *Si caveret, evaderet* and to consider the *et* as due partly to the ending of *caveret*, partly to the preceding sentence: *Si autem crederet, et caveret*. How much better to end: *si caveret, evaderet*! But a copyist with little sense of style might easily repeat the structure which he had just copied. It will deserve serious consideration.

[For 233. 8–10 *ipse*, cf. above, pp. 57–58.]

CHAPTER IX

Quotations from the *De unitate* in Ecclesiastical Literature

THE search for quotations from our treatise in later writers has produced only meagre results. It had been hoped to be able to use them as a check on the MSS of the work itself. But the actual quotations are few, and between them cover only a fragment of the whole. It was difficult enough to trace them at all, and there must certainly be others which have been missed. Those that have been found are given here, not so much for the help they give us in appraising the value of our Cyprianic MSS, but because in a study of this kind to ignore this element in the evidence altogether would be to risk missing something of real importance.

The evidence naturally includes those passages which prove the early existence of the alternative text (PT) in chap. 4, and which were collected by Dom Chapman over fifty years ago. Their importance, especially that of Pelagius II, was made full use of by him and, later, by the present writer, as an important element supporting the genuineness of that version. But we can leave as an open question Dr. Othmar Perler's contention that St. Augustine, too, knew and used that version of chap. 4, for there is no quotation of his so explicit as to have any bearing on the details of its text. Such details are all that we are concerned with here.

In the following list, the authors are arranged chronologically, and besides the reference to the work in which they quote some passage of our treatise, the date of the oldest MS of that work is given, wherever this is available. Our study is at the MS level and we must neither belittle the evidence of such a MS nor, on the other hand, exaggerate it. At best it may be an independent witness to the text of the MS which the author in question used in his day, but he may himself have adapted it to suit his context, or it may have been miscopied by the time our MS of his work was produced; again (though less likely), it may have been 'corrected' according to a Cyprianic MS some time in the interval, or, finally, it may not be correctly reproduced in the printed text which we have had to rely on. But, allowing for all these gloomy possibilities, their evidence can be added to the pool which we are collecting, in the hope that something may come out of it.

AUGUSTINE

214. 7–9   Avelle . . . arescit. *Contra Cresconium* (c. 406), ii. 33. 42[1] (oldest MS 9th cent.).
214. 9–13   Sic . . . extendit. *Contra Cresconium*, iii. 65. 73.[2]
214. 10–15 Ecclesia . . . copiosa. *Contra Gaudentium* (421–2), ii. 2. 2[4] (MS 12th cent.).
214. 10–13 Domini . . . extendit. *Contra Gaudentium*, ii. 13. 14.[5]
214. 12–13 ramos . . . extendit. *Contra Cresconium*, iii. 58. 64.[3]
223. 10   Occidi . . . non potest. Cf. *Ep.* 108. 9.[6]

LEO

213. 2–3   Hoc . . . potestatis. Cf. *Ep.* 14. 11[7] (446).

FULGENTIUS RUSPENSIS (467–533)

214. 17–25 Adulterari . . . evadit. *De remissione peccatorum*, i. 21.[8]
215. 2–6   Qui pacem . . . unum sunt. *Responsio c. Arianos*, 10.[9]

FACUNDUS HERMIANENSIS (fl. c. 550)

215. 4–6   Dicit . . . unum sunt. *Pro defensione trium capitulorum* (547), i. 3.[10]

PELAGIUS I (Papa, 555–61)

212. 18–213. 5 tamen . . . monstretur. Cf. *Ep.* 39 (559)[11] (MS: London, B.M. Add. 8873; c. 1200).

[1] *C.S.E.L.* 52. 401–2.
[2] Ibid. 52. 479.
[3] Ibid. 52. 470.
[4] Ibid. 53. 256.
[5] Ibid. 53. 272.
[6] Ibid. 34. 621.
[7] Migne, *P.L.* 54. 676. Leo does not mention Cyprian, but there is little doubt that he had this passage in mind and was gently correcting Cyprian's statement. The essential phrase is 'quoniam et inter beatissimos apostolos in similitudine *honoris* fuit quaedam discretio *potestatis*'. The brothers Ballerini, in their valuable note (ibid.), do not allude to Cyprian.
[8] Ibid. 65. 544.
[9] Ibid. 65. 224.
[10] Ibid. 67. 536.
[11] Pius M. Gassó and Dom Columba Batlle, *Pelagio I Pp. Epistulae quae supersunt*, Montserrat (1956), p. 112. The text revises that of Loewenfeld, but his faulty punctuation is retained. It should obviously read: 'Sed idcirco uni primum, quod daturus est etiam [in] omnibus, dedit ut, secundum beati Cipriani martyris id ipsum exponentis sententiam, una esse monstretur ecclesia.'

PELAGIUS II (Papa, 579–90)

Epistula II ad episcopos Histriae (584–9)[1] (MS: Paris, Lat. 1682, 9th cent.):

TR 213. 4	Exordium . . . proficiscitur. ⟨Et⟩+
PT213. 2–12	primatus . . . confidit.
219. 24–220. 2	Ad pacis . . . ruperunt.
221. 23–222. 10	Ad sacrificium . . . derelinquit.
223. 5–10	Cum Deo . . . non potest.
226. 2–8	An ⟨esse⟩ sibi . . . aliud altare.
PT 227. 9–22	Peius . . . pervenire.

ISIDORUS ARCHIEP. HISPALENSIS (*c.* 560–636)

De ecclesiasticis officiis, ii. 5.[2]

The use of *De unitate,* chap. 4, is clear from the combination of Matt. 16. 19:

212. 9–11 Tu es Petrus . . . et portae inferi *non vincent eam,* with

213. 2–3 . . . siquidem *et ceteri apostoli* cum Petro *pari consortio honoris et potestatis* effecti sunt.

LIBER SCINTILLARUM ('DEFENSORIS') (*c.* 700)

215. 2–3 Qui pacem . . . facit (ii. 53).[3]
223. 4–7 Deus inquid . . . unianimis noluerunt (iii. 63).[4]
231. 17–18 Pacem quaerere . . . pacis (ii. 54).[5]
231. 18–19 Ad disensionis malum (!) . . . caritatis (i. 46).[6]

BEDA VENERABILIS (675–735)

PT 212. 15+213. 1–7. Cf. Homil., ii. 22[7] (MS: latter half of 9th cent.).

---

[1] *M.G.H.,* Epist. II (L. M. Hartmann), p. 448, and (more accurately, but with over-sceptical comments) *A.C.O.* iv. ii (E. Schwartz), pp. 110–11. The importance of this letter for the early dating of the 'Conflated Text' in chap. 4 was underlined by Dom Chapman and was reassessed by the present writer in '*De un.* MSS', pp. lxxii–lxxiv and 48–51. All the variants in the passages quoted by Pelagius have been included in the critical apparatus here under the siglum *Pel.*

[2] Migne, *P.L.* 83. 781–2.
[3] *Corpus christianorum,* cxvii (H. M. Rochais), p. 12.
[4] Ibid., p. 17.
[5] Ibid., p. 12.   [6] Ibid., p. 6.
[7] *Corpus christianorum,* cxxii (D. Hurst), p. 347; Migne, *P.L.* 94. 218–19: 'Quod enim Petro dictum est *pasce oves meas,* omnibus utique dictum est. Hoc namque erant ceteri apostoli quod fuit Petrus, sed primatus Petro datur ut unitas ecclesiae commendetur. Pastores sunt omnes, sed grex unus ostenditur qui ab apostolis omnibus tunc unanima consensione pascebatur et deinceps a successoribus communi cura pascitur. . . .' This clearly depends on our chap. 4, not as TR has it, but either in the pure PT form, or in the Conflated Text—there is nothing to indicate which.

FLORUS, DIACONUS LUGDUNENSIS (*c.* 800–*c.* 860)

Oratio in Concilio Carisiacensi (Kierzy) *habita* (Sept. 838) (MS: 10th cent.):

    214. 1–16   Episcopatus . . . animamur.[1]
    215. 4–216. 17 Ego et Pater . . . ecclesiam Christi.[2]

HINCMARUS EP. RHEMENSIS (*c.* 806–82)

    232. 22–24 Nemo . . . *De praedestinatione diss. post.* 1.[3]

After this, there is little evidence till we come to the Gregorian reform movement which began in the middle of the eleventh century. Nearly all the great collections of canons preceding (and including) that of Gratian largely depended for their quotations of Cyprian on the *Collection in 74 Titles* (*c.* 1050)—which has never been edited, in spite of its widespread influence.[4] Van Hove's judgement of it is severe: 'Textus quidam sunt interpolati, alii mutilati, quidam mutati.'[5] However, even if the Cyprianic quotations that we find in the Canonists do not distort the original, their verbal changes and omissions make them too unreliable guides for establishing the text of the Cyprianic MSS from which they were drawn.[6]

Of the works produced during the investiture contest, there is, however, one that can retain our attention, since its dependence on previous collections is clearly supplemented by the direct use of a Cyprianic MS:

WALRAMUS EP. NIENBURGENSIS

Liber de unitate ecclesiae conservanda (1090–3) [*M.G.H., Libelli de Lite,* ii. 173–284 (W. Schwenkenbecher)]. [MS of Fulda, extant 1519, now lost.]

---

[1] *M.G.H.,* Legum, sect. III, tom. II, ii, pp. 775–6. As we know that Florus used S, and as he here (776. 6) has the omission of *et* which is peculiar to S (214. 10), he was probably using S for the second passage too, which occurred in the folios of S which today are lost.

[2] Ibid., pp. 774–5. These readings may be noted: 215. 12 domini nostri (with GB); 215. 15 indivisa (with most of the MSS).

[3] Migne, *P.L.* 125. 136 (written before 863).

[4] Cf. '*De un.* MSS', pp. lxix ff.; also the next note below.

[5] A. Van Hove, *Prolegomena ad codicem iuris canonici,* ed. alt. (1945), p. 323, where the relevant bibliography will be found.

[6] A few of their characteristic readings in chap. 4 have been entered under the siglum *Can.*

211. 13–212. 2 videns . . . frustrentur [p. 267; cf. p. 233].
212. 18–213. 5 ut unitatem . . . monstretur [p. 214].
213. 14–16   unitatem . . . probemus [p. 214; pp. 235–6].
215. 2–4   Qui . . . spargit [pp. 193–94].
215. 9–10   Unitatem . . . salutem [pp. 185, 194, 217, 264].
215. 11–23   tunica Christi . . . obtinebat [pp. 215–16 (the passage is abridged and paraphrased)].
216. 15–17   Quis ergo . . . Christi [p. 216].
217. 24–218. 9 Haec est . . . iactantur tempestate [p. 276].
218. 14–16   perversa . . . unitatem [p. 276].
220. 10–221. 3 Si duobus . . . postulant [p. 257 (abridged and rearranged)].
222. 2–5   Quam sibi . . . colliguntur [p. 193].
223. 5–10   cum Deo . . . uon potest [p. 257].
223. 8–10   animas . . . non potest [p. 194 (rearranged)].
224. 8–16   Unitatem . . . pernicies [p. 252].
225. 24–226. 11 Aversandus . . . punitur [p. 254].
227. 2–20   Filii Aaron . . . peccat [p. 271].
229. 18–20   unitatis . . . mutavit [p. 253].
230. 14–231. 12 Opto equidem . . . amittit [p. 255].

No other author has made such liberal use of our treatise, and we can safely say that the MS he was drawing from belonged to our group **L**. Its characteristic variants are included here in the apparatus under the siglum *Wal*.

CHAPTER X

The Evidence of the Text as a Whole

i. *The MSS chosen for collation*

THE survey of selected 'crucial passages' in an earlier chapter has prepared the way for the choice of the MSS to be fully collated. In certain cases, no doubt was left as to the true reading, and if this was a *lectio difficilior*, those MSS which kept it could receive a good mark, whereas a group which perpetuated an obvious blunder deserved a bad mark.

Sometimes, the different ways in which the *lectio difficilior* was 'corrected' gave useful indications of the different groupings of the MSS. This was so in I, but especially in XVI, where the variety of the insertions (*ad praemium Christi, ad Christum, ad regnum Dei*, and *ad Deum*), and of the place of insertion, showed both the connexions and the disconnexions between the MSS. Some of the bad marks were found to be peculiar to MSS already known to be connected. And in certain cases, little light was thrown on our problem: Which MSS were specially good? Which could be used, at least as being fair representatives of others?

On the basis of the presence of good readings and the avoidance of bad, m and p head the list, followed by B and h. Y, W, and T come next, but after that, the marking needs supplementing by other considerations. H almost qualifies by its marks alone, but must be included in any case for its evidence (along with T and h) to the PT tradition. To this tradition M and Q do not really contribute, and as their marking is not good can be omitted.[1] G and L have fair marking, and they, together with the pair P and k, seem required in order to decide whether they are derived from the same first volume as YW (viz. Ur-Ho). It will be remembered in this connexion that L and Pk agree substantially with the *second* volume of Ur-Ho.

Of the rest, only R and D have fair marking, and other considerations must decide the inclusion or exclusion of the rest. The 'Cistercians' can generally be classed with D, but some notice of them is called for.

---

[1] It is not only the marking of the 'crucial passages' which has led to their omission, but also their general corruption. Anyone who doubts the justice of this verdict need only work through Hartel's *apparatus criticus* (which could be added to) and he will recognize that the rare good reading is swamped by a mass of unintelligent and gratuitous readings which point to a predecessor both difficult to read and probably already hopelessly corrupt. Their variants are given only in chapters 4 and 19.

Similarly, μ and its fellows can generally be classed with YW. **E** shows itself in many ways independent of the other families, and its probably close dependence on the old BM fragments ensures its selection.

As between O and 59, which have certain affinities, O was chosen because though 59 had fairly good marks (especially over *unianimis*), it was disqualified by its many outrageous mistakes. K was similarly disqualified, and b would have suffered the same fate if it had not been the only extant MS which had an obvious relationship with Latini's lost Verona MS (V).

No excuse is required for including S in our selection, though its fragmentary character prevents our learning much from the few chapters of our treatise which it contains. And perhaps the number already selected is sufficiently large to allow us to dispense with the help of 110, 225, and Ho, though these are at least as good as some of them.

ii. *The collation: its presentation, the sigla, and their meaning*

The MSS selected in the previous section have been collated fully with a view to establishing the best text possible. How far this has been successful can be tested by the critical apparatus, taken in conjunction with the foregoing studies.

For facility of reference, the text is here presented so as to correspond line by line with Hartel's edition (*C.S.E.L.*), the pages of that edition being indicated throughout. One exception has been made for chap. 4, where, because of their importance, both editions have been printed side by side. However, even here, Hartel's lineation has been indicated for the *Textus Receptus*.

At the end (Appendix I) will be found the other variations which can be estimated to belong to the first edition (in addition to chap. 4).

The critical apparatus is made up of the evidence of three classes of MSS, roughly distinguished from one another. The first of these classes consists of MSS for which there is prima facie evidence that they all came from a very ancient collection of treatises, and differ among themselves (in several subgroups) owing presumably to the vagaries of transcription. The second class forms no such unity. It contains a couple of subgroups, but apart from these, there is nothing at all obvious which would justify their being referred to an original collection. As yet, there is no reason for suggesting that any of them is derived from the same collection as the first group; there is also the possibility that some of them are the result of the comparison of older MSS among themselves, and are therefore 'contaminated'; they have to be treated, for the moment, as more or less independent witnesses.

The third class consists of the chief MSS that preserve the tradition of the first edition (the 'PT' MSS).

The first class, all presumably derived from Ur-Ho, is collated in the following order:

M	the resultant of	Mantua, B III 18	m
		Vatican, Lat. 202	p
	with subsidiary help from Oxford, New Coll. 132		577
W	the resultant of	Würzburg, Univ., Theol. fol. 145	W
		Munich, Lat. 4597	Y
G	St. Gallen 89		G
L	the resultant of	Admont, 587	a
		Admont, 381	207
	with subsidiary help from	Vienna, Lat. 850	205
		Admont, 136	206

(*Note.* **L** (–a) means that a has not got the reading there ascribed to the other three.)

P	the resultant of	Paris, Lat. 1647A	P
		Metz, 224	k
	with subsidiary help from Vat., Reg. lat. 117		110
	Turin, D IV 37		216
	and Escorial, S.I. 11		370

The second class is collated as follows:

S	Paris, Lat. 10592	S
R	Vatican, Reg. lat. 116	R
J	Angers, 148	J
O	Oxford, Add. C 15	O
D	readings common to Oxford, Laud Misc. 451	D
	and the 'Cistercians', viz. Berlin, Th. lat. fol. 700	201
	Dijon, 124	233
	Paris, Nouv. acq. lat. 1792	229
	and also Bamberg, Patr. 64	101

(*Note.* This group, important in other respects, depends on a less good tradition of the text and its collation need only be partial. **D** will represent readings common to them all; D, readings of the Oxford MS, with or without the corroboration of one or two 'Cistercians'. It will be remembered that the later members of the group have been 'improved' by contamination.)

B	Bamberg, Patr. 63		B
E	the resultant of	Brit. Mus., Royal 6 B XV	e
		Brit. Mus., Arundel 217	250

with subsidiary help from Oxford, Bod. 210   *255*
     Lambeth, 106   *253*
   and Oxford, New Coll. 130   *354*
(*Note.* Though e may be mentioned alone in the apparatus, it is generally accompanied by 250. **E** (–e) means that e has not got the reading ascribed to the rest.)

b Berne, Bibl. Bongarsiana 235   b
   with subsidiary help from V (the collations of the sixth (?)-century Verona MS made by Latino Latini in the sixteenth century, in so far as these can be recovered from his corrections of the current editions, surviving either in separate MSS or in the margins of those editions. Their full reconstruction (if worth it) would require a monograph to itself). Only readings which are quite certain have been entered here.

The third class (**H**) has been collated as follows:

H Paris, Lat. 15282   H
T Vatican, Reg. lat. 118   T
   with subsidiary help from Oxford, Laud Misc. 105   U
h Leyden, Voss. lat. oct. 7   h
   with subsidiary help from Madrid, Bibl. Nac. 199   270
   H indicates that H, T, and h are in agreement; if they are not, each is treated separately.
   (*Note.* The members of this class not only provide evidence for the reconstruction of the first edition (especially in chaps. 4 and 19), but also for the treatise as a whole, wherever the two editions were in agreement. In this way, they take their place, whether agreeing among themselves or not, alongside the members of the first two classes.)

Note. Where a MS is adorned with a power (e.g. P^2 or k^1), it is an indication that the word or phrase has been corrected. Thus, k^1 means the reading before correction and, if no k^2 follows, the correction made agrees with the resultant text. P^2 (without P^1 alongside) means the reading of the correction, and what the first hand wrote *either* agrees with the resultant text *or* was not legible. As no critical apparatus can hope to convey all that the MSS present, the omission of such further refinements may perhaps be pardoned. Similarly, no attempt has been made to distinguish corrections made by the scribe himself, by a contemporary, or in later centuries. A small space separates the the sigla of class 1 from the rest. This may help the eye; but the classification proved premature (cf. chap. XI).

iii. *The resultant text, with critical apparatus*

The text corresponds line by line with Hartel's edition, the pages of that edition being indicated in the outer margin. In chap. 4, where the two versions are printed side by side, each line of Hartel's edition (TR) is marked off and numbered separately.

P. 209 *1* Incipit DE ECCLESIAE CATHOLICAE UNITATE

Cum moneat Dominus et dicat: *Vos estis sal terrae,*
cumque esse nos iubeat ad innocentiam simplices et tamen cum
simplicitate prudentes, quid aliud, fratres dilectissimi, quam
providere nos convenit et sollicito corde vigilantes subdoli hostis   5
insidias intellegere pariter et cavere, ne qui Christum sapien-
tiam Dei Patris induimur minus sapere in tuenda salute videamur?
Neque enim persecutio sola metuenda est ea quae sub-
ruendis ac deiciendis servis Dei aperta inpugnatione grassatur.
Facilior cautio est ubi manifesta formido est, et ad certamen   10
animus ante praestruitur, quando se adversarius confitetur. Plus
timendus est et cavendus inimicus cum latenter obrepit, cum
per pacis imaginem fallens occultis accessibus serpit, unde et
P. 210 nomen Serpentis accepit. Ea est eius semper astutia, ea est cir-
cumveniendi hominis caeca et latebrosa fallacia: sic ab initio
statim mundi fefellit, et verbis mendacibus blandiens rudes ani-

---

209 2 Matt. 5. 13   3 *cf.* Matt. 10. 16   6 *cf.* I Cor. 1. 24   **210** 1 *cf.* Gen. 3. 1 *ff.*

---

209 1 de eccl. cath. unit.] **L H**; *add.* in Christo Iesu J; *add.* adversus hereticos et scismaticos B; de cath. eccl. unit. (In Christo perseveres qui legis. Amen *add.* **M**) **MW** SD; de unit. eccl. cath. O; (adversus Novatianum scismatum *praef.* P) de eccl. unit. GP b; (adversus Novatum scismaticum *praef.* k) de unit. eccl. k **RE** 2 commoneat Y   dn̄s S   3 esse] *om.* b   nos esse **M**   et] *om.* Y   4 dilectis si W¹; karissimi G; delectissimi P¹; dilictissimi S   5 et] ut S   6 insidias] *om.* **L**   cavere] *add.* insidias **L**; *add.* vel pavere O   7 Domini. R   induimus **P** SJDVH   in intuenda J²; induenda O¹   8 ea] **E**; sed ea m²; ac non ea H¹T; *om.* **L** J²; et ea *cett.*   subvertendis **M** RbH   9 ac deiciendis] *om.* pL; diciendis S¹   Dei servis **P**   crassantur p T²; grassantur m G SR¹J¹H¹T¹h; crassantur **LP** R²Bb 10 manifesta] manesa S   11 praestruitur] praestruitur G¹; *add.* quam R²; praesti-tuitur D   adversarius] adversa prius Y; *add.* palam **L**   12 metuendus **P**   est] *om.* G h   cavendus est et timendus b   cavendus] *add.* est G² h   obripit **L** JE; obrepat k; *add.* quam R²   **210** 1 accipit D   eius] *om.* **M** h   semper eius Y¹L ea est *alt.*] et b   est *alt.*] *om.* R; *add.* eius G   circumveniendis G   2 homines **M** JT²; hominibus G²   tenebrosa **E**   sic] si J¹   3 statum G²   mundi] *add.* hominem b   et] *om.* H¹T   rude anima S

mas incauta credulitate decepit; sic Dominum ipsum temptare
5 conatus quasi obreperet rursus et falleret, latenter accessit: in-
tellectus tamen est et retusus, et ideo prostratus quia agnitus
adque detectus.

    Unde nobis exemplum datum est veteris hominis viam fugere,   2
vestigiis Christi vincentis insistere; ne denuo incauti in mortis
10 laqueum revolvamur, sed ad periculum providi accepta inmortalitate potiamur. Inmortalitate autem potiri quomodo possumus,
nisi ea quibus mors expugnatur et vincitur Christi mandata ser-
vemus, ipso monente et dicente: *Si vis ad vitam venire*
serva mandata, et iterum: *Si feceritis quod mando*
15 *vobis, iam non dico vos servos sed amicos?* Hos denique fortes dicit et stabiles, hos super petram robusta mole fun-
datos, hos contra omnes tempestates et turbines saeculi inmobili
et inconcussa firmitate solidatos: *Qui audit* inquit *verba*
mea et facit ea, similabo eum viro sapienti qui
20 *aedificavit domum suam super petram: descendit*
pluvia, advenerunt flumina, venerunt venti et in-
pegerunt in domum illam, et non cecidit; fundata
enim fuit super petram. Verbis igitur eius insistere, quaecumque et docuit et fecit discere et facere debemus. Ceterum
25 credere se in Christum quomodo dicit, qui non facit quod Christus
facere praecepit? Aut unde perveniet ad praemium fidei, qui fidem   **P. 211**
non vult servare mandati? Nutet necesse est et vagetur et, spiritu

---

210 4 *cf.* Matt. 4. 3 *ff.*   8 *cf.* Eph. 4. 22; Col. 3. 9   13 Matt. 19. 17   14 Io.
15. 14 *f.*   18 Matt. 7. 24 *f.*

    210 4 incaute D   credulitate mY²G²P² JO²DTh; credelitate Y¹G¹; crudelitas R²;
crudelitate *cett.*   decipit G¹   dōm S; Deum HT   5 conatus] *add.* est **L**
JHT   obriperet   SRJT; obseperet b²   6 et *pr.*] *om.* b   retusus
DBEbT²   et ideo . . . detectus] *om.* p   ideo] *add.* et h   agnitus] *add.* et te Y¹;
add. est R   7 detectus] *add.* est **BH**   8 exemplum nobis **L**   fugite Y¹
9 vestigii **W**¹   nec G   10 ad] a J¹   11 inmortalitatem (imm-) **P** SJ¹VH¹T¹   possi-
mus W¹ b¹   12 ea] *add.* a **P**; in HTh¹   expugnatur] et pugnatur J¹   13 vis]
add. inquid b   pervenire R   14 quod] quae p S¹O   15 dicam **E**(−e)*Vg*   denuo
R   16 supra **G P**   robusta] robustam O¹bT¹   17 turbi-
dines B   immobiles **M**   18 Qui] quid R¹   19 eum] illum R   qui]
quia D¹   20 aedificat W; aedificabit S   super] supra **MWP** OBE; su Y
descendit . . . petram (*l.* 23)] *om.* e   descendet m¹; discendit S   21 advenerunt]
et venerunt **P** *Vg*; et advenerunt J; venerunt O   flaverunt p²G OEbH*Vg*   inpigerunt SJ¹H¹T¹   22 in] *om.* m¹p   23 erat fuit Y¹; erat OEH*Vg*   supra WP B¹b
eius igitur R   insistere] *add.* et **E**   24 et *prim.*] *om.* **L** Eb   fecit et docuit V
fecit] *add.* et J   25 in Christo **GP** SRJOEbV   **211** 1 fieri RObV   unde] *om.* p
perveniat b   2 Mandat G   Nutet] *om.* B   et *pr.*] *om.* B   vacetur m¹p; evagetur B

erroris abreptus, velut pulvis quem ventus excutit, ventiletur;
nec ambulando proficiet ad salutem, qui salutaris viae non tenet
veritatem.   5
3 Cavenda sunt autem non solum quae sunt aperta adque manifesta, sed et astutae fraudis subtilitate fallentia. Quid vero astu-
tius quidve subtilius quam ut, Christi adventu detectus ac prostratus inimicus, postquam lux gentibus venit et sospitandis hominibus salutare lumen effulsit—ut surdi auditum gratiae spiri-   10
talis admitterent, aperirent ad Deum oculos suos caeci, infirmi
aeterna sanitate revalescerent, clodi ad ecclesiam currerent, muti
claris vocibus et precibus orarent—videns ille idola derelicta et,
per nimium credentium populum, sedes suas ac templa deserta,
excogitaverit novam fraudem ut sub ipso christiani nominis   15
titulo fallat incautos? Haeresis invenit et schismata quibus sub-
verteret fidem, veritatem corrumperet, scinderet unitatem. Quos
detinere non potest in viae veteris caecitate, circumscribit et decipit; novi itineris errore rapit de ipsa ecclesia homines et, dum
sibi adpropinquasse iam lumini adque evasisse saeculi noctem   20
videntur, alias nescientibus tenebras rursus infundit ut, cum
evangelio Christi et cum observatione eius et lege non stantes,
christianos se vocent, et ambulantes in tenebris habere se lumen
existiment: blandiente adversario adque fallente qui, secundum
apostoli vocem, transfigurat se velut angelum lucis, et ministros   25
subornat suos velut ministros iustitiae, adserentes noctem pro
die, interitum pro salute, desperationem sub obtentu spei, per-

211 9–13 *cf.* Isai. 42. 6*f.*; 35. 5*f.*   13–212 2 *Wal.*, p. 267   25 *cf.* II Cor.
11. 14*f.*

211 3 errores S   excuti G   ventuleltur S   4 proficiat D   vite B   6 sunt]
om. **M**   7 et] *om.* **L** h¹   astutiae **L** J¹O   fallent. Iam quid **L**   8 quid vero
SJ   ut] *om.* **M** O   hac b¹   promptus R¹   9 lugentibus O¹   sospitandis]
sospitantibus **M**; sospitantis a¹; sopitis a²; hospitandis B   10 efulsit W   surdi]
add. ad G²   11 aperirent] *om.* R   ad Deum] *om.* D   Dominum **WL**; dōm **L**
oculos suos ad Dominum J   suos] *om.* S   12 sanitate] salute E   clodi] G¹a¹
SRJ¹ODBT¹h; claudi *cett.*   current S   14 ac] et S   15 excogitaverat
G; excogitavit O²BE   et ut D   16 heresis m¹W¹**L** SRBVH; haereses *cett.*
17 fidem] et fidei **H**   et scinderet DHT   18 detenere S   via b   lieteris S
cecitatem B   decepit m O¹H¹h¹   19 iteneris S   errorem B   dum] cum S
20 lumina G; lumen RObH   adquae G¹   evasisse] *add.* se **M**   21 rurrus G
infudit G¹   ut] et **M** S   22 evvangelio S   Christi] *om.* **L** *Wal.*   et *pr.*] ut
W   cum] *om.* **L** *Wal.*   non stantes] monstrantes m   23 se et vocent **M**
vocant H¹T   se *alt.*] *om.* b   24 existimant m¹Y¹G HT   26 suos subornat
G **DH**   suos] *add.* si S   minostros S¹   27 diem SB   salutem S   obtentum
G¹; tentu a

fidiam sub praetexto fidei, antichristum sub vocabulo Christi; P. 212
ut dum verisimilia mentiuntur, veritatem subtilitate frustrentur. Hoc eo fit, fratres dilectissimi, dum ad veritatis originem
non reditur, nec caput quaeritur, nec magistri caelestis doctrina
5 servatur.

Quae si quis consideret et examinet, tractatu longo adque ar- *4*
gumentis opus non est. Probatio est ad fidem facilis conpendio
veritatis; loquitur Dominus ad Petrum: *Ego tibi dico* inquit
quia tu es Petrus et super istam petram aedificabo
10 *ecclesiam meam, et portae inferorum non vincent*
eam. Tibi dabo claves regni caelorum, et quae liga-
veris super terram erunt ligata et in caelis, et quae-
cumque solveris super terram erunt soluta et in caelis.

Et idem post resurrectionem suam	Super unum aedificat ecclesiam et,
15 dicit illi: *Pasce oves meas.* Super	quamvis apostolis omnibus |[15] post
illum aedificat ecclesiam et illi	resurrectionem suam parem po-
pascendas oves mandat et, quamvis	testatem tribuat et dicat: *Sicut* |
apostolis omnibus parem tribuat	[16]*misit me Pater et ego mitto vos.*
potestatem, unam tamen cathedram	*Accipite Spiritum* | [17]*sanctum: si*
20 constituit et unitatis originem	*cuius remiseritis peccata remittentur*|
adque rationem sua auctoritate	[18]*illi; si cuius tenueritis tenebuntur,*

212 8 Matt. 16. 18 *f.*   15 (PT) Io. 21. 17; *cf.* Beda, *Hom.* ii. 22   15 (TR) Io.
20. 21–23   18–**213** 5 (TR) Pelagius I, *Ep.* 39; *Wal.*, p. 214

212 1 praetextu **MW**[2]**P** J[2]O[2]**DEH**[2]T[2]; praetecto S   antichristi tum S; antichristo
b**T**[1]   2 ut] et R   veris similia b   subtibiatebe R[1]; subtili arte R[2]   frustentur
W[1] O[1]**D**[1]   3 eo fit] ideo B   aderitatis G[1]   originem] ordinem G   4 redi-
tur] revertitur D   nec *alt.*] *om.* R   magisterii SJEb**V**   doctrine b   6 Quae] quod
J; quem B; quam h   quis] *add.* non G   consideratur S[1]; consideretur S[2]   examinet]
exm∗∗∗ **Y**[1]; aminet k   tractu **M** RE; tracto S; tractatum h[1]   longo] *om.* G   argu-
mento **E**   7 facilius D   compendium G[2]**L** T[2]   8 dm̄s S   dico tibi RB*Vg*
inquit dico tibi petre T   inquit dico G   inquit] *add.* petre JHh   9 quia] qui **W**[1]
istam] hanc OB**T**[2]*Vg*   petram istam h   10 et portae . . . in caelis (*l.* 13)] *om.*
Can.   inferi k*Vg*   11 eam] *add.* et JEbHh*Vg*   dabo] *om.* k[1]   dabo tibi SJ
clavos b   12 et *pr.*] *om.* S   caelo O   13 super] in S   caelis] caelo O; *add.*
Et eidem (ideo J; idem **E**) post resurrectionem suam dicit Pasce oves meas k JOBEb**V**
14 eidem Hh[2]   15 illi] *om.* H[2]T[2]h[2]   14 aedificavit **E**   ecclesiam] *add.* et illi pa-
16 illum] unum M[2]   aedificavit M[1]Q   scendas (*add.* tuendasque O) oves mandat
19 potestatem] *add.* (*ex TR*) et dicat   k JOEb   15 suam] *om.* B   tribuat pote-
(*l.* 15) . . . manifestaret (213 *l.* 1) h   statem **E**   16 Pater] *om.* J[1]   accipe S
tamen] *om.* h   21 adque] *om.* M[2]Q[2]   17 si] *om.* D   si cuius] si cui **L** SR[2]T[2]h[2];
rationem] orationis MQ   suae M[1]Q   sicut R[1]   remeseritis S[1]   remittuntur
                                                        YL ROh*Vg*   18 illi] *om.* G; ei T; illis
                                                        P[1] J[2]DMQ   si] *om.* D   sicut R[1]; si cui R[2]
                                                        retinueritis p E*Vg*   retenta sunt E*Vg*

De ecclesiae catholicae unitate

P. 213 disposuit. Hoc erant utique et
ceteri quod fuit Petrus, sed primatus Petro datur et una ecclesia
et cathedra una monstratur; et
5 pastores sunt omnes, sed grex unus
ostenditur qui ab apostolis omnibus unianimi consensione pascatur.
Hanc Petri unitatem qui non tenet,
tenere se fidem credit? Qui cathe-
10 dram Petri, super quem fundata
ecclesia est, deserit, in ecclesia se esse confidit?

tamen, ut unita|¹tem manifesta-
ret, unitatis eiusdem originem ab
uno incipientem | ²sua auctoritate
disposuit. Hoc erant utique et
ceteri apostoli | ³quod fuit Petrus,
pari consortio praediti et honoris
et potestatis, | ⁴sed exordium ab
unitate proficiscitur ut ecclesia
Christi una mon|⁵stretur. Quam
unam ecclesiam etiam in Cantico
Canticorum Spi|⁶ritus sanctus ex
persona Domini designat, et dicit:
*Una est co|⁷lumba mea, perfecta
mea, una est matri suae, electa* |
⁸*genetrici suae.* Hanc ecclesiae uni-
tatem qui non tenet, te|⁹nere se
fidem credit? Qui ecclesiae reniti-
tur et resistit, in eccle|¹⁰sia se esse
confidit, quando et beatus aposto-
lus Paulus hoc idem | ¹¹doceat et

---

213 3–12 (PT) Pelagius II, *Ep.* 2 (= *Pel.*)   2–3 (TR) Leo I, *Ep.* 14. 11
4 (TR) *Pel.*   6 (TR) Cant. 6. 8 (9)   11 (TR) Eph. 4. 4–6

---

213 1 et] *om.* T   2 ceteri] *add.*
apostoli h   fuit] *add.* et h; *om.* MQ
Petrus] *add.* (*ex TR*) pari (*l.* 3) . . . proficiscitur (*l.* 4) h   sed] et h *Pel.*   3 et]
ut hM²Q² *Pel.*   una] *add.* Christi h *Pel.*
4 una] *om. Pel.*   monstretur MQ *Pel.*
7 unianimi *Pel.*   8 Hanc . . . confidit (*l.* 12)] *om. hoc loco* T (*cf. TR l.* 9)
Petri] ecclesiae suae H; et Pauli MQ;
ecclesiae *Pel.*   10 quem] quam MQ
Pel.   fundatam M¹Q¹   ecclesia fundata *Pel.*   11 ecclesiam M¹Q¹ de-
serit] *add.* et resistit *Pel.*   ecclesiam M¹Q

ut] et a¹   unitatem ut T   animitatem
J¹; unanimitatem J²
213 1 manifestaret] manifestet R; *add.*
et J   eiusdem] eius L RD *Wal.*   inci-
piente W¹Yk OBbQ²   2 utique] *om.*
T   et] *om.* R   3 fuit] *add.* et G DB
Petrus fuit *Can.*   4 sed] *om.* M
unitate] uno M D; ineunte b   profici-
scitur] exoritur T   ut] *om.* R¹   Christi]
Dei M; *om.* V   monstretur] *add.* sed . . .
monstretur (*iterum*) m; mostretur S; mon-
straretur B; monstraetur M¹   5 Quam
. . . suae (*l.* 8)] *om.* M   ecclesiam] *om.*
L   etiam] *om.* ST   cantica DT
6 dm̄i S   designat et] de ecclesia G
dicat S   7 mea *alt.*] *om.* T   matris
8 genetricis k ODB; genetri
T   qui non . . . quando et (*l.* 10)] *om. Can.*   tenet] *om.* R   9 se] *om.* J¹b

Lk ODE*Vg*   electa] *om.* S; *add.* est et B; *add.* est E
T   qui non . . . quando et (*l.* 10)] *om. Can.*   tenet] *om.* R   9 se] *om.* J¹b
fidem se L   ecclesiae . . . resistit] (*ex PT*) cathedram Petri super quem fundata
ecclesia est deserit T   10 Paulus apostolus J   idem] *om.* P

sacramentum unitatis ostendat
dicens: *Unum corpus* | ¹²*et unus*
Spiritus, una spes vocationis ve-
strae, unus | ¹³*Dominus, una fides,*
unum baptisma, unus Deus? |
¹⁴Quam unitatem tenere firmiter 5
et vindicare debemus maxime |
¹⁵episcopi, qui in ecclesia prae-
sidemus, ut episcopatum quoque |
¹⁶ipsum unum adque indivisum
probemus. Nemo fraternitatem |
¹⁷mendacio fallat, nemo fidei veri-
tatem perfida praevaricatione |
¹corrumpat.

}P. 214

Episcopatus unus est cuius a singulis in solidum pars
tenetur. Ecclesia una est quae in multitudinem latius incremento
fecunditatis extenditur: quomodo solis multi radii sed lumen
unum, et rami arboris multi sed robur unum tenaci radice funda-
5 tum, et cum de fonte uno rivi plurimi defluunt, numerositas
licet diffusa videatur exundantis copiae largitate, unitas tamen
servatur in origine. Avelle radium solis a corpore, divisionem
lucis unitas non capit; ab arbore frange ramum, fractus germi-
nare non poterit; a fonte praecide rivum, praecisus arescit. Sic
10 et ecclesia, Domini luce perfusa, per orbem totum radios suos por-

---

213 14–16 (TR) *Wal.*, pp. 214, 235–6   214 1–16 Florus, *oratio in conc.*,
pp. 775–6   7–9 Aug., *c. Crescon.* ii. 33. 42   9–13 Aug., *c. Crescon.* iii. 65. 73
9–15 Aug., *c. Crescon.* iii. 58. 64   10–15 Aug., *c. Gaudent.* ii. 2. 2; 13. 14

213 11 ostendit T¹   Unum . . . vestrae (*l.* 12)] *om.* D   12 et] *om.* L   unum spiritum
R¹   spiritus] *add.* una fides J; *add.* et b   vestrae] nostrae G E   13 Dominus] dm̄s
S; Deus T   baptisma] *add.* et Bb; baptismum T¹   Deus] Dominus T   14 tenere]
om. B   maxime] *add.* nos *Can. Wal.*   maxime . . . praesidemus (*l.* 15)] *om.*
T   15 ecclesiam G¹ O¹   quoque] *om.* m¹   16 individuum M; invisum
W¹M¹   comprobemus M   fraternitate B   17 mendacio . . . veritatem] *om.* T
fidem veritatis S   perfidiae V   214 1 episcopus T¹   insolitum S   2 et
ecclesia b   est] *om.* G   quae] quam Dominus in Christo instituit. Haec M; quem
B   multitudine G OD   incrementum R   3 funditatis G   solis] sol in* G;
soli** H¹; sol iste T   multis radiis G H¹T   sed] et H¹T   unum lumen L
4 robor WP¹ SH (arbor h²)   una h   tenet B   fundata h   5 defluant O²   6 scilicet
difusa G; effusa S   copia R   largitatem G   7 originem RO¹D¹   corpore] *add.*
et V   divisionem] *add.* corpore h   8 fructus p   9 fronte Y   10 et] *om.*
S *Flo.*   ecclesiam B   dm̄i S

rigit, unum tamen lumen est quod ubique diffunditur nec unitas
corporis separatur; ramos suos in universam terram copia uber-
tatis extendit; profluentes largiter rivos latius spandit, unum tamen caput est et origo una, et una mater fecunditatis successibus
copiosa: illius fetu nascimur, illius lacte nutrimur, spiritu eius   15
animamur.

6   Adulterari non potest sponsa Christi, incorrupta est et pudica:
unam domum novit, unius cubiculi sanctitatem casto pudore
custodit. Haec nos Deo servat, haec filios regno quos generavit
adsignat. Quisque ab ecclesia segregatus adulterae iungitur, a   20
promissis ecclesiae separatur, nec perveniet ad Christi praemia
qui relinquit ecclesiam Christi: alienus est, profanus est, hostis
est. Habere iam non potest Deum patrem qui ecclesiam non habet
matrem. Si potuit evadere quisque extra arcam Noe fuit, et qui
extra ecclesiam foris fuerit evadet. Monet Dominus et dicit: *Qui*   25
P. 215 *non est mecum adversus me est, et qui non mecum*
colligit spargit. Qui pacem Christi et concordiam rumpit,
adversus Christum facit; qui alibi praeter ecclesiam colligit,
Christi ecclesiam spargit. Dicit Dominus: *Ego et Pater unum*
sumus, et iterum de Patre et Filio et Spiritu sancto scriptum   5
est: *Et tres unum sunt.* Et quisquam credit hanc unitatem
de divina firmitate venientem, sacramentis caelestibus cohaeren-

---

214 17 *cf.* II Cor. 11. 2 *et* Eph. 5. 23–32   17–25 Fulgent., *remiss. pecc.* i. 21
24 *cf.* Gen. 7. 23; I Pet. 3. 20   25 Matt. 12. 30   215 2–6 Fulgent.,
resp. c. Arian. 10   4 Io. 10. 30   4–6 Facund. Herm., *defens. tri. capit.* i. 3
4–216 17 Florus, *orat. in conc.*, pp. 774–5   6 I Io. 5. 8

---

214 11 defunditur P; difunditur k   12 ramos] *folia seqq. deperd.* S   copiam
H¹T¹   copia vobistatis D¹   13 profluens M; profluente G²; profluenter
R   spandit] MW¹G¹ O¹BbT¹h; pandit W²YG²LP SJO²e *Flo.*; expandit RDHT²
14 et *pr.*] *om.* h   una origo L   et una] *om.* M   15 gloriosa bV   tutrimur
G¹   17 adulterare T¹   est] *om.* b   18 cubili W O¹; cubilis O²   19 Domino
RD   regno] *om.* b   generat R   20 quisquis b   ecclesia] *add.* eius H
segregatur eTh   21 separetur m   Christi] *om.* GL   praemia Christi E   praemium HT   22 relinquet m; reliquit G; dereliquit DE   ecclesia R   est *pr.*]
add. et D   profanus est hostis est] *om.* L   23 iam] *om.* WGP ROE   Dominum p   non habet . . . ecclesiam (*l.* 25)] *om.* L   24 quisque] quisquam p¹ J²B;
quisquis p²; quis Y²P²; *add.* qui MY²P² J²E; *om.* T¹   si extra arcano efuit R   arca
B; archam E; archa b   25 ecclesiae P   fores P²   fuerit foris G; extra fuerit
foris L   fuerit] fuerint T¹; *om.* h¹   evadet MP²k JE; evadit *cett.*   et dicit] dicens B
215 1 adversus] adversum WL ODbH; contra B*Vg*   mecum non OBb   colligit
mecum L   2 dispargit L RO¹; dispergit O²   conclcordiam Y   3 praeter]
add. Christum H   ecclesiam] *add.* Christi G   4 dispargit O¹; dispergit O²
6 Et *pr.*] *om. Flo.*   tres] hi tres b   7 de] *om.* T¹h

tem, scindi in ecclesia posse et voluntatum conlidentium divortio
separari? Hanc unitatem qui non tenet non tenet Dei legem,
10 non tenet Patris et Filii fidem, vitam non tenet et salutem.
    Hoc unitatis sacramentum, hoc vinculum concordiae insepara-   7
biliter cohaerentis ostenditur quando in evangelio tunica Domini
Iesu Christi non dividitur omnino nec scinditur sed, sortientibus
de veste Christi, quis Christum potius indueret, integra vestis
15 accipitur et incorrupta adque indivisa tunica possidetur. Loquitur ac dicit scriptura divina: *De tunica autem, quia de
superiore parte non consutilis sed per totum textilis fuerat, dixerunt ad invicem, 'Non scindamus
illam sed sortiamur de ea cuius sit.'* Unitatem ille por-
20 tabat de superiore parte venientem, id est de caelo et a Patre venientem, quae ab accipiente ac possidente scindi omnino non po-
terat, sed totam semel et solidam firmitatem inseparabiliter obtinebat: possidere non potest indumentum Christi qui scindit et
dividit ecclesiam Christi. Contra denique cum, Solomone moriente,
regnum eius et populus scinderetur, Achias propheta Hieroboam   P. 216
regi obvius factus in campo in duodecim scissuras vestimentum
suum discidit, dicens: *Sume tibi decem scissuras quia
haec dicit Dominus, 'Ecce scindo regnum de manu
5 Solomonis, et dabo tibi decem sceptra, et duo sceptra*

---

215 9–10 *Wal.*, pp. 185, 217, 264   16 Io. 19. 23 *f.*   **216** 3 III Reg. 11. 31 *f.*, 36

---

215 8 sindi m   ecclesias **M**; ecclesiam **L** O[1]   posset **L**   voluntate p[1]G T[1];
voluntatem **WP** DBbHT[2]   et collidentium **L**; conludentium DH; confidentium B
conlidentium . . . unitatem] *om.* T   9 qui] *om.* Y   non tenet] *om.* W E   non
tenet Dei legem] *om.* DHT *Can. Wal.*   legem Dei O   10 non] qui non J[2]   non
tenet] *om.* T   fidem] Dei R[2]   fidem vitam] debitam T   vitam] unitatem **WP** B;
et veritatem **E**   11 unitas Gk[1]   sacramentum] *om.* G[1]   12 coherenti **WP**;
cohaerens R   evvangelio m   Domini] *add.* nostri G B *Flo.*   13 dividatur Y[1]   nec]
non J   14 quis] qui J   Christum potius] potius Christum G; Christi vestem
L   induceret R   15 et] *om.* **P**   adque] et R   individua **WP** B   16 ac]
et R   adicit G[1]   divina] *om. Flo.*   De *pr.*] *om.* R   17 superiora G; superiori
b   non consutilis] inconsutilis **L***Vg*; non cossutilis R; non consubtilis D[1]; *add.*
erat **E**   per] super R[1]   19 sortiemur Y   ea] illa p[1] OD   ille] illa m[2]W[2]
20 superiori Rb   venientem *pr.*] *om. Flo.*   a] *om. Flo.*   veniente R   21 acci-
dente b   ac] et **W**   22 totam] *add.* sed totam G[1]   simul Y O[2]   et] *om.* G
RJOeb   solidam et semel firmatam **L**   solida firmitate G   23 poterit R   qui
. . . Christi] *om.* R   24 divid✳✳ m[1]   Christi] *om.* B   Solomone p[1]G; Salemone **L** O;
Salomone *cett.*   **216** 1 populum RB[2]   Acazias R   Iheroboam G   2 obviam
G   duodecim] xii pWL DBe   scissuris **E**; cissuras b   3 discindit R; scidit
JBHT   decem] x pWL; *om.* J   4 Dominus] dñ W   regnum] *add.* meum H
5 Solomonis HT; Salemonis **L** O   decem] x W; *om.* **L**   sceptra decem R

erunt ei propter servum meum David et propter
Hierusalem civitatem, quam elegi ut ponam nomen
meum illic.' Cum duodecim tribus Israel scinderentur, vestimentum suum propheta Achias discidit; at vero quia Christi
populus non potest scindi, tunica eius per totum textilis et   10
cohaerens divisa a possidentibus non est: individua, copulata,
conexa ostendit populi nostri, qui Christum induimus, concordiam cohaerentem; sacramento vestis et signo declaravit ecclesiae unitatem.

8   Quis ergo sic sceleratus et perfidus, quis sic discordiae furore   15
vesanus, ut aut credat scindi posse aut audeat scindere unitatem
Dei, vestem Domini, ecclesiam Christi? Monet ipse in evangelio
suo et docet, dicens: *Et erunt unus grex et unus pastor,*
et esse posse uno in loco aliquis existimat aut multos pastores
aut greges plures? Apostolus item Paulus hanc eandem nobis   20
insinuans unitatem, obsecrat et hortatur et dicit: *Obsecro in-*
quit *vos, fratres, per nomen Domini nostri Iesu*
Christi, ut id ipsum dicatis omnes, et non sint in vo-
bis schismata, sitis autem compositi in eodem sensu
et in eadem sententia; et iterum dicit: *Sustinentes in-*   25
P. 217   *vicem in dilectione, satis agentes servare unitatem*
Spiritus in coniunctione pacis. Stare tu et vivere putas
posse de ecclesia recedentem, sedes sibi alias et diversa domicilia
condentem, cum dictum sit ei in qua praeformabatur

---

216 15–17 *Wal.*, p. 216   18 Io. 10. 16   21 I Cor. 1. 10   25 Eph. 4. 2 *f.*

---

216 6 ei] et **M**; *om.* W¹   propter *pr.*] *add.* propter G¹   David servum meum Gk
7 Iherusalem G   ut] *om.* **M**   ponat R   8 ibi k   Cum ... Israel] *om.* R   duo-
decim] xii pW**L** DBe   tribus] *om.* W   Israhel **P** OT; *om.* J   scinderetur R
9 Achaias R¹   scidit BEH²T²h; dicit b; scindit H¹T¹   at vero] A clero **M**; Ad vero
J¹   10 scindi non potest **E**   texilis O   11 coherentes G¹; quoerens D
a] *om.* b   individuam copulatam V   12 conexam V; contexta *Flo.*   induimus]
induimur h; *om.* e   13 coherentes R; coherente O   declaruit W¹; declarat
b   15 sceleratus Y   et] ac J   et perfidus] *om.* **L** *Wal.*   perditus O²   16 ut]
qui **M**; *om.* H¹   credat aut T²   17 dominicam G   18 et *prim.*] *om.*
R   erit GP² ROBb   19 posse] se R; *om.* e   uno posse b   in uno loco m**L**
exestimet G¹   20 item] idem b; autem V   21 et dicit] dicens **D**; et docet J;
et docet dicens **H**   vos inquit **L**   22 per] propter W   nostri] *om.* **M** J¹O; n P
23 ipsum] ipsut R; *om.* b; ipsum id H¹   24 schismata] chismata Y; dissensiones
D   25 sustinetis W¹; sustinentibus B   **217** 1 dilectionem bH; delictionem T¹
2 coniunctione] vinculo Y; coniunctio R¹   tu] *om.* G; te R; te tu B¹   posse putas **M**
3 ecclesiam O¹   recedente b   sedes] sed et R   domicilia diversa b   4 condentes
R; concedentem O   ei] **M** Dh; ad Raab (*aut simile aliquid) cett.*   praeformatur b

5 ecclesia: *Patrem tuum et matrem tuam et fratres tuos*
et totam domum patris tui colliges ad te ipsam in
domum tuam: et erit, omnis qui exierit ostium do-
mus tuae foras, reus sibi erit; item sacramentum Paschae nihil aliud in Exodi lege contineat quam ut agnus, qui in
10 figura Christi occiditur, in domo una edatur? Loquitur Deus dicens:
In domo una comedetur: non eicietis de domo car-
nem foras. Caro Christi et sanctum Domini eici foras non potest, nec alia ulla credentibus praeter unam ecclesiam domus est.
Hanc domum, hoc unianimitatis hospitium designat et nuntiat
15 Spiritus sanctus in Psalmis, dicens: *Deus qui inhabitare*
facit unianimes in domo. In domo Dei, in ecclesia Christi
unianimes habitant, concordes et simplices perseverant.

Idcirco et in columba venit Spiritus sanctus. Simplex animal   9
et laetum est: non felle amarum, non morsibus saevum, non
20 unguium laceratione violentum; hospitia humana diligere, unius
domus consortium nosse; cum generant simul filios edere, cum
commeant volatibus invicem cohaerere; communi conversatione
vitam suam degere, oris osculo concordiam pacis agnoscere, legem circa omnia unianimitatis inplere. Haec est in ecclesia no-
25 scenda simplicitas, haec caritas obtinenda: ut columbas dilectio
fraternitatis imitetur, ut mansuetudo et lenitas agnis et ovibus

---

217 5 Ios. 2. 18 *f.*   11 Exod. 12. 46   15 Ps. 67 (68). 7   18 *cf.* Matt. 3. 16;
Marc. 1. 10; Luc. 3. 22; Io. 1. 32   24–**218** 9 *Wal.*, p. 276

---

217 5 et *alt.*] *om.* R   6 colligis H¹T¹h   ipsum G¹   in] *om.* W¹   7 erit]
om. **M**   hostium Yk DbH   8 foras] *om.* Y; foris **P**   tibi **M**   item] *add.*
cum ad **M**; *add.* de **L**; *om.* JT¹h   sacramentum] sacramento L; *add.* quoque H
9 legem BH¹   contine✳t J; continet **H**   10 Loquitur . . . comedetur (edatur?)] *om.*
L   Deus] Dominus **D**   11 comedetis O²; edatur mY¹ H¹; edetur JH; *add.* et O
eicitis G   carnem de domo R   12 carnem p   13 ulla] una **E**   14 Anc
D¹   domum hanc W   unitatis **L** J²; unitas J¹; unianimitatis D¹BHT¹; unanim-
cett. (*sicut pluries infra*)   denunciat **WGP** ROBbh²   denunciat et designat B
15 Spiritus . . . Psalmis] *om.* R   psalmo T   dicens] *om.* b   habitare HT   16 unianimes YG¹ RDEH   domo *pr.*] *add.* Dei **M**   In domo *alt.*] *om.* R   17 unianimes
YG¹ RDEHT¹   habitent G; inhabitant b   et concordes habitant J   18 columbam
DV   19 et le✳tum G; electum **L**   est] *om.* **P**   saevum] servum D¹   20 laceratio-
bus k¹   hospitia] *add.* consuevit **E**   21 consortia **E**   dum b   congene-
rant Y¹; cum gerant D   sedere W¹Y B   filio sedere H¹   cum *alt.*] *om.* W¹G;
com Y¹   22 commoneant H¹; commeat T¹   volatilibus W¹Y BH¹T; volantibus
k **D**   23 diligere k H¹   pacis] facis T¹; *om.* T²   24 unianimitatis implere]
om. Y   una animitatis B¹   noscendi R; nocenda b¹   25 haec caritas] et **L** *Wal.*
columbae b   dilectionem G¹   26 et *pr.*] ut **M**

aequetur. Quid facit in pectore christiano luporum feritas et ca-
P. 218 num rabies et venenum letale serpentium et cruenta saevitia
bestiarum? Gratulandum est cum tales de ecclesia separantur,
ne columbas, ne oves Christi saeva sua et venenata contagione
praedentur. Cohaerere et coniungi non potest amaritudo cum dul-
cedine, caligo cum lumine, pluvia cum serenitate, pugna cum   5
pace; cum fecunditate sterilitas, cum fontibus siccitas, cum
tranquillitate tempestas. Nemo existimet bonos de ecclesia posse
discedere: triticum non rapit ventus, nec arborem solida radice
fundatam procella subvertit; inanes paleae tempestate iactantur,
invalidae arbores turbinis incursione vertuntur. Hos execratur et   10
percutit Iohannes apostolus, dicens: *Ex nobis exierunt, sed*
non fuerunt ex nobis; si enim fuissent ex nobis,
mansissent nobiscum.

10   Hinc haeresis et factae sunt frequenter et fiunt, dum perversa
mens non habet pacem, dum perfidia discordans non tenet uni-·   15
tatem. Fieri vero haec Dominus permittit et patitur manente pro-
priae libertatis arbitrio ut, dum corda et mentes nostras veritatis discrimen examinat, probatorum fides integra manifesta
luce clarescat. Per apostolum praemonet Spiritus sanctus et dicit:
Oportet haeresis esse ut probati manifesti sint   20
in vobis. Sic probantur fideles, sic perfidi deteguntur, sic et
ante iudicii diem hic quoque iam iustorum adque iniustorum

---

218. 11 I Io. 2. 19   14–16 *Wal.*, p. 276   20 I Cor. 11. 19

---

217 27 adequetur G E   christiano pectore k   ferocitas k   rabies canum G
218 1 rabies et venenum] *om.* R   serpentum WGP JD; serpentinum H¹   cruen-
tum k¹; cruentarum k²   3 ne *pr.*] nec b   ne *alt.*] neve J; nec b   sua] *om.* D
venerata T¹   4 coerere W¹; cohereri B   coniugi G¹a¹; coniungere b¹   dulcedine]
add. et L; dulcedinem B   6 faecunditatem O¹   sterelitas k¹ J¹ObT¹   pontibus
p¹; potibus p²; fontium H¹   7 extimet R   bonum D   discedere posse J
8 non] cu W¹; *om.* G¹   arbore B   9 subverti R   tempestates R   iactantur]
add. et DVH   10 turbines R   incussione G   vertentur V   hoc k¹   11 iohannis J¹B   dicit apostolus L   *ierunt G   12 si enim] nam si J*Vg*; si b
fuissent ex nobis] ex nobis essent J; ex nobis utique fuissent O   13 mansissent]
permansissent E*Vg*; *add.* utique JB*Vg*   14 Hinc] *add.* et WG   haeresis] heresis
W¹G¹ RB; h(a)ereses *cett.*   et *pr.*] *om.* J   et factae] effecte B   frequenter et
factae sunt E   dum] cum D   15 habet... non] *om.* e   cum R   16 vero]
om. h   hoc R   17 ut dum corda] *om.* G   corda et] *om.* L   vestras L   avertitis
L   18 discrimine ObH   19 clarescit M; clarescant Y²   20 Oportet] *add.*
et m²pWGP RJET*Vg*   h(a)eresis WP¹ B; hereses *cett.*   esse] *om.* G; *add.* et
scismata bV   probati] *add.* in H¹T¹   21 in] *om.* B   perfidiae L   22 quoque
iam] pro quaedam b

animae dividuntur, et a frumento paleae separantur. Hi sunt
qui se ultro aput temerarios convenas sine divina dispositione
25 praeficiunt, qui se praepositos sine ulla ordinationis lege constituunt, qui nemine episcopatum dante episcopi sibi nomen adsu-
munt; quos designat in Psalmis Spiritus sanctus: *Sedentes in pe-*
stilentiae cathedra: pestes et lues fidei, serpentes ore fallentes P. 219
et corrumpendae veritatis artifices, venena letalia linguis pesti-
feris evomentes; quorum sermo ut cancer serpit, quorum trac-
tatus pectoribus et cordibus singulorum mortale virus infundit.
5   Contra eiusmodi clamat Dominus, ab his refrenat et revocat 11
errantem plebem suam, dicens: *Nolite audire sermones*
pseudoprophetarum, quoniam visiones cordis eorum
frustrantur eos; locuntur sed non ab ore Domini.
Dicunt eis qui abiciunt verbum Domini: 'Pax erit vobis
10 *et omnibus ambulantibus in voluntatibus suis';*
omni qui ambulat errore cordis sui: 'Non venient
super te mala.' Non locutus sum ad eos, et ipsi pro-
phetaverunt. Si stetissent in substantia mea et
audissent verba mea, et si docuissent populum meum,
15 *convertissent eos a malis cogitationibus eorum.* Hos
eosdem denuo Dominus designat et denotat, dicens: *Me dereli-*
querunt fontem aquae vivae, et effoderunt sibi lacus
detritos qui non possunt aquam portare. Quando aliud

---

218 23 *cf.* Matt. 3. 12   27 Ps. 1. 1   219 3 *cf.* II Tim. 2. 17   6 Ier.
23. 16 *f.*   12 Ier. 23. 21 *f.*   16 Ier. 2. 13

---

218 23 animi E   a] *om.* O   paleae] plagae H   Hi] Hinc WGP JDH; Hii k Bb
24 se] *om.* G   aput W   convenias R; convenisse T¹   dispositione] *add.* se G;
disputatione R; dispensatione JOH¹   25 qui se] *om.* J¹   ordinationis] m²;
ordinationes R¹; dispositionis Ob   26 adsumunt] imponunt b¹   27 quod Y
R¹   in Psalmis] *om.* b   spalmis G   219 1 cathedram WP O¹Bb; cathedras E
fide m²p   serpentes m²pG¹ J; serpentis *cett.*   fallentis Y¹   2 corrumpenda
B   lotalia O¹   3 tractatibus m¹p   4 pectoris D   infundit] *add.* contra
virus infundit R   5 huiusmodi R¹   Dominus] *add.* et H   et] ei R   7 illorum b   8 frustantur O¹   illos b   sed] et E   9 eis] eius W¹   adiciunt W¹;
habitiunt D   Domini] Dei WP OBEb   vobis] *add.* vobis G   11 omni] REH;
omnibus G; omnis *cett.*   ambulat] *add.* in P² RDBE(−e)H; ambulant J; ambulant
in G   12 te] eum O²   sum locutus G   et] sed R   13 substantia mea et]
substantiam exeant R   14 si] *om.* M; sic P   meum] *add.* legem meam O ; *add.*
et E   15 converterem M; convertissem GP Oh; non vertissent D   eorum] e✱✱✱ G¹
16 eodem D¹   Dominus denuo k   derelinquerunt mWG BH¹h   17 vitae
GP bVT¹   et effoderunt] et offoderunt G¹; et foderunt EVh; et effonderunt T¹
18 detrictos D   *in marg.* de baptismo mW (*add.* hereticorum W)

baptisma praeter unum esse non possit, baptizare posse se opinantur; vitae fonte deserto, vitalis et salutaris aquae gratiam pol-   20
licentur. Non abluuntur illic homines sed potius sordidantur, nec
purgantur delicta sed immo cumulantur; non Deo nativitas illa
sed diabolo filios generat: per mendacium nati veritatis promissa
non capiunt, de perfidia procreati fidei gratiam perdunt. Ad pacis
P. 220 praemium venire non possunt qui pacem Domini discordiae furore
ruperunt.

12   Nec se quidam vana interpretatione decipiant quod dixerit
Dominus: *Ubicumque fuerint duo aut tres collecti in*
nomine meo, ego cum eis sum. Corruptores evangelii ad-   5
que interpretes falsi extrema ponunt et superiora praetereunt,
partis memores et partem subdole comprimentes; ut ipsi ab
ecclesia scissi sunt, ita capituli unius sententiam scindunt. Dominus enim, cum discipulis suis unianimitatem suaderet et pacem,
Dico inquit *vobis quoniam si duobus ex vobis con-*   10
venerit in terra de omni re quamcumque petieritis,
continget vobis a Patre meo qui in caelis est. Ubi-
cumque enim fuerint duo aut tres collecti in no-
mine meo, ego cum eis sum: ostendens non multitudini
sed unianimitati deprecantium plurimum tribui. *Si duobus* in-   15
quit *ex vobis convenerit in terra*: unianimitatem prius
posuit, concordiam pacis ante praemisit, ut conveniat nobis fideliter et firmiter docuit. Quomodo autem potest ei cum aliquo

---

219 24–220 2 *Pel.*   220 4 Matt. 18. 20   10 Matt. 18. 19 *f.*   10–221 2 *cf. Wal.*,
p. 257

---

219 19 posse] *om.* W J   se posse b   se] *om.* ROh   20 deserti G¹   aquae]
add. et Y   21 Non ... sordidantur] *om.* G   abluuntur] lavuntur R   22 immo
cumulantur] potius sordidantur b   cumulantur] maculantur **WP** DB   Deo]
Domini R; Domino **D**   ista **H**   23 zabulo L; diaboli R¹   filio H   generant
O¹   nati] Nam **L**; nativitatis O   nati veritatis] nativitatis G¹   220 1 pervenire
Pel.   qui] quia M¹Q *Pel.*   3 ne D   quidem DH   decipiat **L D**   dilexerit G¹
4 aut] *om.* J¹   5 ego] eo D¹   eis] illis **P**   7 partis] partim GP² DbH²; partem B   partem] partim **WP Db**   8 scindit **L**   9 suis] *om.* h   una animitatem RH¹T¹; unanimitatem *cett.*   suaderet] suam deseret R   pacem] *add.* ait
W¹Y; *add.* dixit h   10 vobis inquit R   quoniam] *om.* G   duobus] *add.* inquit
H¹T¹; duo m²L(−a)   convenerint m²L(−a) BH¹   11 quacumque G   12 con-
tingnet m; contingent **L**(−a) H¹   est] *add.* et Y   13 aut] vel ET   14 cum eis]
om. L   15 unianimitati R; unanimitate G¹ J¹; unitati **L**; unamitati h; unianimitati
cett.   depraecanti B   plurimum] *om.* Y   tribus m¹p   duo m²L(−a)   16 convenerint m²L(−a)   terram HT   unianimitatem R; unanimitatem *cett.*   18 potest
autem O   ei] *om.* BT¹

convenire, cui cum corpore ipsius ecclesiae et cum universa fra-
20 ternitate non convenit? Quomodo possunt duo aut tres in nomine
Christi colligi, quos constet a Christo et ab eius evangelio separari? Non enim nos ab illis, sed illi a nobis recesserunt et, cum
haeresis et schismata postmodum nata sint dum conventicula
sibi diversa constituunt, veritatis caput adque originem relique-
25 runt. Dominus autem de ecclesia sua loquitur, et ad hos qui sunt
in ecclesia loquitur ut, si ipsi concordes fuerint, si secundum
quod mandavit et monuit, duo aut tres licet collecti unianimiter P. 221
oraverint, duo aut tres licet sint, inpetrare possint de Dei maie-
state quod postulant. *Ubicumque fuerint duo aut tres,*
ego inquit *cum eis sum.* Cum simplicibus scilicet adque
5 pacatis, cum Deum timentibus et Dei praecepta servantibus, cum
his duobus vel tribus licet esse se dixit; quomodo et cum tribus
pueris in camino ignis fuit et, quia in Deum simplices adque
inter se unianimes permanebant, flammis ambientibus medios
spiritu roris animavit; quomodo apostolis duobus in custodia
10 clausis, quia simplices, quia unianimes erant, ipse adfuit; ipse
resolutis carceris claustris, ut verbum quod fideliter praedica-
bant multitudini traderent, ad forum rursus inposuit. Quando
ergo in praeceptis suis ponit et dicit: *Ubi fuerint duo aut*
tres, ego cum eis sum, non homines ab ecclesia dividit, qui
15 instituit et fecit ecclesiam; sed, exprobrans discordiam perfidis et

---

221 6 *cf.* Dan. 3. 49–51 (LXX et *Vg*)   9 *cf.* Act. 5. 19–21

220 19 cui] qui m² RD   20 non convenit] *om.* R   possunt] *add.* Christi in
nomine **L**   in nomine Christi] *om.* **L**   21 collegi J¹   constat YG¹ JET²
evangelio] aecclesia Y   22 recessunt H   23 hereses pY²LP² JOEbH²T²h
postmodum nata] *om.* HT   sunt Rh   dum] cum W HT   conventiculas m¹W
24 diversas W   relinquerunt m¹ R²; reliquerint G   25 autem . . . collecti (221,
l. 1)] *eadem manu super rasur.* R   et] sed O; ei D   et . . . sunt] ut si ipsi et ad eos
qui R   hos] *add.* loquitur O   sunt] *om.* b   26 in ecclesia] *om.* m¹p; *add.* sunt R;
add. sua sunt b   loquitur] *om.* JO   ut] et G¹   ut si ipsi] *om.* R   **221** 1 duo]
quo D   duo . . . oraverint] *om.* a¹   licet] *om.* **L**   collecti] *om.* H¹   unianimiter RD;
unanimiter *cett.*   2 duo . . . sint] *om.* M H²T   possunt b   ad Dominum maiestatis
R   3 Ubicumque] *add.* inquit J   tres] *add.* collecti O; *add.* collecti in nomine
meo b   4 inquit] *om.* J   5 paccatis YG¹; peccatis H¹   Deum] Dominum **M**k
RV; Dei   a; Domino D   6 his] is B   licet] *om.* **L**   se] *om.* W¹ J¹   7 Deo
L; Domino **DV**   8 inter se] *om.* k   unanimes G¹ D   ambeuntibus O   medio
GL RJODBbh; *add.* fornaci a²; *add.* fornacis **L**(−a)   9 spiritu] *om.* J   quomodo]
add. et E   apostolus O¹   custodiam m   10 unianimes G¹ DB; unames
Y¹; unanimes *cett.*   11 resolvit **L**; solutis **H**   carceribus b   claustra **L**   verum
B   feliciter a   12 ad] *om.* J²   13 ergo] ego b   14 tres] *add.* collecti B
15 exprobrans] W¹; probans Y¹; exprobans mW² RO¹h

fidelibus pacem sua voce commendans, ostendit magis esse se
cum duobus aut tribus unianimiter orantibus quam cum dissiden-
tibus plurimis, plusque inpetrari posse paucorum concordi prece
quam discordiosa oratione multorum.

13   Ideo et, cum orandi legem daret, addidit dicens: *Et cum ste-*   20
teritis ad orationem, remittite si quid habetis ad-
versus aliquem, ut et Pater vester qui in caelis est
remittat peccata vobis; et ad sacrificium cum dissensione
venientem revocat ab altari et iubet prius concordare cum fratre,
tunc cum pace redeuntem Deo munus offerre; quia nec ad Cain   25
munera respexit Deus, neque enim habere pacatum Deum po-
P. 222   terat qui cum fratre pacem per zeli discordiam non habebat.
Quam sibi igitur pacem promittunt inimici fratrum? Quae sacrificia celebrare se credunt aemuli sacerdotum? Secum esse Christum,
cum collecti fuerint, opinantur qui extra Christi ecclesiam colliguntur?   5

14   Tales etiam si occisi in confessione nominis fuerint, macula
ista nec sanguine abluitur: inexpiabilis et gravis culpa discordiae
nec passione purgatur. Esse martyr non potest qui in ecclesia non
est; ad regnum pervenire non poterit qui eam quae regnatura
est derelinquit. Pacem nobis Christus dedit, concordes adque uni-   10
animes esse praecepit, dilectionis et caritatis foedera incorrupta
adque inviolata mandavit. Exhibere se non potest martyrem qui

---

221 20 Marc. 11. 25   23 *cf.* Matt. 5. 23–24   23–222 10 *Pel.*   25 *cf.* Gen.
4. 5   **222** 2–5 *Wal.*, p. 193   10 *cf.* Io. 14. 27

221 16 infidelibus b   suam GL   ostendit] *add.* se h²   se esse bT²   se] *om.* BT¹h
17 unianimiter W²; una miter W¹; unanimiter *cett.*   dissedentibus a; dissentienti-
bus Bh   18 pluribus **ML** OEbV   pacificorum R   concordi prece paucorum
E   concordiae RO; concordium B   19 discordiae RO; discordi J   orationem R
20 ideo] *om.* E   et *pr.*] *om.* **M** D   dicens] *om.* H   21 adversum D   22 et]
om. b   23 remittet W   peccata] *add.* vestra L J *Vg*   vobis peccata E *Vg*   vobis]
om. J   24 veniente *Pel.*   altare **L**; altario R   iubet] *add.* hunc **M** HT   con-
cordari Y **DB**; reconcordare P; recordare R   fratre] *add.* et O²   25 cum] *om.* J
redeunte J² *Pel.*   Domino W¹? **D** *Pel.*   offere m; offerret D¹   Cayn b   26 pec-
catum m¹ **B**¹; paccatum Y; placatum EH   Dominum **DV** *Pel.*   **222** 2 Quae]
qui p   3 aemuli] *add.* verorum a²; aemulii R   4 opinantur] *add.* Hii B;
add. hi *Pel.*   Christi] *om.* *Pel.*   colligunt R; colleguntur J¹   6 confessionis
nomine m¹p   nominis] *add.* Christi O² *Pel.*   7 discordiae] *add.* quae *Pel.*
8 ecclesia] *add.* Dei J; *add.* sancta *Pel.*   9 poterit] *add.* non poterit B   quae]
qui G¹   10 dereliquit mp² WP JBbT; reliquit R   nobis pacem R   concordas
D¹   unianimes D; unanimes *cett.*   11 phedera b   12 inviolata] *add.*
servari DH²; *add.* servare **E**   se] *om.* D

fraternam non tenuit caritatem. Docet hoc et contestatur Paulus
apostolus, dicens: *Et si habuero fidem ita ut montes*
15 *transferam, caritatem autem non habeam, nihil sum;*
et si in cibos distribuero omnia mea, et si tradidero
corpus meum ut ardeam, caritatem autem non ha-
beam, nihil proficio. Caritas magnanima est, cari-
tas benigna est; caritas non aemulatur, non infla-
2c *tur, non inritatur, non agit perperam, non cogitat*
malum; omnia diligit, omnia credit, omnia sperat,
omnia sustinet. Caritas numquam excidet. 'Numquam'
inquit 'excidet caritas': haec enim semper in regno erit, haec
in aeternum, fraternitatis sibi cohaerentis unitate, durabit. Ad re-
25 gnum caelorum non potest pervenire discordia; ad praemium
Christi, qui dixit: *Hoc est mandatum meum ut diligatis*
invicem quemadmodum dilexi vos, pertinere non po-   P. 223
terit qui dilectionem Christi perfida dissensione violavit. Qui
caritatem non habet, Deum non habet; Iohannis beati apostoli
vox est: *Deus* inquit *dilectio est, et qui manet in Deo,*
5 *in dilectione manet, et Deus in illo manet.* Cum
Deo manere non possunt qui esse in ecclesia Dei unianimes noluerunt: ardeant licet flammis, et ignibus traditi vel obiecti bestiis
animas suas ponant, non erit illa fidei corona sed poena perfi-

---

222 14 I Cor. 13. 2–5, 7–8   26 Io. 15. 12   223 4 I Io. 4. 16   5–10 *Pel.*
8–10 *cf. Wal.,* p. 194

---

222 13 tenet ROEb   hoc] *om.* R   contestatur] hortatur R; testatur H
14 habuero] *add.* inquit O   16 si *pr.*] *om.* D¹   cibos] *add.* pauperum pk² Jb
divisero D   omnia mea] animam meam b   17 ardeat Rb   autem] *om.* b
habeo W¹   18 proficio] sum M   magnissima R¹; magnanimis B; magna b   est]
om. G   19 aemulatur] *add.* non zelat B   non inflatur] *om.* EH   20 non inritatur... perperam] *om.* R   cogitat] *add.* proximo D   21 malum] *add.* non
gaudet iniustitiam R; *add.* non gaudet super iniustitiam (bV), conlaetatur autem in
veritate b   omnia diligit] *om.* HT   22 excidit G¹ J²DBeH*Vg*; excedit k² J¹O¹;
excedet O²   Numquam . . . erit (*l.* 23)] *om.* k   23 excedit J¹; excedet H¹;
excidit J² DBeh*Vg*   haec *pr.*] *add.* est h   semper] *add.* et RbTh   24 duravit O¹B
25 venire B   discordia] *add.* non L; *add.* nec P RJDEbH; *add.* et O   26 qui dixit]
dicentis R; monuit dicens b   meum] Dei R   223 1 dilexit D¹   vos] *add.* Ad
Christi praemium m²; *add.* ad regnum Dei L; *add.* ad Deum R; *add.* ad Christum
DH   pertinere] pervenire JO   poterit] potuit W; *add.* ad praemium Christi WP
JBE; *add.* ad Christi praemium Ob   2 Christi] Dei O   3 Deum] Christum
H   Iohannes R   beati] *om.* MG   4 Deo in dilectione] dilectione in Deo
ODE(−e)VT*Vg*   5 et...manet] *om.* GL V,*fort. recte*   Deus] Dominus D   6 Deo]
Domino DB   unianimes] G RD; unianimiter *Pel.*; unanimes *cett.*   7 ardent
D   obiectis b¹H *Pel.*   8 animam suam *Pel.*   illi a¹   fides b   perfidiae poena E

diae, nec religiosae virtutis exitus gloriosus sed desperationis in-
teritus. Occidi talis potest, coronari non potest. Sic se christianum   10
esse profitetur quomodo et Christum diabolus saepe mentitur,
ipso Domino praemonente et dicente: *Multi venient in no-*
mine meo dicentes: 'Ego sum Christus', et multos fal-
lent. Sicut ille Christus non est, quamvis fallat in nomine, ita
nec christianus videri potest qui non permanet in evangelii eius   15
et fidei veritate.

15   Nam et prophetare et daemonia excludere et virtutes magnas
in terris facere sublimis utique et admirabilis res est, non tamen
regnum caeleste consequitur quisque in his omnibus invenitur,
nisi recti et iusti itineris observatione gradiatur. Denuntiat Do-   20
minus et dicit: *Multi mihi dicent in illo die: 'Domine,*
Domine, nonne in tuo nomine prophetavimus et in
tuo nomine daemonia exclusimus et in nomine tuo
virtutes magnas fecimus?' Et tunc dicam illis: 'Num-
quam vos cognovi; recedite a me qui operamini inius-   25
titiam.' Iustitia opus est ut promereri quis possit Deum
iudicem; praeceptis eius et monitis obtemperandum est ut acci-

P. 224   piant merita nostra mercedem. Dominus in evangelio, cum spei
et fidei nostrae viam conpendio breviante dirigeret: *'Dominus*
Deus tuus' inquit *'Dominus unus est, et diliges Do-*
minum Deum tuum de toto corde tuo et de tota

---

223 10 Aug., *Ep.* 108. 9   12 Matt. 24. 5   21 Matt. 7. 22–23   **224** 2 Marc.
12. 29–31

---

223 9 religiosae virtutis] *om. Pel.*   exitus] exigitur *Pel.*   11 et] se HT
zabulus **L**; zabolus R   saepe] se saepe **L**k²   12 promonente D¹   Multi] *add.*
enim **E**   veniunt **L**   13 dicentes] *add.* quia **E**   14 Christi R   nomine]
homine D   ite G¹   15 nec] *add.* hic V   videri] *add.* non Y¹**L**(−a) evangelio
MG RO   17 eicere b   18 sullimis **E**   et] *om.* a   est res k   19 quisquis
b   his] *om.* G¹   omnibus his O   20 observatione] observationis via m²**D**; obsecra-
tione B   gradiantur B   21 mihi] *add.* et a   illa ROEbVH*Vg*   22 Domine]
om. G   nonne] *om.* B   tuo nomine] nomine tuo GL DH   tuo . . . in] *om.* e   pro-
phetamus P¹   et . . . exclusimus] *om.* h   23 tuo nomine] nomine tuo m ODbH
daemonia nomine a   nomine tuo] tuo nomine **W** Bb   24 magnas virtutes **W**
multas HT*Vg*   25 novi b*Vg*   me] *add.* omnes V   operabamini **P E**   iniusti-
tiam] iniquitatem **WG**P JBb*Vg*   26 iustitia] *add.* piis m²; iustia Y¹; iustitiae P
O²; iustitiam D²   opus] operatus D   Dominum possit R   Deum] *om.* Y; Dominum J; Domino D   **224** 1 Dominum m¹   evangelio] *add.* suo OV   cum
spei] dicit cum ipse R   2 et] ac **L**   conpendio] *add.* et **M**; *add.* veritati Y¹
brevitate p²   dirigeret] redigeret **M**; redirigeret m²; *add.* audi inquit Israel J*Vg*
3 inquit] *om.* RJ   Dominus] Deus **L** O²**D**(*om.* D)H*Vg*   unus est] *om.* W¹   diligis
J¹   4 de *alt.*] ex **L***Vg*

5 *anima tua et de tota virtute tua.' Hoc primum, et se-*
cundum simile huic: 'Diliges proximum tuum tam-
quam te.' In his duobus praeceptis tota lex pendet
et prophetae. Unitatem simul et dilectionem magisterio suo
docuit; prophetas omnes et legem praeceptis duobus inclusit.

o Quam vero unitatem servat, quam dilectionem custodit aut cogitat qui, discordiae furore vesanus, ecclesiam scindit, fidem de-
struit, pacem turbat, caritatem dissipat, sacramentum profanat?

Malum hoc, fidelissimi fratres, iam pridem coeperat sed   *16*
nunc crevit eiusdem mali infesta clades, et surgere ac pullulare
15 plus coepit haereticae perversitatis et schismatum venenata pernicies, quia et sic in occasu mundi oportebat, praenuntiante per
apostolum nobis et praemonente Spiritu sancto: *In novissimis*
inquit *diebus aderunt tempora molesta; erunt homi-*
nes sibi placentes, superbi, tumidi, cupidi, blas-
20 *phemi, parentibus indictoaudientes, ingrati,*
impii, sine adfectu, sine foedere, delatores, incon-
tinentes, inmites, bonum non amantes, proditores,
procaces, stupore inflati, voluptates magis quam
Deum diligentes, habentes deformationem religio-
25 *nis, virtutem autem eius abnegantes. Ex his sunt*
qui repunt in domos et praedantur mulierculas
oneratas peccatis, quae ducuntur variis desideriis,   **P. 225**
semper discentes et numquam ad scientiam veri-
tatis pervenientes. Et quomodo Iamnes et Mambres

---

224 8–16 *Wal.*, p. 252   17 II Tim. 3. 1–9

---

224 5 et . . . tua] *om.* R   virtute] mente b[1]   Hoc] *add.* est **L** DH   et *alt.*] *om.* b
6 simile] *add.* est **L** H; similem B   huic] illi b*Vg*   diligis J[1]B   tuum] *om.* G; tibi O
7 te] *add.* ipsum **L** JBbH*Vg*   mandatis H   9 omnes prophetas m   10 quam
alt.] *add.* vero b   dilectione B   custodiat R[1]   11 quis W   ecclesiam] *add.* Dei
E   sindit m   13 hoc] *om.* R   fidelissimi] dilectissimi RJOV   14 crevit] *add.*
et R   cladis P J[1]   et surgere] exsurgere **L** OEbH *Wal.*   ac] et p J   pululare
W   15 cshismatum G   16 et] *om.* **M D**   sic et R   occasum LP JO[1]DEb
18 temporalia b   molesta] *add.* et J[2]   19 cupidi] *om.* GL J   20 parentibus] arentibus D[1]; parcentibus H[1]   indicto odientes m[2]   indicto] *add.* non W[2]GL R[2]O[2]b*Vg*;
om. k De   audientes] obedientes **L** R[2]*Vg*; inoboedientes **P**; *om.* e; inaudientibus D[1];
inaudientes D[2]**H**   21 adfectione **P** *Vg*   foedere] *add.* proditores procaces O; fide
HT   incontinentes] inertes HT   22 non] *om.* W[1] J[1]   proditores procaces] *om.*
O   23 voluntates D[1]; voluntates suas D[2]; voluntatem J; voluptatem HT   magis
voluntates **L**   24 Dominum **M**k O   diligentes] amantes b   deformationem
religionis habentes **E**   religionis] pietatis b*Vg*   25 virtutes D   **225** 1
honeratas Yk[2] D[1]b   2 dicentes R[1]H[1]   3 Iannes Wa VT[1]   Mampres W[1]

restiterunt Mosi, sic et hi resistunt veritati; sed
non proficient plurimum, imperitia enim eorum ma- 5
nifesta erit omnibus, sicut et illorum fuit. Adimplen-
tur quaecumque praedicta sunt et, adpropinquante iam saeculi fine,
hominum pariter ac temporum probatione venerunt. Magis ac
magis adversario saeviente, error fallit, extollit stupor, livor in-
cendit, cupiditas excaecat, depravat impietas, superbia inflat, 10
discordia exasperat, ira praecipitat.

17   Non tamen nos moveat aut turbet multorum nimia et abrupta
perfidia, sed potius fidem nostram praenuntiatae rei veritate corroboret: ut quidam tales esse coeperunt quia haec ante praedicta
sunt, ita ceteri fratres ab eiusmodi caveant quia et haec ante 15
praedicta sunt, instruente Domino et dicente: *Vos autem ca-*
vete: ecce praedixi vobis omnia. Vitate, quaeso, vos eiusmodi homines, et a latere adque auribus vestris perniciosa con-
loquia velut contagium mortis arcete, sicut scriptum est: *Saepi*
aures tuas spinis et noli audire linguam nequam; 20
et iterum: *Conrumpunt ingenia bona confabulationes*
pessimae. Docet Dominus et admonet a talibus recedendum:
Caeci sunt inquit *duces caecorum: caecus autem*
caecum ducens simul in foveam cadent. Aversandus
est talis adque fugiendus quisque fuerit ab ecclesia separatus: 25
P. 226 perversus est huiusmodi et peccat, et est a semetipso damnatus.

---

225 16 Marc. 13. 23   19 Ecclus. 28. 28 (*Vg*; 28. 24 LXX)   21 I Cor. 15. 33
23 Matt. 15. 14   24–226 11 *Wal.*, p. 254

---

225 4 resiterunt m¹   Mosi] W; Moysy Y; Moisi b; Moysi *cett.*   sic] ita b V *Vg*
hii W¹Y J¹bHT; isti R; ii E   resistent m¹pW   5 proficent m¹; proficiunt OH¹T¹
illorum p   6 et] *om.* W H   7 praedicata L   et] *om.* B   adpropinquat B
finem R¹   8 probationes m¹pL VT²   venerunt] *add.* et D   9 saeviente]
veniente b   libor P¹ J¹   10 excedat G   12 moneat D¹   aut] au k; ac J
turbat WY¹   rupta L; arrupta R; aperta J   13 vestram M   praenunciata L R;
renunciante D; praenuntiatam B; praenunciante H¹   rei] *om.* R   veritatis m¹;
veritas p   corroboret] roboret M   14 ut] et m¹pP D; *add.* quoniam JH   quidem O
tales] fallaces D; *add.* fallaces B   15 ita . . . praedicta sunt] *om.* W b   eius
modica veniant J¹   et] *om.* M R   haec et L   16 instruente] stestante H¹;
struente T; testante H²   Dominum R¹   vos . . . cavete] cavete autem
vos J   17 omnia] *om.* k h   Vita W¹; Vigilate D   vos quaeso M   vos] *add.* fratres D
18 adque] *add.* ab OEbVH   vestris] *om.* E   21 et iterum] *om.* O¹   ingenia bona]
mores bonos J *Vg*   confabulationis G¹   22 Docet] *om.* L   et] *om.* R¹   monet
B   talibus] *add.* esse V   recedendum] *add.* esse b   23 inquit] autem R   24 cadunt
LP ODB¹ b *Vg*   adversandus m O¹DbH   25 quisquis G   226 1 et *pr.*]
om. G   semetipsa J¹   damnatus] *add.* A semetipsis dampnati sunt qui se ab aecclesia
Christi separant M

An esse sibi cum Christo videtur qui adversum sacerdotes Christi
facit, qui se a cleri eius et plebis societate secernit? Arma ille
contra ecclesiam portat, contra Dei dispositionem repugnat.
5 Hostis altaris, adversus sacrificium Christi rebellis, pro fide perfidus, pro religione sacrilegus, inobsequens servus, filius impius,
frater inimicus, contemptis episcopis et Dei sacerdotibus dere-
lictis constituere audet aliud altare, precem alteram inlicitis vocibus facere, dominicae hostiae veritatem per falsa sacrificia pro-
10 fanare, nec scire quoniam qui contra ordinationem Dei nititur
ob temeritatis audaciam divina animadversione punitur.

Sic Chore et Dathan et Abiron, qui sibi contra Mosen et Aaron   *18*
sacerdotem sacrificandi licentiam vindicare conati sunt, poenas
statim pro suis conatibus pependerunt: terra compagibus ruptis
15 in profundum sinum patuit, stantes adque viventes recedentis soli
hiatus absorbuit. Nec tantum eos, qui auctores fuerant, Dei indi-
gnantis ira percussit, sed et ceteros ducentos quinquaginta participes eiusdem furoris et comites, qui coagulati cum isdem simul
ad audaciam fuerant, exiens a Domino ignis properata ultione
20 consumpsit: admonens scilicet et ostendens contra Deum fieri
quicquid inprobi fuerint ad destruendam ordinationem Dei humana voluntate conati. Sic et Ozias rex, cum turibulum ferens et

---

226 2–8 *Pel.*   12 *cf.* Num. 16. 1–35   22 *cf.* II Par.(Chron.) 26. 16–21

226 2 An] in D   esse] *om. Pel.*   videatur J   adversus RJOb *Pel.*   sacerdotem
G¹ J   3 facit] *add.* Cum Christo esse non videbitur, qui contra sacerdotes Christi
facit **M**   clerici m¹   secernit] *add. longam rasuram* m   illa J¹   4 Dei] Domini
D   disp**tionem R¹; dispositione b   5 Hostis] *add.* est B   altaris] *om.* D;
add. et B   Christi sacrificium RB   Christi] Dei J   rebelis G   pro fide] provide **L**
6 relione a¹   inobsequens] *add.* Dei **M**   7 delictis W¹   8 audeat G
9 domestice b   hostiam G   per] *om.* J   falso sacrificio J²   10 nec scire]
nescire m¹p**L** T² *Wal.*; nescit m²; nesciens O²   quoniam] *om.* G   quoniam qui]
quia D   ordinem O   Dei] Domini R   11 ob] ac D   temeritatis] *add.* suae bV
audacia Rb   animi adversione h   ponitur m¹; puniatur b   12 Core G RD¹BT¹; ore
a¹   et *prim.*] *om.* O   Datan P b   Habiron G   sibi] *om.* m¹   Mosen P; Moysen *cett.*
13 sacerdotes **W** REh   sunt] *add.* Hic **M**   poenam b   14 rependerunt MP²k RD;
penderunt G¹; expenderunt G²; dependerunt J; prependerunt B; perpenderunt
H   15 sinus R   rapuit b   recedentes P¹ O¹DT¹; cedentes R; recedentibus
omnibus h   solis **W** B; solii R¹   16 fatus R¹; iatus R²; hiatibus T   obsorbuit
m; adsorbuit R   Nec] non b   tantummodo bV   fuerant] fuerunt R; *add.* eiusdem
dementiae bV   17 et] ad D   ceteros] illos R   ccl m J¹H   ducentos] *add.* et
O   quinquaginta] l **W**   18 comitis G   coagolati D¹   hisdem pP **D**BHT²;
iisdem h   19 ad audaciam] audacia p; *rasura* m   exigens G   operata D   20 con-
sumsit W¹Y   admonet R   Deum] Dominum **D**   21 improbi] *om.* m¹   fue-
rint] fecerint b   22 et *pr.*] ergo Y; *om.* R

contra legem Dei sacrificium sibi violenter adsumens, resistente
sibi Azaria sacerdote, obtemperare nollet et cedere, divina indi-
gnatione confusus et leprae varietate in fronte maculatus est, ea   25
P. 227 parte corporis notatus, offenso Domino, ubi signantur qui Dominum promerentur; et filii Aaron, qui inposuerunt altari ignem
alienum quem non praeceperat Dominus, in conspectu statim
Domini vindicantis extincti sunt.

19   Quos imitantur scilicet adque sectantur qui, Dei traditione con-   5
tempta, alienas doctrinas adpetunt et magisteria humanae insti-
tutionis inducunt; quos increpat Dominus et obiurgat in evangelio suo, dicens: *Reicitis mandatum Dei ut traditionem
vestram statuatis.* Peius hoc crimen est quam quod admisisse lapsi videntur, qui tamen in paenitentia criminis consti-   10
tuti Deum plenis satisfactionibus deprecantur. Hic ecclesia quaeritur et rogatur, illic ecclesiae repugnatur; hic potest necessitas
fuisse, illic voluntas tenetur in scelere; hic qui lapsus est sibi
tantum nocuit, illic qui haeresin vel schisma facere conatus est
multos secum trahendo decepit; hic animae unius est damnum,   15
illic periculum plurimorum. Certe peccasse se hic et intellegit et
lamentatur et plangit, ille tumens in peccato suo et in ipsis sibi

---

227 2 *cf.* Lev. 10. 1–2   2–20 *Wal.*, p. 271   8 Marc. 7. 9   9–22 (PT) *Pel.*

---

226 23 sibi] *om.* G   resistens ibi R¹; resistenti R²   24 sibi] illi R²; *om.* B
Azarias R¹; Azariae R²   sacerdoti R²   nollit J¹   et cedere] et credere Wa² J; et
ceteri R¹; *om.* R²; et cedere vel credere a¹; et secedere B   divina] *add.* Dei b   25 con-
fusus] *add.* est **L** H   et] *om.* P²   lepraae W; lebrae J¹   ea] et m   **227** 1 corporis]
add. scilicet V   notatus] *add.* est **M**   offensio D¹   ubi . . . qui] qua salvari obtemperantes **H**   signantur] signa R   Dominum] Deum **L**; Domino D¹HT   2 et]
om. **L**   filiis p   aron Y   altaria R¹   3 praecerat Y   statim] *om.* b   Domini statim
GP²   4 dm̄i S   5 adque] que **M**   Dei] Domini DH   temptata B   7 in-
ducant G   abiurgat D   evvangelio k   8 reicistis RD   9 vestram] *om.*
WY²   Peius] eius D¹   hoc] schismatis *Pel.*   quod] *add.* hi qui sacrificaverunt
(-arunt h) **H** *Pel.*   amisisse Re; ammisisse Dh¹; ammississe H   admisisse lapsi videntur]
om. Pel.   10 lapsi] lapsum H¹T²; *om.* h   paenitentiam RB   11 Deum] Dominum
L DBV *Wal.*   plenissimis *Pel.*   Hic] in **L**; hinc k; *add.* et B; illic **HMQ** *Pel.*
12 illic] hic **HMQ** *Pel.*   ecclesia RB   hic] illic **HMQ**   hic . . . scelere] *om. Pel.*
13 illic] hic **HMQ**   hic] hinc V; illic **HMQ**   qui lapsus est] lapsum R   tantum
sibi **E**   14 illic] hic **HMQ** *Pel.*   heresim pP JDBEH; eresim b   haeresin vel]
om. Pel.   hereses et scismata **L** *Wal.*   scismata T¹   schisma facere] schismata agere
b   15 se contrahendo T¹   decipit G *Pel.*   hic] illic **HMQ** *Pel.*   16 illic] *om.*
m¹; hic **HMQ** *Pel.*   plurimorum periculum B   plurimorum] multorum **L D**   peccasse se] se peccasse p; peccans **L** *Wal.*   se] *om.* m¹W   hic] ille **HMQ** *Pel.*   et *pr.*]
om. B *Pel.*   17 lamentat k   ille] hic **HMQ** *Pel.*   tumens] *add.* et inflatus B   in
alt.] *om. Pel.*   sibi] suis b

delictis placens a matre filios segregat, oves a pastore sollicitat,
Dei sacramenta disturbat; et cum lapsus semel peccaverit, ille
20 cottidie peccat; postremo lapsus martyrium postmodum consecutus potest regni promissa percipere, ille si extra ecclesiam
fuerit occisus ad ecclesiae non potest praemia pervenire.

Nec quisquam miretur, dilectissimi fratres, etiam de confes-   20
soribus quosdam ad ista procedere, inde quoque aliquos tam
nefanda, tam gravia peccare. Neque enim confessio inmunem   **P. 228**
facit ab insidiis diaboli, aut contra temptationes et pericula et
incursus adque impetus saeculares adhuc in saeculo positum per-
petua securitate defendit: ceterum numquam in confessoribus
5 fraudes et stupra et adulteria postmodum videremus, quae nunc
in quibusdam videntes ingemescimus et dolemus. Quisque ille
confessor est, Solomone maior aut melior aut Deo carior non est,
qui tamen quamdiu in viis Domini ambulavit tamdiu gratiam
quam de Domino fuerat consecutus obtinuit; postquam dere-
10 liquit Domini viam, perdidit et gratiam Domini. Et ideo scriptum est: *Tene quod habes, ne alius accipiat coronam
tuam,* quod utique Dominus non minaretur auferri posse coronam iustitiae, nisi quia recedente iustitia recedat necesse est et
corona.

15   Confessio exordium gloriae est non meritum iam coronae, nec   21

---

228 11 Apoc. (Rev.) 3. 11

---

227 18 diliciis T[1]; deliciis T[2]   plangens W[1]   filio segregato vel R[1]; filium segregat
oves R[2]   19 sacramentum R   disturpat W   ille] hic HMQ *Pel.*   21 potest
regni] post reni W[1]; postest regni W[2]   ille] illic R[1]M[1]Q; hic H *Pel.*   si] *om.* O
ecclesiam] *add.* si O[2]   22 occissus H   praemia non potest JO   potest] post
W[1]   primia G   venire O   23 ne k[1]   etiam] *add.* et V   24 ista] star G[1]; instar
G[2]   praecedere m; prosilire bV   inde quoque aliquos] *om.* R[1]; ideoque aliquos
b   228 1 nefaria tamque V   peccata DH; peccasse b   2 fassit R[1]   diaboli]
zabuli L   aut] ut R[2]   3 saecularis J[1]   in] *om.* D   4 securitatis R[1]   detendit
B   5 strupra G[1] H   viderimus G   quod k   6 ingemiscimus MP[1]k
B[1]EbHT[2]h[2]   et] ut G[1]   et dolemus] *om.* M   quisquis G   7 confessus
D   est] *add.* et R[2]   Salemone L(−a) O; Salamone P T   aut *pr.*] et L   aut melior]
om. b   audeo k[1]   Deo] Domino R; *om.* D; eo HT   non] *om.* P[1]   8 quamdiu]
tamdiu G   ambulabat M   9 postquam] *add.* autem E; *add.* vero T[2]   derelinquit
G R; direliquit B[1]   10 Dominum M[1] b   Domini viam] viam Domini L E; diu
fama R[1]   Et ideo] sicut V   Et ideo ... est] *om.* G   ideo] idcirco b   11 est] *add.*
et excitavit Dominus Sathan (Satanan V) ipsi Salomoni. Et ideo in Apocalipsi Dominus
ad Iohannem graviter cominatur et dicit bV   12 Domini B[1]   nominaretur
G[1]L   posset R[1]   13 quia] *om.* M; qui W[1]   recedente] *add.* a L; recedet
W[1]   recedat] reddat G[1]   15 meritum] praemium b   iam] *om.* h[1]   coronae iam M

perficit laudem sed initiat dignitatem; cumque scriptum sit:
Qui perseveraverit usque ad finem hic salvus erit,
quicquid ante finem fuerit, gradus est quo ad fastigium salutis
ascenditur, non terminus quo iam culminis summa teneatur.
Confessor est: sed post confessionem periculum maius est, quia   20
plus adversarius provocatus est; confessor est: hoc magis stare
debet cum Domini evangelio, per evangelium gloriam consecutus
a Domino. *Cui multum datur multum quaeritur ab*
eo, et cui plus dignitatis adscribitur plus de illo
P. 229 *exigitur servitutis.* Nemo per confessoris exemplum pereat,
nemo iniustitiam nemo insolentiam nemo perfidiam de confessoris moribus discat; confessor est: sit humilis et quietus, sit in
actu suo cum disciplina modestus ut, qui Christi confessor di-
citur, Christum quem confitetur imitetur. Nam cum dicat ille: 5
Qui se extollit humiliabitur et qui humiliat se
exaltabitur, et ipse a Patre exaltatus sit quia se in terris
sermo et virtus et sapientia Dei Patris humiliavit, quomodo potest extollentiam diligere qui et nobis humilitatem sua lege mandavit, et ipse a Patre amplissimum nomen praemio humilitatis   10
accepit? Confessor est Christi: sed si non postea blasphemetur
per ipsum maiestas et dignitas Christi. Lingua Christum confessa
non sit maledica, non turbulenta, non conviciis et litibus per-
strepens audiatur, non contra fratres et Dei sacerdotes, post verba
laudis, serpentis venena iaculetur. Ceterum si culpabilis et de-   15

---

228 17 Matt. 10. 22 *et* 24. 13   23 *cf.* Luc. 12. 48   **229** 6 Luc. 14. 11 *et*
18. 14 (*cf.* Matt. 23. 12)   8 *cf.* I Cor. 1. 24   10 *cf.* Phil. 2. 8–9

228 16 perficit] *add.* iam b   initiat] inhiat **M**; initia et R¹   17 ad] in **M**Wk
DBEHT¹h¹*Vg*   hic] is WP; *om.* D   18 quicquid] quisquis in bono T²   gradus]
gratum **L**   quo] per quem **M**; quod P¹ D¹T¹; qui b   salvus B   19 non] *add.*
iam p; con D   20 Confessor ... provocatus est] *om.* **M**   quia] *add.* est J¹   21 pius
R¹   adversa prius Y   provacatus W¹   confesso h¹   hoc] *om.* HT   magis] *add.*
est hoc magis Y   22 Dominus m   gloriam con-] *om.* Y¹   cum secutus k
23 a Domino] Dominum **L**; * Domini R; *add.* ait enim Deus **DH²**   quaeretur
MW²P RB²bT¹h*Vg*   ab eo] habeo D; a domino b   24 et] *om.* D   **229** 2 iniu-
stiam W   confessoribus G   3 est] *add.* Christi RB   sit *pr.*] si R   4 actus vocum
W¹   moderatus Y   ut qui] hoc D   5 quem confitetur] confitentem m¹p
imiturum R¹; imitatur T¹   cum] *om.* R¹   ille dicat O   ipse b   6 exaltat k
se humiliat **M** ODH; se humiliaverit b   7 sit] est **D**   quia] qui E   se] ipse **L**(−a:
in se); *om.* h¹   terris] *add.* et J   8 patientia T¹h   huliavit W¹   9 diligere]
docere T¹   humilitate Ga   11 sed] *om.* **L**   blasphetur Y¹   12 magestas
Y   13 maledicta H¹   comviciis P; convivis J¹; cum viciis H   15 laudis]
add. et confessionis V   et detestabilis] *om.* **M** bV

testabilis postmodum fuerit, si confessionem suam mala conversatione prodegerit, si vitam suam turpi foeditate maculaverit,
si ecclesiam denique ubi confessor factus est derelinquens, et unitatis concordiam scindens, fidem primam perfidia posteriore mu-
20 taverit, blandiri sibi per confessionem non potest quasi electus
ad gloriae praemium, quando ex hoc ipso magis creverint merita
poenarum.

Nam et Iudam inter apostolos Dominus elegit, et tamen Do-   *22*
minum Iudas postmodum prodidit; non tamen idcirco aposto-
25 lorum firmitas et fides cecidit quia proditor Iudas ab eorum
societate defecit. Sic et hic: non statim confessorum sanctitas et
dignitas conminuta est quia quorundam fides fracta est. Beatus
apostolus loquitur in epistula sua, dicens: *Quid enim si ex-*   P. 230
ciderunt a fide quidam illorum? Numquid infideli-
tas illorum fidem Dei evacuavit? Absit: est enim
Deus verax, omnis autem homo mendax. Stat confes-
5 sorum pars maior et melior in fidei suae robore et in legis ac di-
sciplinae dominicae veritate, nec ab ecclesiae pace discedunt qui
se in ecclesia gratiam consecutos de Dei dignatione meminerunt;
adque hoc ipso ampliorem consecuntur fidei suae laudem quod
ab eorum perfidia segregati, qui iuncti confessionis consortio fue-
10 runt, a contagione criminis recesserunt. Vero inluminati evangelii

---

229 18–20 *Wal.*, p. 253   23 *cf.* Marc. 3. 13, 19   230 1 Rom. 3. 3–4

---

229 16 mala] macula **L**   malam conversationem **R**[1]   17 prodegerit] protegerit
W; prodigerit G[2]P[2]; prodiderit k[2] O[2]ET[2]; perdiderit D[2]; *om.* R   18 denique] *add.*
ipsam b**V**   est] *om.* **L**   derelinquere m[1]   19 posteri* Y[1]; posteriori Y[2]; posteri-
orem H[1]T[1]   mutuaverit B; vitaverit T[1]   21 ad] aut **M**   praemium] primum
G[1]   hoc] hinc b[1]   merita] praemia D   23 Iuda W[1]; Iudan W[2]   et *alt.*] sed
J   Dominum] *om.* OB   24 postmodum] *add.* Dominum OB   tradidit **W** B; prodit G   non tamen] *om.* H[1]   25 Iudas] *om.* J[1]   26 defecit] *om.* H[1]   dignitas et sanctitas G   27 comminutas R[1]; commutata H   est *pr.*] *om.* R[1]
cor unda D[1]   fracta] peracta **L**   **230** 1 apostolus] *add.* Paulus B**V**   in epistula
sua loquitur D   si] sic R   2 a fide] *om.* W[1]   quidam illorum a fide **J**   in-
credulitas J*Vg*   3 eorum G   evacuabit m[1]pWY[1]GLP[1]k OEb*Vg*   Absit] *om.*
G   enim] autem **L** J*Vg*   4 autem] *om.* k   Stat] *add.* autem B   5 maior
et] maiora G   in *pr.*] et B; *om.* **D**   robore] robur m; *add.* stat B   in *alt.*] *om.*
V   lege p[2]   disciplina p; disciplinam G   6 dominicae] *om.* b   veritatis m[1]p
discedunt] d**dunt k[1]   qui se in] quis un J[1]   7 ecclesiam G BH[1]T[1]   dignatione]
add. me m[1]   meminerint **L**; eminerunt P[1]   8 ampliorem] maiorem V   fidem
P[1]   laudem] *add.* imo ampliorem b**V**   quo h   9 perfidiam B[1]   segregat **W**
iunctis confessionibus G   confessionis] *om.* **L**   fuerant h   10 contagione m**YL**
ROD[2]b; confessione J; contagio *cett.*   recesserunt] *add.* hi R[2]   inluminati vero
O   evangelio Pk[1]; evangelico k[2]   lumine evangelii **E**

lumine, pura et candida Domini luce radiati, tam sunt in conservanda Christi pace laudabiles quam fuerunt in diaboli congres-
sione victores.

23 Opto equidem, dilectissimi fratres, et consulo pariter et
suadeo ut, si fieri potest, nemo de fratribus pereat, et consentientis   15
populi corpus unum gremio suo gaudens mater includat. Si
tamen quosdam schismatum duces et dissensionis auctores, in
caeca et obstinata dementia permanentes, non potuerit ad salutis
viam consilium salubre revocare, ceteri tamen vel simplicitate
capti, vel errore inducti, vel aliqua fallentis astutiae calliditate   20
decepti, a fallaciae vos laqueis solvite; vagantes gressus ab erro-
ribus liberate; iter rectum viae caelestis adgnoscite. Contestantis
apostoli vox est: *Praecipimus vobis* inquit *in nomine Domini
Iesu Christi ut recedatis ab omnibus fratribus ambulantibus inordinate et non secundum traditio-*   25
P. 231 *nem quam acceperunt a nobis*; et iterum dicit: *Nemo
vos decipiat inanibus verbis: propterea enim venit
ira Dei super filios contumaciae. Nolite ergo esse
participes eorum.* Recedendum est a delinquentibus vel immo
fugiendum ne, dum quis male ambulantibus iungitur et per   5
itinera erroris et criminis graditur, a via veri itineris exerrans
pari crimine et ipse teneatur. Unus Deus est et Christus unus, et
una ecclesia eius et fides una, et plebs in solidam corporis

---

230 14–231 12 *Wal.*, p. 255   23 II Thess. 3. 6   231 1 Eph. 5. 6–7

---

230 11 lumini D   Domini] Dominum m¹a; *om.* k¹   tam] iam B   12 pace]
luce G   fuerant Rbh   diaboli fuerunt in D   zabuli L   confessione B   14 Opto]
hortor V   equidem] *om.* m; et quidem L   15 suado R¹   ut] *om.* H¹T   con-
sentienti R¹   16 corpus] *om.* J; *add.* in J²   includat Y¹   17 dissensiones m¹;
discensionis W¹; dissensionum D   in] *om.* ML   18 caeca] *om.* L   obstinata]
add. in caeca L   permanetes b   19 consilio p¹   revocari R¹   ceteris O²;
ceterum b   tamen] *om.* O²h   20 captis O²   induti k¹; inductis O²   aliqua]
aqua Y¹   fallentes a¹; fallentia R; fallendi b   austutiae k¹   astutia calliditatis G
21 deceptis O²   a] *om.* OH¹   gressum D   22 libertate D¹   rectum] *add.* hinc
M   vitae M H   assumite E   23 inquit vobis EbH   inquit] *om.* WP¹k Th
Domini] *add.* nostri Lk JbVTh*Vg*; *add.* Dei R   24 omnibus] hominibus m¹
fratribus] *om.* WP¹k B   25 non] *om.* R   231 1 accepistis GLP²b   dicit]
om. J   3 esse] fieri O   4 relinquentibus b   vel] *om.* m²p T²   5 per]
perit W   6 iti⁕nera P   trahitur L *Wal.*   a] *om.* R   aberrans k; exarrans R¹
7 Deus unus H   est Deus E   unus Christus L *Wal.*   unus *alt.*] *add.* est H   et
tert.] est O   8 eius] *om.* J   plebs] *add.* una bVH   in] *om.* M   solida M DHT;
add. et M

unitatem concordiae glutino copulata. Scindi unitas non potest
10 nec corpus unum discidio compaginis separari, divulsis laceratione visceribus in frusta discerpi; quicquid a matrice discesserit,
seorsum vivere et spirare non poterit: substantiam salutis amittit.
Monet nos Spiritus sanctus et dicit: *Quis est homo qui*   24
vult vitam et amat videre dies optimos? Contine
15 *linguam tuam a malo et labia tua ne loquantur in-*
sidiose; declina a malo et fac bonum, quaere pa-
cem et sequere eam. Pacem quaerere debet et sequi filius
pacis, a dissensionis malo continere linguam suam debet qui
novit et diligit vinculum caritatis. Inter sua divina mandata et
20 magisteria salutaria, passioni iam proximus, Dominus addidit
dicens: *Pacem vobis dimitto, pacem meam do vobis.*
Hanc nobis hereditatem dedit, dona omnia suae pollicitationis
et praemia in pacis conservatione promisit. Si heredes Christi
sumus, in Christi pace maneamus; si filii Dei sumus, pacifici
25 esse debemus: *Beati* inquit *pacifici, quoniam ipsi filii*
Dei vocabuntur. Pacificos esse oportet Dei filios, corde mites,
sermone simplices, adfectione concordes, fideliter sibi unianimi-   **P. 232**
tatis nexibus cohaerentes.
Haec unianimitas sub apostolis olim fuit: sic novus credentium   25
populus Domini mandata custodiens caritatem suam tenuit. Pro-

231 13 Ps. 33(34). 13–15   21 Io. 14. 27   25 Matt. 5. 9

231 9 unitate **M DH**T; firmitatem V   concordi J   glutinae R¹; glutine R²
Scindi] *add.* enim k   unitas] divinitas Y   10 ne G   separari] separare Y¹; *add.*
nec RObVT²   divulsas J¹; divulsus H¹T¹   11 frustra mW¹Gk¹ RJ¹OB¹bH¹T¹h¹
discerpit **M**   matre J²   12 poterit] *add.* nec **D**; *add.* sed T²   ammittit P¹;
admittit **D**   13 nos] *add.* in psalmis bV   14 optimos] bonos k **D***Vg*   contineat b   15 suam b   sua b   insidiose] iniquitatem **M** h; desidione G; dolum
JH*Vg*   16 bonum] quod bonum est Ob   17 sequere] consequeris **L**; in-
venies J; consequere V   filius] *add.* est G; filios **L**   18 contingere b¹   suam]
om. J   19 sua] *add.* denique V   20 passionis Y H¹   Dominus] *om.*
M   21 Pacem] *add.* meam JB   dimitto vobis E₁HT   remitto b   22 vobis Y¹
23 conversatione **L** O   24 pace Christi D   Christi pacem abeamus P¹; Christo
pacem habeamus P²   si] *om.* G   fili HT¹   25 debeamus m   ipsi] *om.* k
JODb*Vg*   26 vocantur W¹   esse] *om.* R¹   oportet esse J   **232** 1 sermones
m¹   sermone simplices] *om.* G   concordes] *add.* fidei stabiles B   unianimitatis
J¹H¹; unanimitates Y¹; unanimitatis *cett.*   2 conherentes Y¹   3 unianimitas P¹
J¹; unanimetas R¹; unanimitas *cett.*   apostolos b   4 Domini] Dei R   suam]
om. R   probrat G¹; proba D

bat scriptura quae dicit: *Turba autem eorum qui credide-*   5
rant anima ac mente una agebant, et iterum: *Et erant*
perseverantes omnes unianimes in oratione cum mu-
lieribus et Maria, quae fuerat mater Iesu, et fratri-
bus eius. Et ideo efficacibus precibus orabant, ideo impe-
trare cum fiducia poterant quodcumque de Dei misericordia   10
postulabant.

26   In nobis vero sic unianimitas deminuta est ut et largitas opera-
tionis infracta est. Domos tunc et fundos venundabant et the-
sauros sibi in caelo reponentes, distribuenda in usus indigentium
pretia apostolis offerebant. At nunc de patrimonio nec decimas   15
damus et, cum vendere iubeat Dominus, emimus potius et auge-
mus. Sic in nobis emarcuit vigor fidei, sic credentium robur
elanguit, et idcirco Dominus, tempora nostra respiciens, in evangelio suo dicit: *Filius hominis cum venerit, putas in-*
veniet fidem in terra? Videmus fieri quod ille praedixit: in   20
Dei timore, in lege iustitiae, in dilectione, in opere fides nulla
est. Nemo futurorum metum cogitat; diem Domini et iram Dei
et incredulis ventura supplicia et statuta perfidis aeterna tor-
menta nemo considerat. Quicquid metueret conscientia nostra
si crederet, quia non credit, omnino nec metuit; si autem cre-   25
deret, et caveret; si caveret, evaderet.

---

232 5 Act. 4. 32   6 Act. 1. 14   12 *cf.* Act. 4. 34–35   13 *cf.* Matt. 6. 20
16 *cf.* Marc. 10. 21   19 Luc. 18. 8   22–24 Hincmar, *praedest. diss. post.* 1

---

232 5 scriptura] *add.* divina V   autem] *om.* J¹   crediderunt Y¹k¹; crediderat J¹
6 animam O²   ac] et **ML DH**   mentem unam O²   agebat W¹ D; habebant
O   iterum] *add.* dicit O   Et *alt.*] *om.* G   7 omnes] *om.* Eb   unianimes J¹; *om.* b;
unanimes *cett.*   oratione] *add.* simul b   9 precibus] verbis R   orabant] orantes
M; *add.* et R   ideo *alt.*] Deum **M** b   10 de] *om.* J¹   Domini D   12 nobis]
novis b   unianimitas H¹; unanimitas *cett.*   diminuta pLk² JOET²; domini R   et ut R
13 est] sit **ML** HT; esset b   thensauros W²Y¹; tensauros P¹   15 At] et R   de-
trimonio G¹; de patrio k¹   16 iubeatur domus **L**; Dominus iubeat H   eminus m
potius] *om.* k¹   17 in] *om.* m¹p   marcuit P¹k   vigor] fervor k   rubor G¹; robor
H¹T¹   18 et languit G   Dominus] *add.* noster **M**   nostra] *om.* **M**   19 dixit
L; dicens H¹   20 terram JBh   21 Domini RJ   timore Dei O   et in
dilectione et **H**   22 metu futurorum **E**(−e)   metum] metu pGLk R²Eb; *add.*
nemo **D**; *add.* cogitat. Nemo **H**   diem] metum b   et iram Dei] *om.* D   Dei] *om.*
R   24 Quicquid] quo id G; quod **LP**; quid O; quae quidem J²; qui quod b; quae
V   metuerat mp¹; meruerit h   25 crederet *pr.*] *add.* et caveret J¹   et . . .
credit] *om.* J²   quia . . . crederet] *om.* B   credit] credet m¹; credidit Wk R   omnino
nec metuit] *om.* J   nec] non **E**   si autem] salutem **L**   crederes **M**; metueret J
26 et . . . si] *om.* H¹   caveret *pr.*] caveres **M**; *add.* et Y   si caveret] sic averi∗∗ W¹;
et Ob   caveret *alt.*] caveres **M**; *add.* et GL RBEHT¹   evaderes **M**

Excitemus nos quantum possumus, dilectissimi fratres, et   27
somno inertiae veteris abrupto ad observanda et gerenda Domini
praecepta vigilemus. Simus tales quales esse nos ipse praecepit,   **P. 233**
dicens: *Sint lumbi vestri adcincti et lucernae ar-*
dentes, et vos similes hominibus expectantibus do-
minum suum quando veniat a nuptiis ut, cum ve-
5 *nerit et pulsaverit, aperiant ei. Beati servi illi*
quos adveniens Dominus invenerit vigilantes. Ad-
cinctos nos esse oportet ne, cum expeditionis dies venerit, inpe-
ditos et inplicitos adprehendat. Luceat in bonis operibus nostrum
lumen et fulgeat, ut ipse nos ad lucem claritatis aeternae de
10 hac saeculi nocte perducat. Expectemus solliciti semper et cauti
adventum Domini repentinum ut, quando ille pulsaverit, evi-
gilet fides nostra, vigilantiae praemium de Domino receptura. Si
haec mandata serventur, si haec monita et praecepta teneantur,
opprimi dormientes diabolo fallente non possumus: servi vigiles
15 Christo dominante regnabimus.

DE ECCLESIAE CATHOLICAE UNITATE explicit.

---

233 2 Luc. 12. 35–37   8 *cf.* Matt. 5. 16

---

232 27 excimus G¹   28 somno∗∗∗ G   veteris inertiae m¹   obrupto **M**   et
gerenda] *om.* h¹   **233** 1 vigilemus] iubilemus Y²   tales] stabiles H¹T   esse]
om. JBb   nos ipse esse O; ipse nos esse V   praecepit] praecipit m² H; *add.*
esse J   2 Sin G   praecincti Lk bTh¹ *Vg*   ardentes] *add.* in manibus vestris Ob *Vg*
3 vos] tuos G¹   4 ad nuptias b   ut] et a J¹   5 et] *om.* m   epulsaverit
m   ei] Et **M** J¹; ei Et **L**   6 accitos R; accintos H   7 expeditionibus B;
perditionis h   inpeditos] *add.* nos Ob   8 inplicitos] implictos G¹; *add.* nos JV
apprehendant k¹   Luceat] *om.* b   in] *add.* nobis D   vestrum m   lumen nostrum
JE(−e)   9 et fulgeat] effulgeat b   ut] et mp¹   ipse **M** H; ipsut R; ipsum *cett.*
ad ipsum nos lumen O   10 hac] ac B¹h¹   semper] *om.* b   11 evigilet] *add.*
et **W**; vigilet R**D**; evigiles J¹   12 receptura de Domino J   si . . . serventur] *post*
teneantur **L**   13 servantur G   et] *om.* W¹   teneantur] *om.* G   14 zabulo
L; diaboli T¹   fallente diabolo p; *om.* h¹   non] *om.* G²   possumus] *add.* sed D²T²
15 dominante Christo **E**   dominante regnabimus] *om.* h¹   regnavimus (*add.* Amen R)
RO¹   16 Cecilii Cypriani de catholicae ecclesiae unitate explicit **M**; De catholicae
eclesiae unitate explicit W; Explicit de eclesiae unitate Y; Explicit epistola Cecilii
Cypriani de ecclesiae unitate G; De ecclesyae unitate explicit P; Adversus Novatum
explicit k; De unitate ecclesiae explicit R; Caecili Cypriani de ecclesiae catholicae
unitate finit J; Cecilii Cypriani de ecclesiae unitate explicit O; *om. cett.*

CHAPTER XI

The Interrelations of the MSS revealed by the Text

i. *The comparison of variants*

I T is one thing to have made a first selection of MSS, and from them to have reconstructed the text with full critical apparatus; it is quite another to make use of this evidence so as to establish the relationship between the MSS themselves. One has only to turn over the preceding pages and note the different ways in which the MSS group themselves, in order to appreciate the complexity of the problem. We may notice a little group of two or three repeated a number of times, and think we can safely assert interdependence for those two or three MSS; and then we find them parting company and each becoming equally friendly with some other MS or MSS, which are in turn mostly independent of each other. If one considers the MSS by centuries, one finds an early MS apparently depending on a later one, and one can attempt to correct this by postulating a common ancestor older than both. When one has done that a number of times, to fit a number of refractory cases, one only suc-ceeds in building up a genealogy of fantastic proportions, whose value depends on a succession of hypotheses of ever-increasing fragility.

However, if the incidence of individual readings seems unable to lead us to any solid conclusion, an overall comparison by MSS may be more rewarding. The results are given in the chart following, which will be the basis of our final conclusions.

The chart records the number of readings which any one MS has in common with any other—the readings being confined to those which do *not* occur in the resultant text; in other words, to those that appear in the critical apparatus. [There are a few exceptions, viz. those readings which have been adopted for the resultant text though only present in a few MSS. These were entered in the apparatus and have been included here because of their textual importance. On the other hand, where a great number of MSS go against the resultant text, these readings have been omitted, as unlikely to help much in grouping the MSS.]

Readings which occur only in one MS have been omitted; also those which occur *only* in one of the portmanteau sigla: **H** (i.e. H, T, and h), **M** (m and p), **W** (W and Y), **P** (P and k), **L**, **D**, or **E**. For the association that exists between the MSS covered by each of these sigla is known to be so close as to make any further investigation about it superfluous. So too HT, when found alone, has been neglected. But whenever any of these portmanteau sigla (and HT) occurs along with other MSS, it is broken up into its component parts (viz. H, T, and h; m and p, &c.).[1]

All corrected readings (e.g. P²) have been neglected, and only the first thing written has been taken into consideration on the ground that a copyist copies more often correctly than not. In other words, it is assumed (and the assumption may, of course, be wrong in any particular case) that a correction is not a reading of the immediate model (restored by the writer himself or by another), but the substitution of a fresh reading, either from another MS or by conjecture, wise or unwise. This is one of the several reasons why the chart is at best only an approximation, but as a whole it can claim to present an adequate overall picture of the evidence provided by the critical apparatus.

The absurd industry and ridiculous patience involved in preparing the chart seemed at first to be out of all proportion to the results which it might produce. It involved, for each MS in turn, going through the whole of the apparatus criticus, and wherever that MS appeared along with one or more others, putting down these MSS as agreeing with it in some variant. The number of these common variants is indicated by the power attached to the MS on the left of the chart. Then the number of times *each* of the other MSS appeared in association with that MS was counted, to provide the powers attached to each of the MSS in the corresponding line of the chart. Finally, these latter were arranged in descending order of frequency.

Actually, every common variant in each pair of MSS was dealt with twice, according as one or the other MS was having its variants listed (i.e. according as one or the other is now to the left of the chart). This was a useful cross-check, enabling the correction of any oversight or other carelessness in making out the lists.

But the labour was not a waste of time, even if the results are less

---

[1] This has been done consistently in spite of its drawbacks. In a few cases the sigla do not in fact represent the *same* reading in each of the MSS which they severally represent, but only the *resultant* reading—i.e. what was estimated to be the reading of the common source. But this is exceptional and should not notably affect the totals involved.

The Interrelations of the MSS revealed by the Text

spectacular, or even definite, than had been hoped for. Perhaps their being unexpected shows that we are on the right lines, and it looks as if they may have an application to MSS other than those of Cyprian.

Chart of number of variants common to each pair of MSS

1

H^{81}	$T^{45}\ h^{30}\ D^{27}\ J^{23}\ b^{20}\ m^{18}\ BE^{16}\ GO^{15}\ pW^{14}\ LR^{13}\ Y^{12}\ k^{10}\ P^8$
T^{72}	$H^{45}\ h^{33}\ Db^{20}\ J^{19}\ mROB^{16}\ E^{14}\ pk^{13}\ WGP^{12}\ LY^{10}$
D^{74}	$H^{27}\ T^{20}\ pP^{16}\ k^{15}\ RB^{14}\ mWOE^{13}\ YL^{11}\ Gbh^{10}\ J^9$
m^{54}	$p^{43}\ HT^{18}\ h^{14}\ kODb^{13}\ R^{10}\ L^9\ WPJE^8\ B^7\ G^6\ Y^3$
p^{54}	$m^{43}\ kD^{16}\ H^{14}\ Tb^{13}\ EL^{12}\ JO^{11}\ Ph^{10}\ WB^8\ GR^7\ Y^2$
L^{58}	$H^{13}\ pJ^{12}\ Dbh^{11}\ GT^{10}\ m^9\ ROE^8\ WB^7\ Y^6\ P^4\ k^3$
h^{53}	$T^{33}\ H^{30}\ RJ^{16}\ b^{15}\ mOBE^{14}\ L^{11}\ pD^{10}\ WGk^9\ YP^7$
J^{71}	$H^{23}\ T^{19}\ b^{18}\ k^{17}\ h^{16}\ PB^{15}\ O^{14}\ G^{13}\ LRE^{12}\ pW^{11}\ D^9\ mY^8$

2

O^{73}	$b^{31}\ E^{19}\ R^{18}\ kB^{17}\ T^{16}\ H^{15}\ Jh^{14}\ mGD^{13}\ pWP^{11}\ L^8\ Y^7$
b^{63}	$O^{31}\ kE^{22}\ HT^{20}\ R^{19}\ JB^{18}\ W^{17}\ P^{16}\ h^{15}\ Y^{14}\ mp^{13}\ G^{12}\ L^{11}\ D^{10}$
R^{69}	$b^{19}\ O^{18}\ Th^{16}\ G^{15}\ DE^{14}\ BH^{13}\ J^{12}\ m^{10}\ k^9\ YL^8\ pW^7\ P^6$
E^{52}	$b^{22}\ O^{19}\ k^{17}\ H^{16}\ PRTh^{14}\ D^{13}\ pGJB^{12}\ Y^9\ mL^8\ W^7$
G^{56}	$RH^{15}\ B^{14}\ JO^{13}\ EbT^{12}\ WY^{11}\ LkD^{10}\ Ph^9\ p^7\ m^6$

3

W^{60}	$Y^{31}\ B^{26}\ P^{21}\ k^{19}\ b^{17}\ T^{14}\ D^{13}\ H^{12}\ GJO^{11}\ h^9\ mp^8\ LRE^7$
Y^{49}	$W^{31}\ P^{17}\ kB^{15}\ b^{14}\ H^{12}\ GD^{11}\ T^{10}\ E^9\ RJ^8\ Oh^7\ L^6\ m^3\ p^2$
B^{66}	$W^{26}\ b^{18}\ kO^{17}\ HT^{16}\ YPJ^{15}\ GDh^{14}\ R^{13}\ E^{12}\ p^8\ mL^7$
P^{48}	$k^{32}\ W^{21}\ Y^{17}\ Db^{16}\ JB^{15}\ E^{14}\ T^{12}\ O^{11}\ p^{10}\ G^9\ mH^8\ h^7\ R^6\ L^4$
k^{53}	$P^{32}\ b^{22}\ W^{19}\ JOBE^{17}\ p^{16}\ YD^{15}\ mT^{13}\ GH^{10}\ Rh^9\ L^3$

In order to appreciate the significance of the evidence provided by this chart, one is forced to a reconsideration of what we mean by the 'dependence' of MSS on one another, and of the significance to be attached to the readings which they have in common.

The starting-point must be the double fact that, because in some particular passage two MSS have the same reading, it does not follow that there is any dependence or even close connexion between those MSS; nor does it follow that they are *not* connected if in that passage they show different readings.

Two MSS come to have the same reading in various ways: (1) by direct transmission; (2) by dependence on a common source, near or remote; (3) by direct borrowing (i.e. MS Y is making a copy of MS X, but in this passage writes in a reading from MS Z); (4) through marginal borrowing (i.e. the reading from MS Z has already been written in the margin of MS X and is now adopted by MS Y. This is not quite the same as the preceding case: see below); (5) by a conjecture or a slip (which happens to agree with the reading of another MS); (6) by two identical conjectures or slips.

No doubt the first two ways are the most common, but they must not be allowed to make us forget the other possibilities. Some striking reading found in a few MSS may tempt us either to group them into one family, or, if the reading looks genuine, to consider it as surviving in those particular MSS (already known to belong to different families) in direct dependence on the archetype or the autograph itself. Occasionally the latter seems to be the only possible explanation, instanced in our MSS by *ei* (at 217. 4) and by *indictoaudientes* (at 224. 20). But before any such conclusion is arrived at, the likelihood of borrowing or, as it is often called, *contamination* must first be excluded.

But, before passing on, a word must be added about a marginal reading in one MS which has been taken from another.[1] What happens at the next stage? There are three possibilities. The MS may be copied as it stands, i.e. the original text is reproduced and the marginal reading is again copied into the margin.[2] Or the MS may be copied and the marginal reading simply ignored. Or, lastly, the new MS may replace the original reading by the marginal reading. In this last case, we arrive at an agreement with the MS from which the marginal reading originally came, without any indication where it came from. And, in general, the recognition of these three distinct possibilities issuing from a marginal reading suggests caution in conjecturing the reading of a MS's immediate predecessor.

Returning to the six ways in which two MSS can come to have a common reading, we need to give expression to the platitude that they can occur both when the common reading is correct *and* when it is not—though the likelihood is not always quite the same. Mistakes (including lacunae) may originate either because the model is difficult to read; or

---

[1] We are not here considering marginal headings or additions which were *not* taken from another MS. These are generally obvious: cf. 226. 1 and 226. 3 in **M**, and 228. 11 in b**V**.

[2] The fourteenth-century MS from the Benedictine Abbey of Abingdon (now Camb., Corpus Christi Coll. 25) is a copy of the twelfth-century MS from the Cistercian Abbey of Buildwas (now Camb., Pembroke Coll. 154). It enters alternative readings in the margin in precisely the same way; verification would probably show that they were simply transferred from one to the other.

because the scribe is careless, or weary, or both; or because of misunderstanding (perhaps a word is unusual, or the lack of punctuation leads to a false appraisal of the sentence), leading either to nonsense or to a 'learned' correction. Here it must be noted that a 'learned' correction has as much chance of survival as a sound reading; but that this is not true of nonsense. Nonsense itself provokes learned corrections: in fact it may lead to different 'learned' corrections—and to 'unlearned' corrections too. Lastly, just as one can have two identical conjectures, so one can have two identical slips.

We have therefore a number of different ways in which two MSS can have a common reading—correct or incorrect. But whether correct or not, and whether recognizably correct or not, a great number of such common readings reveals a *connexion* between those two MSS, either by direct transcription or by borrowing, whereas a small number of such common readings indicates little or no connexion. This is because the likelihood of accidental agreements is comparatively small: most agreements will be due to transmission or to borrowing in one form or another. But, it must be added at once, this borrowing may have originally occurred a long way back, among the ancestors of our surviving MSS, themselves already belonging to different families, and there may have been multiple borrowing between them. To take a simple example, a member of one family may have passed on a reading to members of another family, which in turn has passed it on to a third. Even if those three families have preserved their separate identities among our surviving MSS, they will each show a common reading which strictly belonged only to one of them. The other two families may have lost their original reading altogether, and if this has occurred a sufficient number of times, the identity of the three families will have become irrecoverable by us. They will seem to be one family instead of three.

This and other similar possibilities suffice to show the extreme difficulty of sorting out the precise relationship existing between our different MSS. We shall have to be content with a few generalizations, which, however, are not without their value. First, as we have just said, where two MSS have a large number of common readings, we can presume a 'connexion' between those MSS, even though we may be unable to specify the nature of that connexion. Secondly, where on other grounds we have been able to distinguish distinct families, or MSS showing independence, then *the more widely spread* a reading is, the older must have been the borrowing—whether it be the true reading or not. Thirdly, where two MSS have comparatively few readings in common (apart from the standard text), there is no such 'connexion' between them.

If these conclusions are correct, then what is most significant in the lists opposite each MS in the chart are the MSS at the beginning and at the end of each line. The former will have 'connexion' with the MS in question, the latter will not. This will guide us in interpreting the data there given.

ii. *'Connexions'—and the comparison of MSS by medieval scholars*

It is on the basis of the 'connexions' of each MS with others that the chart has fallen into three groups, and the nature of these groups is our first surprise. On the basis of the order of the treatises we had grouped together in our apparatus m, p, W, Y, L, P, and k, together with G, which seemed to have affinities with W and Y. On the other hand, we had treated HTh as forming a distinct group to themselves. We now find these three dominating the first group, which contains m, p, and L, but also D and J; whereas WY and Pk form a distinct group with B linking them. O, b, R, E form the third (middle) group, and G seems closer to it than to either of the others.

Whatever else this grouping signifies, one thing is clear, viz. that whereas identity of order (or its demonstrable rearrangement) is referable to a common source, the MSS issuing from such a common source have here acquired 'connexions' with MSS from other sources. It seems important to call attention to this phenomenon which, it would seem, bears only one explanation, but which has not yet been given the notice which it deserves. We have already had a hint of it when dealing with the MS D, in its relation to what is called the Cistercian group. The MSS of this group (mostly of the 12th cent.) perpetuate a number of readings of D (9th cent.), but have considerably—and in varying degrees—improved its text, by comparing it with that of other MSS, a work on which we know the Cistercians were then actively engaged (cf. *De unitate* MSS, pp. xliv–lvi). That improvement of the text, an improvement at least on some of D's aberrations, has been paid for by the incorporation of some at least of the aberrations of the MSS consulted in the process. The result is a definite general improvement of text, but with it the transference to it of a number of incorrect readings belonging to several different families. In other words, we have, along with real corrections, a fair amount of contamination, varying from MS to MS.

The data on our chart seem to tell the same story. If we consider the

K

first group, and confine our attention to the first few MSS indicated in each case, we notice that H and T rank early throughout; h does so in all except D; D in all except h and J. Now we know, from other data, that whereas H, T, and h have a common source, and derive directly from it (say Ur-H), neither D, nor mp, nor **L**, nor J comes from that source. And yet they have a predominance of correspondences with those three MSS, if in very varying proportions. For all that, they each have eliminated a good number of the characteristic readings of the HTh group. What has been said of this group can be said of D too, when the presence of its readings in the other MSS is considered (except h and J, which have eliminated most of them). The conclusion to which these data seem to point can be expressed in a diagram:

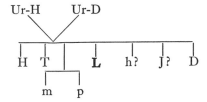

We must suppose two MSS (of which H and D are respectively the closest descendants), both of which are still more corrupt than H and D. Then all the surviving MSS that are mentioned here are the result of different combinations of Ur-H and Ur-D, each correcting the other in varying degrees, or being corrected by whatever other source may have been used in the formation of this or that MS. Possibly h and J should have been omitted: their dependence on Ur-H is obvious, but if they depend on Ur-D at all, they have eliminated its influence almost entirely. (It will be remembered that h (11th cent.) contains the Conflated Text in chap. 4, which goes back at least to the time of Pelagius II in the 6th cent.)

In other words, among the MSS from which our MSS of the ninth and following centuries are derived, some were perhaps even *more corrupt* than these are, and our ninth-century MSS are revisions, which have improved on their sources by the comparison of one with another. For, viewed comprehensively, the transmission of MSS has, after all, depended not only on ignorant monkish scribes, who merely multiplied mistakes from generation to generation, but also at certain periods—and the Carolingian revival was one of them—on scholars of considerable learning and ability who were able in great measure to correct the errors of the past.[1] No doubt they have thereby made it impossible for us to arrange the MSS in neat families, but they have preserved many a correct reading and eliminated perhaps the majority of the errors which had come to them.

This conclusion seems to be confirmed by the fact that we find in the second and third main groups of our chart the same phenomenon which we have considered in the first. In the second, the dominant MSS are O and b, the latter being a very corrupt MS, which, however, stems from the lost Verona MS of the sixth or seventh century. Behind the third group we can clearly discern an Ur-Y and an Ur-P, with perhaps some interference from an Ur-b.

However, even this presentation is an over-simplification. For it is possible to treat most of the MSS of the first group in a different way, omitting D and mp. Then we get this diagram:

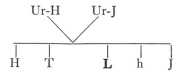

The five MSS concerned have practically as much of J in them as the former collection had of D. Therefore, the complexity of the problem here is obvious, and the same applies to the other two groups.

And this leads us, it would seem, to the conclusion that not only is it today impossible for us to draw up a neat stemma of families (for in no case can we estimate what each of the conjectural Ur-MSS must have contained),[2] but that already before the ninth century the various families, which we may suppose had already come into being in the third and fourth centuries, had contaminated each other in a way similar to that which we have found it necessary to suppose in the ninth century, and of which we have actual evidence in the Cistercian MSS of the twelfth. In other words, there were scholars good or indifferent in the intervening centuries, who had already striven for a pure text and had combined the

[1] Of Servatus Lupus, Abbot of Ferrières, in mid-ninth century, Professor M. L. W. Laistner writes: 'What is unparalleled is his unflagging eagerness to obtain a second manuscript of some work that he already possessed, in order to collate the two and improve his own copy' (*Thought and Letters in Western Europe, A.D. 500–900*, p. 255, cf. pp. 257–8). Perhaps we know of this at all only because of the comparative rareness of MSS of the classical authors, in which we may say Lupus specialized. He may have been writing round so eagerly for such MSS, in order to do for the classics what was already being done for scripture and patristics as a matter of course. The latter called for no particular mention.   [2] See Appendix II.

evidence which they found in different MSS, so that just as we know they kept adding to their collection of Cyprian's letters whenever they found a new Cyprianic MS, they also took the opportunity to revise their own text of the treatises by the fresh readings which the MS at the same time provided.

There is, however, no need to suppose that all our existing MSS are the product of a process of considerable corruption, comparison, and contamination, such as we have just described. It is equally possible that some of them have maintained a comparatively independent tradition, even if we cannot distinguish which these are. If we take h as an example, the difficulty of deciding will be obvious. Leaving aside its already well-proved relationship with H and T (same order of contents; presence of Primacy Text, &c.), we note that the number of its deviations from the resultant text in company with other MSS is strikingly low, ranging from 16 to 7. It is only surpassed by L (13 to 3) and by G (15 to 6). There are two possible explanations of these low figures. *Either* its ancestor shared with H and T not only those readings which h still has in common with them, but also those which are characteristic of H and T, but are no longer in h, having been corrected away with the help of another MS. *Or else* these latter readings did not belong at all to the common ancestors of HTh, but were acquired by some more immediate ancestor of H and T, when it broke away from the tradition which now best survives in h. Either hypothesis will explain the facts: in the one case the purer text is the result of corrections, in the other it is due to a more direct transmission. And as we cannot, at least on the present evidence, prefer one hypothesis to the other, we must be content in practice to accept the evidence of h as being on the whole good, whether it has come to us directly from the early sources, or by the devious way of correction by the comparison of MSS in the distant past.[1]

In the case of h we already knew its close association with H and T, and could neglect the T[33] and H[30] which began its line. But some MSS have low totals throughout, as we have already noticed for G and L. We can add to the number of these by neglecting the associations which a MS has with those MSS which have determined our groups. Those are HT in the first group, ObR in the second, and WP in the third. Agreements with these are only to be expected within each group:

---

[1] In favour of the hypothesis of corrections is the fact that in chap. 4 a second MS was used to create the conflated text. This makes at least probable its use for the revision of the rest of the treatise (and possibly for that of the other treatises too).

what is significant is a low number of agreements with other MSS. The lower the number, the less likely is it that there was regular borrowing between their respective ancestors. This gives us the following list:

Group 1   D, m, **L**, h, J
Group 2   O, R, **E**, G
Group 3   Y, B, P

These MSS, then, show independence, in varying degrees, from the MSS other than those determining their respective groups. By their comparison one with another we can, like our Carolingian forbears, hope to realize a text better than has survived in any of them taken alone. Those most deserving comparison are those which show most independence from one another. Indeed, the 'disconnexions' between our MSS may prove of more practical value to us than the 'connexions' which we have been dealing with.

iii. '*Disconnexions*'

Our chart has already established for us certain unexpected 'disconnexions', which force us to modify some of the conclusions which we came to when dealing with the 'external evidence' and the 'crucial passages'. These led us to treat **M**, **W**, G, **L**, **P** as together constituting one family, or at least one clan, stemming from a common source. (Except for HTh, all the other MSS chosen were treated as independent units whose grouping could not yet be determined.)

However, our chart, which is based chiefly on the 'connexions', presents three main groups and suggests that our original estimate was at least misleading. If there was a common source to the clan—which remains a possibility—its families have not only inter-married but have introduced fresh blood from outside, and even settled down abroad. **M** and **L** remain together, as do **W** and **P**, but they are in separate groups now, and G has little connexion with any. This is confirmed and made very clear by the evidence of disconnexion at the end of each line of the chart, for the MSS there have the fewest variants in common with the MS at the head of the line.

Thus Y (which is the better representative of **W**) is found at the very end of the **M** lines (m and p), and P is fairly low down in both. The connexion, however, of **W** with **P** is manifest in the third group, but mp appear at the end of the WY lines, and almost at the end of the Pk lines. Our first conclusion is that **M** is independent of (or opposed to) **W** and possibly **P**. **L** is likewise opposed to **W** and **P**. As for G, it is definitely opposed to **M** and ranks low in **P**.

The value of establishing these 'disconnexions', or 'oppositions', consists in this—that where there was a common source the fact of general opposition makes it likely that, where they do agree, they are presenting the reading of their common source. And if there is nothing to suggest a common 'source', there is at least a possibility that a good reading preserved in two such 'opposed' MSS is derived directly from the original. At the very least, their general opposition practically ensures that its presence in both is not due to regular borrowing.

In looking for such oppositions in detail, we can expect to find them strongest between members belonging to different groups. As we should expect, **L** is opposed to all in the second and third groups, and G is specially opposed to D, m, and h in the first. **E** is opposed to m in the first and to Y in the third. Y in the third group is opposed to m and h in the first, and to O, R, and **E** in the second. B is opposed to m as well as to **L**.

But there are also oppositions within the first group itself: D against h and J, and J in its turn against m.

The opposition between two MSS only establishes a likelihood in favour of a reading which they have in common. But if the same reading is found in another instance of 'opposed' MSS, the probability is enhanced, and the oftener this occurs the better.

To illustrate the use to which these oppositions can be put in reconstructing the text of the other treatises, let us suppose that we have an unusual, but possible, reading common to **L**, P, and R. In the *De unitate*, according to our chart (p. 126), **L** has 58 variants from the resultant text (apart from those peculiar to itself), and P likewise has 48; but only 4 of these variants are the same in both. Again, R has 69 variants, but of these only 8 agree with those in **L** and 6 with those in P. If we suppose that these figures are representative of the normal relations between these three MSS, then the likelihood of their all three having the same variant can be expressed thus $\dfrac{4 \times 6 \times 8}{58 \times 48 \times 69}$, which is roughly one to 1,000.

In other words, it is extremely unlikely that these three MSS should agree in having a reading *against* the reputedly best text; their common reading is unlikely to be a *variant*, but has every likelihood of being the true reading which has reached each of these 'opposed' MSS in a direct line from the original text. [The example was taken at random.

Subsequent checking showed that the combination **LPR** never occurs explicitly in the critical apparatus. If very occasionally it is, in fact, included under the abbreviation *cett.* (for example, 210.4; 217.4), such rejection of its common reading was based on solid grounds, and exemplifies the one-in-a-thousand exceptions.]

Therefore it may be said in general that whereas any reading in two opposed MSS should be noticed, one that is found in three (or more) mutually opposed MSS will merit special consideration.[1]

[1] See Appendix III.

PART III

CHAPTER XII

The Final Selection of MSS

IF in the course of this study we have roamed about the MSS of St. Cyprian and noted not only the peculiarities proper to such a collection of treatises and letters, but also observed many features which are common to the transmission of ancient authors, and some which may even throw a new light on that of the Latin Fathers in particular, our immediate purpose throughout has been to select a manageable number of MSS which, at least in combination, would promise to establish the best text possible today of the treatises of St. Cyprian. In the last chapter we listed twelve MSS likely to provide checks one against another. A brief survey of the other MSS will suggest which deserve to compete with them for a place in our final list.

V, the lost Verona MS (6th or 7th cent.), whose readings have been entered in the apparatus in so far as they are recoverable from Latini's collations, was omitted from our chart as providing too little material. Its peculiar readings appear most often in b (which is the only MS giving evidence of direct dependence on it) and nearly as often in O and in R.

S was also omitted because it offered only fragments of our treatise and so no sufficient basis for comparison. But if only for its antiquity (about A.D. 500, cf. *C.L.A.* v, no. 602), it calls for complete collation. From the apparatus it will be noticed that it has a number of patent mistakes, but not enough to exclude it from among the MSS that must be consulted. However, its only complete treatises are IV, VI, and VIII; XIII and III are missing; the rest of the treatises all have lacunae owing to the loss of quaternions or single pages.

Coming to the ninth-century MSS, we need to remind ourselves that we eliminated a certain number on the basis of the 'crucial passages'. These were the sister MSS M and Q (about A.D. 800, probably originating from St. Amand or Salzburg, now at Munich and Troyes respectively); K (first half of the century, from the north of France, now in Leyden); 59 (after the mid-century, a French MS, now in Tours). As for 67 (or U, of the second quarter of the century, probably from Lorsch, now in Oxford), we did not so much eliminate as ignore it, because in its treatises it is practically a doublet of its contemporary T, the Vatican MS which has taken up so much of our attention. It seems fully the equal of T for purposes of collation; indeed, it is better written and has not been so tampered with by correctors. But no reason suggests itself for going back on our elimination of the rest.

But our list does not include two other ninth-century MSS which we have constantly used, T itself and W. W (A.D. 820–30), the Würzburg MS by origin and present habitat, is in fact a slightly inferior copy of a MS of which Y is a better copy of about the same date. It can be of use as a check on Y, but if a choice has to be made, Y must be preferred. Lastly, T can safely be sacrificed in view of the many less contaminated MSS in our first group.

Of the MSS later than the ninth century there remain only p, k, H, and b to be considered.

p is a Vatican MS, generally identical with m (both of the 11th cent.). There is not much to choose between them, and if the preference is here given to m, it leaves open the use of p as a check on it, much as W is a check on Y.

k, the Metz MS of the eleventh century too, seems to have been copying the same MS as P had done two centuries earlier. It has at times the better readings and can likewise serve as a check on P.

H, an old friend, with its unique preservation of the Primacy Text in its purity, probably represents best the old MS Ur-H, which has deeply influenced all the first group. That old MS must have gone through a very bad palaeographical period in which many mistakes were made. But it was used as the basis not only of T and U, but also (either itself or an ancestor, as we have seen) of h, the order of its treatises being preserved and its text corrected in places with the help of other MSS. But H itself (second half of the 12th cent., written at Morimond, now in Paris), for all its value in the work of sorting out the MSS, needs too much correcting to be of much use in correcting others.

b, which was only included because of its obvious connexions with V, has proved itself a very bad MS, even though the fact does not manifest itself on the chart. Yet even there its average of common variants is high, and its peculiar readings can be seen in the apparatus to be numerous and mostly worthless. The tradition to which it belongs is obviously responsible for many of the readings in O, and for a good number in R and **E**. These can perhaps be taken as sufficiently representing it.

It must be obvious by now that, if we are to pursue our aim of reducing the number of MSS to manageable proportions, the final choice is not easy. Some of them impose themselves on our choice, but in the case of others the selection must be a little arbitrary, some being equally replaceable by others. But the following team will perhaps be adequate to our purpose.

Y, m, and **E** come first, for their intrinsic merit and their relative independence. Then S, by reason of its age. **L**, h, and G come next (but G only contains five treatises in all, viz. VII, XII, XI, VIII, V). Finally, P, D, and R—ten in all. The inclusion of J, B, and T is optional; each has its own interest and could provide additional checks, but they are not likely to make any substantial contribution. They can, however, act as substitutes for S and G for those treatises or parts of treatises which are wanting in those two MSS.

To the twelve MSS suggested in the last chapter we have added one—S. But we have subtracted three from them, eliminating one altogether (O), and reducing two others to subsidiary positions (J and B) where we have also placed T. B (11th cent., now in Bamberg) which came out well in the study of 'crucial passages', is reduced in status with reluctance, but the third group is already sufficiently represented by Y and P, and these show better oppositions than does B. J (early 9th cent., of Western France, now at Angers) is a mixture of good and bad and deserves at least a subsidiary function. Lastly O (9th cent. too, once at Murbach and now at Oxford) is definitely sacrificed both because of its many errors and because anything it might contribute of good readings or oppositions would seem to be available in R or **E**.

A word must be added with regard to **L** and **E**, each of which represents several MSS. For the first, a is undoubtedly the best, and only occasionally will one of its brethren, e.g. *205* or *207*, throw light on their common source. Similarly, e is the best representative of **E**, but it can at times be checked by *250*.

In fine, for an edition of the treatises of St. Cyprian (excluding III, the *Testimonia*)[1] the following ten MSS are suggested for full collation, to five of which cognate MSS are added for comparison:

MUNICH, Lat. 4597	Y
(Würzburg, Univ., Th. f. 145)	(W)
MANTUA, B III 18	m
(Vatican, Lat. 202)	(p)
BRITISH MUSEUM, Royal 6 B XV	e
(Brit. Mus., Arundel 217)	(250)
PARIS, Lat. 10592	S
LEYDEN, Univ., Voss. lat. oct. 7	h
ADMONT, 587	a
(Vienna, Lat. 850)	(205)
(Admont, 381)	(*207*)
ST. GALLEN, 89	G
PARIS, Lat. 1647A	P
(Metz, 224)	(k)
OXFORD, Bod., Laud Misc. 451	D
VATICAN, Reg. lat. 116	R
(For general subsidiary help):	
(Angers, 148)	(J)
(Bamberg, Patr. 63)	(B)
(Vatican, Reg. lat. 118)	(T)

This may not be the best possible selection and, even from the data provided by this study, scholars may be able to justify a different one. This one is offered as a practical solution, giving a reasonable assurance that with these MSS nothing much is likely to be missed in Cyprian's treatises which has survived until today.

[1] There now seems less reason for omitting IX, the *Ad Fortunatum*. It accompanies the other treatises in all but three of the MSS listed below: it is missing in h, G, and *207*. In S its first folios are missing but three-quarters of the treatise remains. The only other notable MS with IX in a different position is N (cf. above, pp. 30, 32); it may well be worth collating here, though C. H. Turner quite ignored it (cf. *J.T.S.* xxxi (1930) 231 ff.

APPENDIX I

The First Edition of the Treatise

AN attempt is here made to list the readings likely to have been in the edition of the treatise which contained PT in chap. 4. Some of them agree with the readings adopted in the main text, but have been included here because of their special interest. All can be checked by the critical apparatus.

209 1 De Ecclesiae Catholicae Unitate
  9 grassantur
210 3 [et] 4 Deum 5 conatus ⟨est⟩ 7 detectus ⟨est⟩ 11 immortalitatem 12 ea] in 21 flaverunt inpigerunt 23 erat
211 17 et fidei et scinderet 20 lumen 26 suos subornat
212 8 inquit ⟨Petre⟩ 11 eam ⟨et⟩ 14–213. 12 (cf. *totum textum*, *supra*, pp. 99–100, col. 1)
214 4 robor 12 copiam 14 spandit 20 segregatur 21 praemium
215 1 adversum 7 [de] 9 [non tenet Dei legem] 15 indivisa
216 3 scindit 5 Solomonis 9 scidit 21 docet dicens
217 4 dictum sit ei in qua 8 [Item] Sacramentum quoque 9 continet 11 edetur 14 unianimitatis 15 habitare 17 unianimes (*et sic deinceps*)
218 18 discrimine
219 1 serpentis 5 ⟨et⟩ ab 9 Domini 11 omni ⟨in⟩ errore 22 ista
220 23 heresis cum
221 2 [duo . . . sint] 11 solutis 24 iubet ⟨hunc⟩
222 13 testatur 19 [non inflatur] 21 [omnia diligit] 23 semper ⟨et⟩ 25 discordia ⟨nec⟩
223 1 vos ⟨ad Christum⟩ 4 Deo in dilectione 11 et] se 21 illa
224 7 te ⟨ipsum⟩ 14 exsurgere 20 inaudientes (??) 21 foedere] fide incontinentes] inertes 23 voluptatem
225 4 hii 5 proficiunt 6 [et] 14 ut ⟨quoniam⟩ 18 adque ⟨ab⟩
226 17 ccl 18 hisdem
227 1 qua salvari obtemperantes Domino 9–21 Peius hoc crimen est quam quod hi qui sacrificaverunt admisisse lapsi videntur, qui tamen in paenitentia criminis constituti Deum plenis satisfactionibus deprecantur.

Illic ecclesia quaeritur et rogatur, hic ecclesiae repugnatur; illic potest necessitas fuisse, hic voluntas tenetur in scelere; illic qui lapsus est sibi tantum nocuit, hic qui heresim vel schisma facere conatus est multos secum trahendo decepit; illic animae unius est damnum, hic periculum plurimorum. Certe peccasse se ille et intellegit et plangit, hic tumens in peccato suo et in ipsis sibi delictis placens a matre filios segregat, oves a pastore sollicitat, Dei sacramenta disturbat; et cum lapsus semel peccaverit, hic cottidie peccat; postremo lapsus martyrium postmodum consecutus potest regni promissa percipere, ille si extra ecclesiam

228 7 Deo] eo   21 [hoc]
229 8 patientia
230 22 vitae   23 [inquit]
231 7 Deus unus est et Christus unus est   8 plebs una in solida corporis
     unitate   21 dimitto vobis
232 6 ac] et   13 infracta sit   21 ⟨et⟩ in dilectione ⟨et⟩   22 cogitat ⟨nemo cogitat⟩
233 1 tales] stabiles   9 ipse

APPENDIX II

Contamination: Stemmata and 'Connexions'

THE evidence collected in this study makes manifest how contamination has pervaded all the MSS on which we depend for the text of St. Cyprian's works, and few will question the conclusion that 'it is today impossible for us to draw up a neat stemma of families' (p. 131). What we have found is not unlike A. E. Housman's estimate of the MSS of Juvenal: 'Authors like Juvenal, read and copied and quoted both in antiquity and in the Middle Ages, have no strictly separated families of MSS. Lections are bandied to and fro from one copy to another, and all the streams of tradition are united by canals' (*D. Iunii Iuvenalis Saturae*, 2nd ed., 1931, p. xxiv).

Does this mean that we can make no headway at all with the ancestry of our MSS? We have in fact, over and over again, appealed to 'common ancestors' of two or more MSS, and even dubbed them with the pretentious prefix 'Ur-'. Was this merely wishful thinking? At least it was based on concordant readings too numerous to be explained by mere chance. The Ur-MSS can therefore rightly be postulated, provided that we are aware of the limits of their usefulness. For, as we said in explanation of our avoidance of stemmata, 'in no case can we estimate what each of the Ur-MSS must have contained'. Whereas the Ur-MSS can in fact be used to illustrate the 'connexions' that exist between our surviving MSS, we cannot so reconstruct them as to be able to say that *this* reading is derived from this Ur-MS and *that* from that. The diagrams that follow are an attempt to illustrate these two points.

It will be remembered that in dealing with the MSS of the first group in our chart (p. 126), we first derived them from Ur-H and Ur-D (p. 130), but then showed that most of them could have been derived equally well from Ur-H and Ur-J (p. 131). A single diagram can be devised to combine these two results (Fig. 1). Ur-H (which we can here denote by **H**) is represented by the inner circle, and Ur-D(**D**) and Ur-J(**J**) by the incomplete circular rims about it. The eight MSS of our first group (placed outside the circles) are mainly the result of the mutual contamination, in varying degrees, of two (or three) of these Ur-MSS. [a takes the place of **L**, as being the best representative of that family.]

This at least gives us a pictorial representation, easy to grasp, of the presence or absence of Ur-D or Ur-J among the main constituents—along with Ur-H— of all eight MSS. It shows the basic 'connexions' that exist between those eight MSS, without pretending to determine the varying relationships by which **H**, **D**, and **J** came, between them, to produce those eight. **H** need not have been put in the centre: it need not have first contaminated **D**, and then

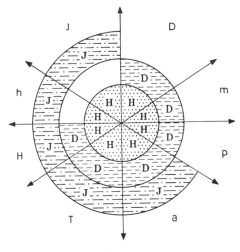

FIG. 1

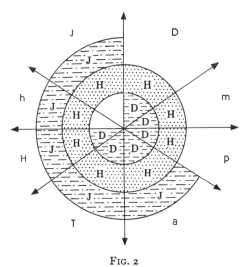

FIG. 2

with **D** have contaminated **J** before producing T. Maybe **D** was in the centre as in Fig. 2, a diagram which in fact says neither more nor less than Fig. 1. Unless other evidence can be found beyond what our chart has given us, we must be content to leave the relationship between our Ur-MSS undetermined.

The reason is, as we said above, that we are not in a position to estimate what any of our Ur-MSS contained. For not only can two MSS produced by the *same* three sources show many *different* readings (as is clear, for example, for H, T, or a), but those two same MSS could have been produced by sources which were quite different from the first three. If this can be shown, it will be clear that neither can we determine the order in which the Ur-MSS contaminated each other, nor assign any reading to one Ur-MS rather than to another. If this is realized, there will be no danger of reading more into our circular diagrams than they are meant to say.

Two more figures should make the matter clear. They are enlargements of the lower section of Figs. 1 and 2, showing how the different readings in the MSS T and a could have arisen from the three Ur-MSS **H, D**, and **J**. For the sake of clarity two other MSS, which we may call F and Z, have been inserted. They do not contribute any new readings, but simply record the effect of **D**'s contamination by **H** or vice versa, before the contamination by **J** took effect.

Eleven words or phrases have been selected, for each of which at least one of our sources (**H, D, J**) differs from the resultant text (here called 'C', for Cyprian (?)). C readings are left white; each of the others is distinguished as before.[1]

In Fig. 3 (which corresponds to the lower part of Fig. 2), **D, H**, and **J** differ from each other in most of the eleven readings, and the final differences between T and a are due to a different choice having been made at the two contaminations. To take the first word: **D** carried the genuine reading, but this was displaced in both F and Z by the reading in **H**. This was passed on to T in spite of **J**'s having the genuine reading, but in a it was the latter which prevailed.

[1] If the variants in each of the three Ur-MSS are indicated by **D, H**, and **J** respectively, and the 'correct' reading by C (and by C *with* **D** or **H** or **J** where either would produce the same result), then the eleven readings are as follows:

FIG. 3

	1	2	3	4	5	6	7	8	9	10	11
Ur-D	C	**D**	C	**D**	C	C	**D**	**D**	**D**	**D**	**D**
Ur-H	**H**	C	**H**	**CH**	**CH**	**H**	**CH**	C	**H**	**H**	**H**
Ur-J	C	**J**	C	**CJ**	**J**	**J**	C	**J**	**J**	**CJ**	**CJ**

It is these *same* readings that give rise to *both* T *and* a.

FIG 4.

	1	2	3	4	5	6	7	8	9	10	11
Ur-H	**H**	C	**H**	C	C	C	C	**H**	**H**	**H**	**H**
Ur-D	C	**CD**	C	**D**	**CD**	**D**	**D**	C	C	**D**	**D**
Ur-J	**CJ**	**J**	**CJ**	**CJ**	**J**	**J**	C	**J**	**J**	**CJ**	**CJ**

The three Ur-MSS are here different from the preceding ones, yet they *equally* can give rise to both T and a.

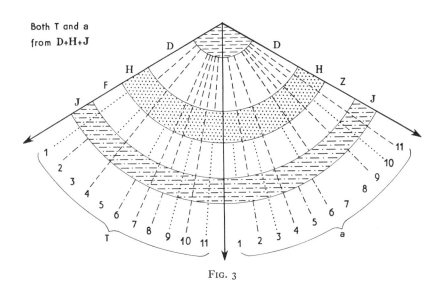

FIG. 3

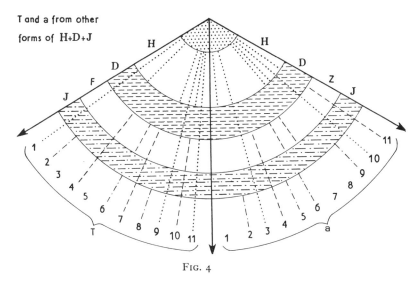

FIG. 4

L

For the second word, **D** had a variation of its own, but **H** had the true reading. This prevailed in F, but yielded to **D** in Z. However, both F and Z were here overborne by **J**, so that T and a are here in agreement, if wrongly, with each other.

These indications will suffice to show how each of the readings in T and a could have arisen from the same three Ur-MSS. In only three cases out of the eleven do T and a agree and, whereas T has two correct readings and a three, these do not correspond. [Extreme examples have been chosen deliberately: on an average, correct readings would predominate, especially in the case of a (cf. **L** on the chart, p. 126).] Therefore there is no difficulty in explaining how two MSS which contain such manifest differences have inherited their respective readings from the same Ur-MSS—and from nowhere else. [And for the sake of simplicity we have neglected the likelihood of fresh mistakes or conjectures being added by F, Z, T, or a, on their own.]

But could T and a have acquired their readings from *other* Ur-MSS than these? Or to put it another way, could **D**, **H**, and **J** have had other readings than those which we have assigned to them? Let us suppose for the moment that each of the variants, which appear in T and a, does in fact derive from the Ur-MS which we have indicated; what of the remaining readings in each of our Ur-MSS? Could they have been different from what we assumed them to be in Fig. 3? That they could is shown in Fig. 4.

Here we have T and a exactly as they were before, but now, in place of **D**, **H** is taken as the starting-point, contaminated successively by **D** and **J** (as in Fig. 1). If we first consider **H**, we notice at once that five of its eleven readings (2, 4, 5, 6, 7) agree with C, whereas in Fig. 3 only two certainly did so (2, 8), with three possibles (4, 5, 7). Therefore, as between Figs. 3 and 4, **H** certainly differed at 6 and 8, and possibly also at 4, 5, and 7. Similarly, whereas in Fig. 3 **D** has four readings of C (1, 3, 5, 6), in Fig. 4 it has four certain such readings (1, 3, 8, 9) and two doubtful ones (2, 5). Therefore **D** differs in the two figures at 6, 8, 9 and possibly also at 2 and 5.

Therefore the three Ur-MSS on which the eleven passages both in T and in a depend might be reconstructed in more than one way, at least so far as this section is concerned. It is obvious that these two figures do not exhaust the possibilities, even if the same orders of contamination, **D–H–J** or **H–D–J**, are preserved. Fresh possibilities are also opened up if **J** is moved up to second or to first place—all moves which are equally legitimate.

It is clear that the consistency of our Ur-MSS is becoming more and more tenuous. A last blow will reduce them to pulp. We have just seen how easily a reading in **D** can be ousted by one in **H** and vice versa. Now **D** is only there at all because of the readings which we find in our surviving MS D. But we know from our critical apparatus that there are 27 variant readings which are *common* to H and D. What, then, is to prevent those 27 readings (or most of them) not being in **D** originally, but entering it by contamination from **H**? Or vice versa? So too with our other Ur-MSS, both those in this group and those in the two other groups. Their relationships within their own groups remain indeterminate: no particular reading can be ascribed to any one Ur-MS rather than to another.

Are we then to say that Ur-H absorbs Ur-D and that we can dispense with Ur-D altogether? By no means. Our Ur-MSS remain essential, for even if the 27 common readings of D and H had all to be ascribed ultimately to Ur-H, there are still 47 variant readings of D which fall outside the scope of Ur-H, and which justify us in retaining Ur-D as one of the sources of at least our first group of MSS.

So that our circular diagram (either Fig. 1 or Fig. 2) can remain as a basic scheme of the connexions of the MSS belonging to group 1. Similar diagrams will represent groups 2 and 3. But the present note will have shown the necessary limitations which the interpretation of these diagrams must respect.

APPENDIX III

'Opposed' MSS

THE preceding Appendix was almost negative in its conclusions, and provided little or no help for choosing between variant readings. But at the end of Part III (p. 135) the possibility suggested itself of turning the 'oppositions' of MSS to good purpose, and it deserves following up. Two MSS are 'opposed' to each other when, though each varies often from the resultant text, their variants agree together only very rarely. In our chart we neglected all those variants which appear in only one MS, but even so we saw that the likelihood of **L**, P, and R having the same variant was roughly of the order one to 1,000. Such a 'variant' would obviously be a rival to the reading of the resultant text. Or to put it more practically: where these three MSS have the same reading, the probabilities are that that reading is the correct one.

Such is the reason for drawing up the following tables. They only consider the ten MSS which we have chosen for the collation of the other treatises, J however replacing S, which does not figure on our chart. In the first table, consisting of circles, each MS is surrounded by those with which it is in opposition, opposition being admitted only where the agreements are less than ten. [The MSS with which they have the *fewest* agreements (6 or less) are to the right of the circle.] Thus one can see at a glance whether the MSS in which a particular reading is found are opposed to one another or not.

In the second table every triangle compares three MSS, each of which is opposed to the other two, and of which at least one pair has less than seven agreements. The number of variants in each MS is indicated, as also the agreements between each pair; and in the centre is placed a figure related to the likelihood of agreement between the three, e.g. in the first: one to 1,000. These figures in the middle must be taken as only indicating very roughly a high degree of unlikelihood, lessening as we go on, but dealing with too many imponderables to claim to be exact estimates. However, they do seem to exclude mutual borrowing between these MSS or between their ancestors, and to suggest that an agreement between the three MSS must be due to some factor other than those responsible for the many variants which occur in them. That factor may well be the transmission of the reading to each of them, direct from the original text.

Therefore any reading found in one of these combinations deserves particular attention.[1]

[It is gratifying to find that the facts agree with these calculations. With four exceptions the critical apparatus never presents triply opposed MSS together.

---

[1] Several more triangles could be added which might at least be suggestive.

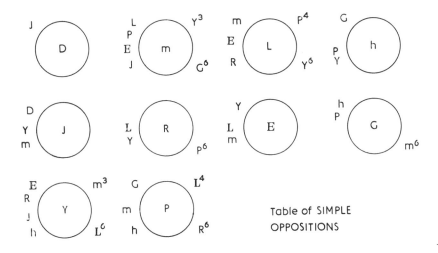

Table of SIMPLE
OPPOSITIONS

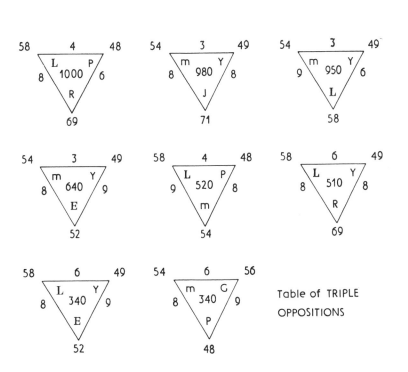

Table of TRIPLE
OPPOSITIONS

The exceptions are interesting. 211. 16 [mYL; LYR] and 232. 26 [mYJ, by implication] have already been adopted in the text. 212. 17 (TR) [LYR] is easily explained by the influence of the Vulgate. We are left with 230. 10 [mYL and LYR], and here alone, on the strength of these oppositions, a last-minute change has been made from *contagio* to *contagione*. Cyprian uses both freely (cf. 225. 19; and Watson, p. 220).]

CORRIGENDUM

On p. 90 the *Liber de unitate ecclesiae conservanda* was ascribed to Walramus Nienburgensis. Printing was too far advanced to correct this. In fact, Schwenkenbecher ascribed it to Walram of Naumburg, but E. Sackur rejected this when he republished it in *M.G.H.* (p. 178 n. 2). There can be little doubt that the author was a monk of Hersfeld, not otherwise known (cf. M. Manitius, *Gesch. d. lat. Lit. des MAs* III pp. 40–43), but the convenient siglum *Wal.* has been retained.

BIBLIOGRAPHY

D. BAINS, *A Supplement to Notae Latinae* (850–1050) (1936), Cambridge; cf. Lindsay.

C. BATLLE, *see* GASSÓ.

G. BATTELLI, *Lezioni di Paleografia* (1949), Vatican.

C. BECKER, *Catalogi bibliothecarum antiqui* (1885), Bonn.

M. BÉVENOT, 'St. Cyprian's "De unitate", 4, in the Light of the MSS', in *Analecta Gregoriana*, 11 (1937), Rome. [Abbr: '*De Un.* MSS'.]

—— 'A New Cyprianic Fragment', in *Bulletin of the John Rylands Library*, vol. 28 (1944) i, 76–82, Manchester.

—— *St. Cyprian: 'The Lapsed' and 'The Unity of the Catholic Church'*, translation and notes, A. C. W. 25 (1957), Westminster, Maryland; London.

—— 'An "Old Latin" Quotation (2 Tim. 3. 2) and its Adventures in the MSS of St. Cyprian's "De unitate ecclesiae", chap. 16', in *T. u. U.* 63, *Studia Patristica*, i (1957) 249–52, Berlin.

B. BISCHOFF, *Die südostdeutschen Schreibschulen und Bibliotheken in der Karolingerzeit*, 1 (1940), Leipzig.

—— 'Paläographie', in *Deutsche Philologie im Aufriß* (1952), pp. 379–451; 2nd ed. revised, published separately (1956), Berlin, Munich.

—— and J. HOFMANN, *Libri S. Kyliani: Die Würzburger Schreibschule und die Dombibliothek im VIII und IX Jahrhundert* (1952), Würzburg.

A. BLAISE and H. CHIRAT, *Dictionnaire latin-français des auteurs chrétiens* (1954), Strasbourg.

A. BRACKMANN, *see* KEHR.

F. DI CAPUA, *Il ritmo prosaico nelle lettere dei Papi e nei documenti della Cancelleria romana dal IV al XIV secolo*, vol. i (1937); vol. ii (1939); vol. iii (1946) [so far to A.D. 523], Rome.

J. CHAPMAN, 'Les Interpolations dans le traité de S. Cyprien sur l'unité de l'Église,' in *Rev. Bén.*, xix (1902) 246–54, 357–73; xx (1903) 26–51, Maredsous.

—— 'The Order of the Treatises and Letters in the MSS of St. Cyprian', in *J.T.S.* iv (1902) 103–23, London.

C. CHARLIER, 'Les Manuscrits personnels de Florus de Lyon et son activité littéraire', in *Mélanges Podechard*, pp. 71–84 (1905), Lyons.

H. CHIRAT, *see* BLAISE.

A. C. CLARK, *The Descent of Manuscripts* (1918), Oxford.

L. DELISLE, *Le Cabinet des manuscrits de la bibliothèque impériale*, 3 vols. (1868–81), Paris.

P. M. GASSÓ and DOM COLUMBA BATLLE, *Pelagio I Pp. Epistulae quae supersunt* (1956), Montserrat.

J. DE GHELLINCK, *Patristique et moyen âge*, vol. ii (1947), Brussels, Paris.

W. HARTEL, *S. Thasci Caecili Cypriani opera omnia*, C.S.E.L. iii. i–iii (1868–71), Vienna.

L. M. HARTMANN, *Epistulae Pelagii iunioris ad episcopos Histriae*, in *M.G.H.*, Epist. II, pp. 442–67 (1899), Berlin.

J. HOFMANN, *see* BISCHOFF.

A. E. HOUSMAN, *D. Iunii Iuvenalis Saturae*, 2nd ed. (1931), Cambridge.

D. HURST, *Bedae Opera*, in *Corpus Christianorum*, 122 (1955), Turnhout.

M. R. JAMES, *A Descriptive Catalogue of the Latin MSS in the John Rylands Library at Manchester*, 2 vols. (1921), Manchester and London.

P. F. KEHR, *Regesta Pontificum Romanorum: Italia Pontificia*, vols. i–viii (1906–35); Id.: *Germania Pontificia* (by A. Brackmann), vols. i–iii (1911–35), Berlin.

N. R. KER, *Medieval Libraries of Great Britain: a List of Surviving Books* (1941), London.

H. KOCH, *Cyprianische Untersuchungen* (1926), Bonn.

—— *Cathedra Petri: neue Untersuchungen über die Anfänge der Primatslehre.* Beiheft zur *Z.N.T.W.* 11 (1930), Giessen.

P. O. KRISTELLER, 'Latin Manuscript Books before 1600, Part I: A Bibliography of the Printed Catalogues of the Extant Collections', in *Traditio*, v (1947), 227–317; Id., 'Part II: a Tentative List of the Unpublished Inventories of Imperfectly Catalogued Extant Collections', in *Traditio*, ix (1953), 393–418, New York.—Also published separately, much enlarged (1960), New York.

M. L. W. LAISTNER, *Thought and Letters in Western Europe, A.D. 500–900*, 2nd ed. (1957), London.

P. LEHMANN, 'Die Bistümer Konstanz und Chur' (1918) and 'Die Bistümer Mainz und Erfurt' (1928), in *Mittelalterliche Bibliothekskataloge Deutschlands und der Schweiz*, Munich.

E. LESNE, *Histoire de la propriété ecclésiastique en France*, vol. iv: *Les Livres, scriptoria, et bibliothèques du commencement du VIIIe à la fin du XIe siècle* (1938), Lille.

W. M. LINDSAY, *Notae Latinae: an Account of Abbreviation in Latin MSS of the Early Minuscule Period* (c. 700–850), (1915), Cambridge. *See also* BAINS.

E. A. LOWE, *The Beneventan Script* (1914), Oxford.

—— 'More Facts about our Oldest Latin MSS', in *Classical Quarterly* xxii (1928) 43–62, Oxford.

—— *Scriptura Beneventana*, facsimiles, 2 vols. (1929), Oxford.

—— *Codices Latini Antiquiores*, vols. i–ix (1934–59), Oxford.

P. MAAS, *Textkritik* (3rd ed. 1957), Leipzig.

—— *Textual Criticism*, translation of preceding (1958), Oxford.

K. MENGIS, 'Ein altes Verzeichnis cyprianischer Schriften', in *Philologische Wochenschrift* 38 (1918) 326–36, Berlin.

G. MERCATI, 'D'alcuni nuovi sussidi per la critica del testo di S. Cipriano', in *Studi e Documenti di Storia e Diritto* xix–xx (1898–9), Rome. Also published separately (1899), Rome; and among the author's collected works in *Studi e Testi*, lxxvii (1937) 152–267, Vatican.

P. A. H. J. MERKX, 'Zur Syntax der Kasus und Tempora in den Traktaten des hl. Cyprian', *L.C.P.* ix (1939), Nijmegen.

C. MOHRMANN, *Études sur le latin des chrétiens* (1958), Rome. *See also* SCHRIJNEN.

G. MORIN, 'S. Augustini Sermones post Maurinos reperti', in *Miscellanea Agostiniana*, i (1930), Rome.

R. B. PALMER, *see* STRECKER.

G. PASQUALI, *Storia della tradizione e critica del testo*, 2nd ed. (1952), Florence.

O. PERLER, 'Le "De unitate" (chap. IV–V) de saint Cyprien interprété par saint Augustin', in *Augustinus Magister*, pp. 835–58 (1954), Paris.

H. PÉTRÉ, '*Caritas*' (1948), Louvain.

H. L. RAMSAY, 'Our Oldest MSS of St. Cyprian, III: The Contents and Order of the MSS LNP', in *J.T.S.* iii (1901–2) 585–94, London.

P. RUF, 'Bistum Augsburg' (1932); 'Bistum Eichstätt' (1933); 'Bistum Bamberg' (1939), in *Mittelalterliche Bibliothekskataloge Deutschlands und der Schweiz*, Munich.

J. SCHRIJNEN and C. MOHRMANN, 'Studien zur Syntax der Briefe des hl. Cyprian', *I, L.C.P.* v (1936); *II, L.C.P.* vi (1937), Nijmegen.

E. SCHWARTZ, *Acta Conciliorum Oecumenicorum* (1914–36), Berlin, Leipzig.

W. SCHWENKENBECHER, 'Liber de unitate ecclesiae conservanda' (Walramus ep. Nienburg.), in *M.G.H. Libelli de Lite imperatorum et pontificum s. XI et s. XII*, pp. 173–284 (1892), Hanover.

H. VON SODEN, 'Die cyprianische Briefsammlung: Geschichte ihrer Entstehung und Überlieferung', in *T.u.U.* 25 (1904), Leipzig.

—— 'Die lateinische Neue Testament in Afrika zur Zeit Cyprians', in *T.u.U.* 33 (1909), Leipzig.

A. SOUTER, 'List of Abbreviations and Contractions in the John Rylands MS. No. 15', in the *Bulletin of the J.R.L.* vol. 5 (1918–19), reprinted separately 1919, Manchester.

—— *A Glossary of Later Latin to 600 A.D.* (1949), Oxford.

K. STRECKER, *Introduction to Medieval Latin* (translated and revised by Robert B. Palmer) (1957), Berlin.

C. H. TURNER, 'The Original Order and Contents of our Oldest MS of St. Cyprian', in *J.T.S.* iii (1902) 282–5, London.

—— 'The Turin and Milan Fragments', ibid., pp. 576–84.

—— 'Prolegomena to the "Testimonia" of St. Cyprian', ibid., vi (1905) 246–70; ix (1907) 62–87; xxix (1928) 113–36; xxxi (1930) 225–46, Oxford.

A. VAN HOVE, *Prolegomena ad codicem iuris canonici*, 2nd ed. (1945), Malines, Rome.

E. W. WATSON, 'The Style and Language of St. Cyprian', in *Studia Biblica*, iv (1896) 189–324, Oxford.

A. WERMINGHOFF, 'Flori diaconi oratio in Concilio Cariacensi habita', in *M.G.H. Legum*, III *Concilia*, II. ii pp. 768–78 (1908), Hanover, Leipzig.

F. WORMALD and C. E. WRIGHT, *The English Library before 1700* (1958), London.

SCRIPTURE INDEX

Scripture Index

INDEX OF MANUSCRIPTS

GENERAL INDEX

Ad Fortunatum (IX), 32, 40, 55, 138.
ad Rhaab or *ei*? 58, 70–72, 127.
Admont, abbey, 43, 62; *see also* Index of MSS.
adversandus or *aversandus*? 82–83.
Aldhelm of Malmesbury, 53.
Ancestors of surviving MSS, contamination among, 6–7, 57, 93–94, 129–32; indicated by common order of contents, 4, 8, 18–19; indicated by lacunae, 4, 5, 36–42; in two volumes, which might separate, 21–24, 32; postulated necessarily, but text indeterminable, 131–2, 142–7; H (twelfth century) linked with F (*c.* 400), 25–28; Ho (fifteenth century) keeps ancient order, 29–35, 44; *see also* contamination, Middle Ages.
Augustine, St., 50, 82, 87, 88.
Avellana, de Fonte, 32.

Bains, D., 151.
Ballerini, P. and J., 88.
Baluze, E., 32.
Battelli, G., 151.
Bec, catalogue, 50.
Becker, C., 51, 151.
Bede, the Venerable, 53, 89.
Bévenot, M.: '*De Un.* MSS', ix, 8, 23, 56, 73, 129, 151; 'A New Cyprianic Fragment', 30, 151; other studies, 151.
Bischoff, B., v, 3, 21, 22, 49, 151.
Blaise, A., and Chirat, H., 68, 151.
Bobbio, 25.
Bonneval, abbey, 49.
Boston, John, of Bury St. Edmunds, 52.
Brackmann, A., 152.

Carolingian Age, 4, 130, 133.
Catalogus scriptorum ecclesiae (by John Boston), 52.
Cena Cypriani, 17, 32, 40.
Chap. 4 of *De un.*: two versions of, PT and TR, viii, 8, 54, 56–59, 93, 99–101; PT, 23, 63, 65, 72, 78, 85, 87, 89, 92, 93, 94, 99–100, 132, 140–1; Conflated Text, 8, 54, 56, 89, 99–100, 130.
Chapman, Dom J., 23, 25, 34, 87, 89, 151.
Charlier, C., 151.
Cheltenham list, fourth-century Cyprianic corpus, 50.
'Cistercian' MSS, 23, 24, 25, 60, 71, 78, 81, 92, 94, 129.

Clarendon Press, v.
Clark, A. C., *The Descent of Manuscripts*, 37, 151.
Cluny, catalogue, 50.
Common variants, *see* Variants common to any two MSS.
Conflated Text, *see* chap. 4 of *De un.*
'Connexion' between MSS, 128, 129–33; *see also* Variants common to any two MSS.
Contamination, 6–7, 57, 79, 93–94, 127, 142–7; true reading due to (or to direct descent?), 57–58, 129–32.
Cornelius, Pope, letters to, 34, 35, 45, 47.
Corpus Christianorum, v, 89.
'Crucial passages', 4, 60–86, 133.
crudelitate or *credulitate*? 65–66.
Cyprianic corpus, 18; in two volumes, 21–24, 25, 28; Cheltenham list (A.D. 359), 50; treatises all together, letters in various incomplete collections, 1–2; *see also* letters, treatises.
Cyprianic manuscripts: collation for critical edition, 1; 'family groups', 8, 9, 14, 15; progressive selection, 2, 55, 92–95, 136–9; *see also* non-extant MSS of Cyprian.

De ecclesiae catholicae unitate, revised text, 96–123.
De laude martyrii (App. iii), 16, 29–30, 34, 35, 39, 40, 45, 46, 47.
Dekkers, E., v.
Delisle, L., 151.
Di Capua, F., 151.
'Disconnexion': ('opposition') between MSS, 129, 133–5; use of 'opposed' MSS in establishing text, 134–5, 148–50; *see also* 'connexion'.

Erfurt, catalogue, 50.
Evidence: 'external' and 'internal', 2–5; 'external', the codices, &c., 3,18–53,133; 'internal', the text, 4, 54–135; majority vote not decisive, 5.

Facundus, Hermianus, 88.
'Family groups', 8, 9, 14–15.
Fleury, 49, 51.
Florus of Lyons, 16, 51, 90, 153.
Fulgentius Ruspensis, 88.